SOVIET ART 1920s-1930s

RUSSIAN MUSEUM, LENINGRAD

ART

1920s-1930s

RUSSIAN MUSEUM, LENINGRAD

INTRODUCTION BY MIKHAIL GUERMAN
CONTRIBUTORS: L. VOSTRETSOVA, N. KOZYREVA, S. LIUBIMTSEV,
AND O. SHIKHIREVA
GENERAL EDITOR: VLADIMIR LENIASHIN

SOVIETSKY KHUDOZHNIK, MOSCOW
HARRY N. ABRAMS, INC., PUBLISHERS, NEW YORK
IN ASSOCIATION WITH
HOFFMANN UND CAMPE VERLAG, HAMBURG
MEULENHOFF/LANDSHOFF, AMSTERDAM
PENGUIN BOOKS LTD, HARMONDSWORTH

Front cover: Kazimir Malevich. *Torso in a Yellow Shirt*, 1928—32 (plate 54)
Back cover: Natan Altman. *Petrocommune*, 1921 (plate 12)
Page 2: Nikolai Suetin. Detail from "Design for a mural," 1920 (plate 59)

Project director: Andreas Landshoff
English-language editor: Phyllis Freeman
Designer: Mikhail Anikst
Translated from the Russian by Sharon McKee

Copyright © 1988 by Sovietsky Khudozhnik, Moscow

Harry N. Abrams, Inc., edition:
Library of Congress Cataloging-in-Publication Data:
Soviet art 1920s—1930s / introduction by Mikhail Guerman.
256 p. 24×32.8 cm
Designed to serve as a catalogue for an exhibition being mounted by the Russian
Museum in Leningrad.
ISBN 0—8109—2399—8 (pbk.):
1. Art, Russian—Exhibitions. 2. Constructivism (Art)—Soviet Union—Exhibitions.
3. Suprematism in art—Exhibitions. 4. Art, Modern—20th century—Soviet
Union—Exhibitions. 5. Gosudarstvennyĭ russkiĭ muzeĭ (Leningrad, R.S.F.S.R.)—
Exhibitions. I. German, Mikhail IUr'evich. II. Gosudarstvennyĭ russkiĭ muzeĭ
(Leningrad, R.S.F.S.R.)
N6988.5.C64S67 1988   88—3371
759.7'074—dc19   CIP

Penguin Books edition:
Published by the Penguin Group
27 Wrights Lane, London W8 5TZ, England
Viking Penguin Inc., 40 West 23rd Street, New York, New York 10010, USA
Penguin Books Australia Ltd, Ringwood, Victoria, Australia
Penguin Books Canada Ltd, 2801 John Street, Markham, Ontario, Canada L3R IB4
Penguin Books (NZ) Ltd, 182—190 Wairau Road, Auckland 10, New Zealand
Penguin Books Ltd, Registered Offices: Harmondsworth, Middlesex, England

Published in West Germany by Hoffmann und Campe, Hamburg
Published in the Netherlands by Meulenhoff/Landshoff, Amsterdam

Originated and designed in the USSR
Printed and bound in Finland

Contents

■■■■■■■■■■■■ This volume is the result of a ruthless process of elimination, whereby from the best the very best were chosen, and of the best the absolutely essential. Nevertheless, in the end many of the absolutely essential had to be left out ■ In the years after the Revolution and later, as the twenties became the thirties, savage arguments raged in the Soviet art world. Extremism was all but the norm of every artistic program, adversaries were shown no mercy, and sadly, at times no attempt was even made to understand them. But now, decades later, much looks different; some quarrels were clearly forced, some conflicts were imaginary—as, indeed, consensus could also prove to be. The actual battleline was often far away from the polemical front, and there were silent disputes—not between artists but between their works. All of this now needs to be given serious study, as do the paintings, drawings, and prints here gathered together for the first time in many years ■ The aspect of Russian art of the twenties that has probably always been hardest to come to terms with is the perhaps unprecedented ebullience and explosive intensity of artistic life at a time of rapid social change and daily hardship—at a time of hunger, cold, and the absence of elementary materials and proper working conditions. The political changes long awaited in Russia were not just "days that shook the world"; they shook the inner world of artists too. Even those who had looked forward to the Revolution with joy and hope did not find it easy to accept the stark reality. The artist's imagination collided with the here and now. Occasionally the result was tragic. But for many it provided a beneficial albeit painful impetus to innovate and address a new audience ■ Naturally, the events that occurred in Russian art at the start of the twenties were bound up with what had gone before. The art of the first post-Revolutionary decade was created by men and women who had ties with the art of the turn of the century. Many artists' groups not only endured but remained faithful to their previous traditions and continued to influence the direction art took. On the other hand, much of what is now regarded as art of the Revolution—from the patent classicism of Kuzma Petrov-Vodkin's *Bathing the Red Horse* (1912) to the fiery manifestoes of the Futurists to the brave experiments of Kazimir Malevich—appeared before the events of November 1917 ■ The artists' associations singled out for attention in this catalogue had fairly deep roots: witness such illustrious societies as the World of Art, Makovets, and the Society of Moscow Painters (essentially an offshoot of the Cubo-Futurist Jack of Diamonds, that maintained its predecessor's basic traditions and continued its principal line of inquiry). The blossoming of art in the twenties was nourished by the hopes and concerns of the pre-Revolutionary years, while new disputes were really extensions of the disputes of the past—though the actual situation had radically changed ■ Today the verbal cut and thrust between the various groups in the first years after the Revolution demonstrates the situation less clearly than a juxtaposition of specific major works by specific artists. Take *The Violin* by Petrov-Vodkin (1918), with its startling tottering universe, the charm of the play of colors on the crumbling plaster of the dusty window, the poignant defenselessness of the fragile instrument in a deserted and unstable world, the very beauty of that defenselessness asserting how essential and important it is to man. Is this painting, which we have come to regard as a poetic distillation of the era's hopes and confusion, really the antithesis of Natan Altman's or Malevich's bold experiments? Or do these artists, rather, share the same worries and joys, while expressing them differently? ■ However, this catalogue will probably surprise the reader less for the famous avant-garde works heard of but never seen than for the wealth of superb pieces by artists known to few except scholars. Fame eluded these artists because they did not crush their opponents, real or imagined, because they did not sing their own praises while vilifying those who thought differently. Appraising this very important stratum of art is no simple task ■ Such, for instance, is the spell cast by the masterful paintings and drawings of Pavel Filonov. A product of suffering, they reflect the asceticism of an extremist who has become a popular legend over the years. These works probably have an even greater effect now than they did fifty years ago, when they were created. Today we are able not only to give the artist his due but to consider his work objectively and recognize that it is a link in the chain of the development of Soviet painting. Though the phenomenon of Filonov may not seem to fit in the history of art, it has its roots there. They are revealed in the "inflamed conscience" so typical of Russian culture, the gift of foresight which predicates that suffering and evil must be experienced before harmony can be attained, and a rare analytical perception that breaks up the molecules of the visible world, just as Dostoyevsky broke up the yawning depths of the subconscious ■ The hallmarks of Filonov's creativity are the simplicity and wisdom of the parable together with an almost aggressive intrusion into the most profound secrets of matter as well as our conception of it, a distinct tie with primitivism and at the same time with the most daring innovations to be made at the beginning of the century, and encompassing all of this, a mighty and masterful individuality ■ Today we are probably drawn above all to those works by artists such as Filonov or Vasily Kandinsky that contain the most explosive energy in an innovative and independent form. One example is undoubtedly the posters of ROSTA (Russian Telegraph Agency). They preserve the intense excitement of those times, when the most audacious experiments in form were also meant to have a social message. Certainly the vivid temperament of the artists who continued the Jack of Diamonds tradition—such as Piotr Konchalovsky, Ilia Mashkov, and Rudolf Frenz—sheds new light on the viability of that trend, particularly in the twenties, as well as on its reflection of the anxious tempo of the changes then taking place.* ■ Perhaps now, when works by artists from various associations and groups have been brought together, one of the biggest surprises is how little they actually differ in essentials. It is not just that at a time of noisy and merciless debates artists who apparently held diametrically opposed views showed themselves capable of appreciating and understanding one another. Many people do not know, for instance, that Isaac Brodsky thought highly of Filonov and considered it beneficial, indeed essential, that he teach at the Academy. In turn, Filonov praised Brodsky the artist and man. Today, however, the movements Brodsky and Filonov represented and the roles they played in Soviet art are regarded as antagonistic. Admittedly, the truth about the history of Soviet art is only just beginning to come out. Once the facts are told, the proper appraisals should follow ■ Like it or not, the names that were concealed from the public eye and made anathema by sinister labels have a special appeal. The sensation Malevich caused will long continue to reverberate. One of the fathers of the contemporary avant-garde whose art and artistic principles served as a manifesto for generations of abstractionists the world over, Malevich was to the end of his days an artist of Soviet Russia, concerned for its well-being and the dynamism of its art, and to many artists in this country he was a beloved teacher and mentor. A world devoid of volume, shadow, and at times, people is revealed in Malevich's works, but that world possesses a rigorous harmony. His quest was to find the perfect form of expression, free of petty representation and obsession with everyday life. However, in his best paintings there is invariably a threshold, and if the attentive viewer can cross it, he will certainly sense a longing for plastic perfection and the occasional attainment of it akin to great art, along with a sense of the grandeur and significance of everyday life. That is how Malevich perceived the world and that is how he strove to depict it: "To break free of nature's grasp and build a new world...." His art was a paradoxical and tragic combination of knotty theories and a tremendous sense of the new pulse of the times. It is no coincidence that his work of the twenties and thirties is a search for a synthesis of cosmic abstract harmony and the activities of daily life. People are depicted going about their ordinary business but they are invested with a highly significant, solemn impersonality. On occasion he deliberately did not paint faces, merely retaining symbols for people. But his world is meaningful and serious ■ Malevich eagerly sought contact with the present and future, even foreseeing the existence of space satellites (inevitably Suprematist). He dreamed of a new architecture, and his sketches of "planity" (homes of the future) now seem like a leap into the twenty-first century. He also turned his attention to applied arts, for he recognized that his experiments in abstraction needed to be concretized in objects. Moreover, the paintings he did at the end of his life take decided issue with the abstraction of his earlier works ■ Malevich had many pupils and even more followers. It is hard to say whose art was most strongly influenced by Malevich's "force fields": his students—Nikolai Suetin, Lev Yudin, Mikhail Matiushin, Ivan Puni, Alexandra Exter, Anna Leporskaia, Alexander Rodchenko, Natan Altman—his colleagues at the Institute of Artistic Culture (Inkhuk), or simply artists who had contact with him and took a great interest in his art though they were his opponents in many ways ■ This catalogue presents artists by groups. However, the reader will notice that this method of arrangement unfortunately does

<hr />

* It is, incidentally, worth noting that Frenz was never formally a member of the Jack of Diamonds itself or of those associations which took up its search (the Society of Moscow Artists, Society of Moscow Painters, et al.). Though he did not possess the individuality of a Petrov-Vodkin or a Filonov, Frenz brought together the best aspects of many of the movements of the time: Malevich's Suprematist flatness, the erudition of Post-Impressionism, and the Cubists' analytical understanding. However, in Frenz's work, as in the work of most of his contemporaries, all this merged into a lively painterly and plastic entity. Synthesis was very much a feature of the times.

not give sufficient consideration to prominent figures in the avant-garde who attracted a significant number of, particularly, young painters but who did not really belong to any fixed association. Among them was Malevich, who had pupils and like-minded colleagues. Filonov similarly had a small but fanatically devoted following. Vladimir Tatlin took an active part in exhibitions and organizational work and was generally in the thick of artistic life; nevertheless he did not belong to any group. Kandinsky's compositions, with their improvisational fervor, would presumably have more appeal than Malevich's rather cold "mathematical harmony." However, although Kandinsky held important posts as an administrator and teacher, his vision had little impact on the turbulent Soviet art world. In the twenties his art ceased to have any place in that world. In 1921 he and his country parted ways. Perhaps that is why, though his art had its roots primarily in Russia, it came to exhibit certain features that must be traced to other sources ■ The avant-garde usually attracts and shocks. While giving the brave experiments of its celebrated representatives their due, it must be said that beyond the classics of the post-Revolutionary days and the sensational canvases of Lef—a group of artists and writers committed to Constructivist principles—there is a whole stratum of art that, if not entirely unknown, has slipped from view, as it were, during the past forty to fifty years. One of the decisive reasons for this is the widespread belief that 1917 was a watershed in Russian art. This is only partly true. The social situation changed and so, accordingly, did the social and civil content of many artists' work, but naturally the best of what was integral to these artists went unaltered ■ While declaring their loyalty to the problem of form, the members of the Four Arts movement (1924—31)—Petrov-Vodkin, Martiros Sarian, Pavel Kuznetsov, Anna Ostroumova-Lebedeva, Vladimir Favorsky, Alexei Kravchenko, Vladimir Lebedev, Piotr Miturich, Nikolai Tyrsa, Alexei Karev, Nikolai Ulianov—were not just highly cultured (most of them had previously belonged to the *fin de siècle* World of Art or the Blue Rose) but also profoundly serious in their aesthetics and social sensitivity. The compositions of Kuznetsov, executed with such uneasy calm, reveal his meditation on everlasting change through harmony of color. Sarian finds a new pictorial, emotional energy. Watercolors and prints by Ostroumova-Lebedeva, Favorsky, and Kravchenko take up contemporary themes while carefully maintaining the highest technical standards, something by no means alien to the experiments of the new age ■ Petrov-Vodkin's name naturally brings to mind not just the other members of the Four Arts but his pupils or followers. Once again the problem arises: where is it appropriate to speak of a formal group as opposed to a sphere of influence or an innate affinity? Leonid Chupiatov, who is, sadly, still little known, is a good example of an artist who absorbed the plastic ideas of his teacher, Petrov-Vodkin, and was influenced by the complex trends of the time while retaining his individuality, fervid imagination, and heightened sense of the age ■ Soviet painting, drawing, and printmaking of the twenties and thirties had wide links outside the context of the fine arts—with literature, theater, and cinema. The kinship of certain phenomena in terms of both content and form is obvious. Filonov's visual structures and Andrei Platonov's prose have, in all likelihood, a common emotional and imaginative base. Similarly, the prose of the twenties often broke ground in much the same way as Suprematism did. This is exemplified by Victor Shklovsky, with his mathematically constructed phrases, carefully controlled emotion, and vigorous characterization. Matiushin's "romantic" experiments in color and Alexander Tyshler's fantastic compositions may conjure up distant but definite associations with the early prose of Isaac Babel. The traditions of the Jack of Diamonds have direct analogues in the earthy, picturesque prose of Alexei Tolstoi. Despite the lack of precise analogies, these comparisons do illustrate that visual and verbal arts were moving in the same direction ■ Until now little has been said about what are perhaps the decisive media: photography, photomontage, and cinema. Here the figure of Alexander Rodchenko stands out. His photocollages belong to the realm of Filonov's thought, and his sculptures have an affinity with Tatlin's dynamic Monument to the Third International, while some of his photographs are directly in line with the aesthetic of the Society of Easel Artists (OST) in terms of their emotional quality and choice of types. Rodchenko did his work at a time when the cinema was rapidly developing, Sergei Eisenstein was employing unprecedented montage devices, and amazing documentary footage was being shot by Dziga Vertov for his world famous *Cinema-Eye* newsreel (1924), whose basic principle was later borrowed by John Dos Passos. It was perhaps Vertov who best characterized the tangled searches of the twenties and thirties: "Many do not understand that the intricate path I am following will lead in the end to the greatest simplicity, to a simplicity as intricate as a smile or the pulse of a child" ■ Again, the point is not who borrowed from whom or even who was influenced by whom—that question will be addressed in articles and books to come. At present it is what all artists in this period had in common that is under consideration. In this context painters are no longer seen simply as members of individual movements or exemplars of programs, but as products of their time, people caught up in the swift and turbulent current of a shared creative quest ■ These shared artistic experiences are well illustrated by the Society of Easel Artists (OST), which occupies an extremely important place in the history of Soviet art of the twenties and thirties because of both its persistence in attempting to express the new reality in poetic terms and its role in the development of Soviet painting. OST is a typical example of the natural cooperation among very different artists who were neither avant-garde Marxists nor mere recorders of everyday life ■ The history of OST is like a distillation of fruitful and characteristic conflicts, the strivings and attainments of the age in miniature. The overwhelming majority of its members had studied at the Higher Art-Technical Studios, known as Vkhutemas, and withstood the test of being instructed by competing teachers with highly diverse interests: the artistic thought represented on the faculty ranged from Malevich to Piotr Konchalovsky, from Kandinsky to Abram Arkhipov. Though much has been said about the deficiencies of the Vkhutemas education, very high professional standards were maintained there. For several years Vkhutemas was run by Favorsky, whose prestige as an artist and teaching system imparted a respect for the "sacred craft" and an immunity to extremist positions and empty declarations. The classes given by Rodchenko and Lissitzky, with their cult of ascetic graphic and compositional experimentation, and the opportunity for exhaustive study of the Shchukin and Morozov collections of Post-Impressionist painting, provided a solid foundation for attaining creative individuality. The budding artist could familiarize himself with works by "the most modern masters" at the Museum of Artistic Culture, which might rightfully be called the birthplace of OST. "A fusion of contemporary subject matter and contemporary formal means—that was ... what OST set out to achieve. The objective was completely correct in principle and good results were to be expected from it," wrote the critic Yakov Tugendkhold. It should be added that OST's goals challenged both the documentary approach of the Association of Artists of Revolutionary Russia (AKhRR) and the more abstract experiments of the avant-garde ■ OST is most often associated with the name of Alexander Deineka, perhaps due to the magnitude of his talent and to his place in the new art of the post-Revolutionary period. His celebrated work *The Defense of Petrograd* (1927) became a classic of Soviet art. Perhaps because of their monumental size and lucidity, his works have merged with our image of the brave, upbeat motifs of the Soviet arts of the twenties and thirties. *Textile Workers* (1927) is another of Deineka's paintings that has become a standard. It combines a clear awareness of the advances documentary films were then making in the use of foreshortening, contrast, and perspective, the lyricism of lucid coloring, precise shapes faintly "echoing Suprematism," harmonious line, and, finally, a rare compositional exactness tinged slightly with a rational chill. Favorsky's lessons have unquestionably left their mark on the painting, but Deineka contributes his own interpretation of reality, a blend of a poetic and a documentary view; in the blue-gray world of "the ideal shop" the women workers preserve their individuality, intensity, and a character typical of the twenties, which becomes particularly recognizable with the passage of time ■ The world of human activity, the city, the factory, the bustling streets—that was what the members of OST were primarily interested in, though it did not exhaust their supply of themes and motifs. One of the leaders of the group, David Shterenberg, who had been active in organizing artistic life in Petrograd and Moscow in the first years after the Revolution, painted small, even intimate scenes that achieved a universality and solemn significance. Certain elements of his painting hark back to the work of ancient Russian masters: space is compressed, the human figures and objects are depicted with ascetic severity, the world is philosophical and solemn, and everything from human faces to the minutiae of daily life seems to be in a leisurely dialogue with eternity. For all his apparent remoteness from OST's main themes and objectives, Shterenberg was, in fact, very much at one with the group in his rational mastery, keen sense of the times, and finally, his belief in the intrinsic worth of a carefully constructed, meaningful painting ■ But naturally the program and value of OST is most tangible in works where the new realities and dynamics are recognized and embodied in a combination of poetic excitement and fully modern formal experimentation. Alexander Labas's work calls to mind the cinema and literature of the late twenties and early thirties, which evidenced more interest in the almost miraculous symbols of the new age than the fine arts did. Ilya Ehrenburg and many Western writers aestheticized the new world of objects, while film eagerly poeticized it. Thanks largely to OST, the aesthetic value of the machine age was revealed to us. There were artists who subordinated their plastic system to the power of the all-conquering machine. The members of OST, on the other hand, tried to reconcile urbanization and the traditional values of the visual world ■ OST was fairly diverse and tolerant (toward its own). This does not mean, however, that it was disinclined to get involved in debates or at least state its disagreement with other associations, particularly AKhRR. The rivalry of these two influential groups had its roots in their attitudes toward the past (the members of AKhRR regarded themselves as successors to the Peredvizhniki while OST's members objected to the insistence on representation) and in contemporary goals (AKhRR opposed the Leftists—largely those supporting Lef—while OST eagerly employed modern plastic principles). Unfortunately, both groups believed they had an exclusive claim to the truth, though the best works to come out of each did not pose any threat to the other and retained their originality ■ At the 1928 exhibition held to mark the tenth anniversary of the Revolution and of the Red Army's founding, the works displayed by the members of OST failed to win the top prizes or to get a sympathetic reception from the official critics though they included the paintings by Deineka discussed above. Even Tugendkhold caustically noted "a synthesis of the iconic with the American" in the OST works. Hailing the popularity of AKhRR's exhibitions and their attempts to achieve a "heroic realism," he commented that it was "completely natural that people today should want to see the present in the mirror of art" ■ Here we get a glimpse of the drama of the late twenties and early thirties, which, like many other aspects of that time. needs to be analyzed calmly and without bias. The public was indeed looking for a "mirror"; it was not prepared for complex experiments. Every artist has an interest in the public. That is why it is particularly important to understand which artists' work naturally met the expectations of a public that was still naïve but eager to experience beauty, and which artists recognized the way the wind was blowing and trimmed their sails to it. The question is hard to answer. Art historians sometimes underestimate how important the public's trust is to the artist (particularly in periods of fervent optimism), and the effect that trust has on him, sometimes determining the direction he takes ■ Though the best AKhRR works, in their pronounced traditionalism, differed from those to come out of OST, the two groups shared a keen understanding of the swiftly and fascinatingly changing times and types that peopled them. It was during his AKhRR period that Georgi Riazhsky produced *The Delegate* (1927) and *The Chairwoman* (1928). AKhRR's members included Sergei Gerasimov, Mitrofan Grekov, Sergei Maliutin, and Konstantin Yuon, whose works clearly exhibit pictorial freedom, artistry, and sharp perception. As a large influential, active organization, however, AKhRR had certain dictatorial tendencies. At times it was this fact, and not just the association's artistic principles, that prompted many artists and whole groups to declare their opposition to it ■ One of the largest associations outside Moscow, which had much in common with OST in both its history and its views, was the Leningrad Circle of Artists. Eventually the only large association in Leningrad, it really had no one to lock horns with except the ubiquitous AKhRR. Striving, like OST, to create modern works of great artistry, the members of the Circle refused to use painting "to illustrate certain episodes, to capture various moments of present-day life." They sought to achieve (to use their own expression) "a professional maximum." And acquaintance with their work certainly shows that in their search for modern, truly artistic, well-thought-out, and philosophically intelligent painting they had much in common with OST. Perhaps the Circle possessed a greater lyricism. At times the influence of Post-Impressionism was more perceptible, but even the faint reminders of Suprematism were few and far between ■ The best years for the Circle, as for OST, came at the end of the twenties. Between 1927 and 1930 large easel painting flourished. This was the time that saw the works by Deineka mentioned earlier, Petrov-Vodkin's *Death of the Commissar* (1928), Riazhsky's paintings of women, the widely acclaimed *Support Heavy Industry* (1927) by Yury Pimenov (OST), Labas's best works, and Filonov's stunningly dramatic *The Narva Gates* (1929) ■ Again and again we come back to AKhRR. Like the avant-garde, this artists' organization has always been regarded from either an unthinkingly apologetic or a sharply negative point of view. However, now the time has come to make a calm and unbiased reappraisal of the association's role. It must not be forgotten that at a time when the Soviet people were rapidly being introduced to culture, "the general public" was an important indicator of success, success which quite rightly helped the artist gain faith in himself. Today it is hard to imagine the thrill and naïveté with which the new audience discovered art, or the number of misconceptions and judgments we now correctly term "vulgar socialism" that were common among that same "general public" ■ AKhRR was an extremely large, mobile organization. In contrast to most associations (whose exhibitions were confined to a single city), AKhRR continued the Peredvizhniki's tradition of showing its work in many cities. These exhibitions attracted large crowds, so great was the need for an art that replicated life without embellishments. AKhRR's viability and success were predictable: they were the inevitable outcome of historical and cultural processes. Understandably, many associations, even those which opposed AKhRR's artistic program, were drawn to certain aspects of its members' work, not for commercial reasons (although there were, of course, such instances), but out of a desire to feel that they were needed by the public and the times. It is not surprising then that the major exhibitions held at the end of the twenties were sponsored by AKhRR. *Death of the Commissar* by Petrov-Vodkin, who belonged to Four Arts, was one of the works by members of other associations shown at the AKhRR 1928 exhibition ■ The existence of a specific Leningrad school is often disputed. However, the paintings produced by the members of the Circle with their cult of restrained, austere coloring, Nikolai Tyrsa's exquisite and daring paintings, the severe artistry of Nikolai Lapshin's landscapes, the brilliant school of drawing represented by Vladimir Lebedev, Vladimir Konashevich, and Georgi Vereisky, and the celebrated lithograph studio in Leningrad all make up a current that, while perceptibly independent, nevertheless did not go against the tide of Soviet art ■ Still, it must be reiterated that although a large number of paintings were neither "leftist" nor "conservative," their artistic merit established a climate in which more commonly known works appeared ■ The name Sinezubov probably does not evoke any specific associations today. This artist belonged to Makovets, a romantic, fervent group that combined the traditions of Symbolism and primitive painting and played a sizable role in the artistic life of Moscow during the brief years of its existence. Its members included Sergei Gerasimov, Nikolai Chernyshev, Alexander Shevchenko, and Vasily Chekrygin, a brilliantly gifted painter who died young. Nikolai Sinezubov, however, was not one with this group in spirit. His small paintings are eternal, not in the sense that they are great art, but because the motifs he chose and the way he treated them transcended time. These works are in the solid realist tradition and depict a world of objects that is recognizable and uncomplicated but nevertheless filled with a lively and anxious sense of the twentieth century. In the austerity of his cool, calm and slightly mournful colors he is reminiscent of the early Picasso. His *Mother* has absorbed the anxious rhythms of the School of Paris, and they seem to dissolve in a tender trust in life. There is none of the doleful repetitiveness those rhythms took on among the late Peredvizhniki or any flirtation with avant-garde devices: just an idea, love, and first-class painting. Many similar examples exist; we have to accustom ourselves to the idea that we know too little about the artists whose voices were drowned out by the rumblings of competing declarations ■ Few would suppose that the painter of *The Washerwomen* (1930), Ivan Ivanovsky, exhibited with OST. Among the overly familiar or "sensationally unknown" works, this one has attracted attention for the noble mastery of its execution. What sadness there is in the tired figures of the women, what anxious exactness in the use, so uncommon for the time, of the black line to contour the form (reminiscent of Daumier).

The work contains no pathetic element nor is it strikingly experimental, but it bespeaks pain in life and delight in it. The qualities of great art live in this canvas ■ Many, many more such examples could be cited, but at present it is more important to become oriented in this vast material in order to gain at least a rough idea of the relative strength of the various groups in the art world at the start of the thirties, on the eve of the decree of the Central Committee of the All-Union Communist Party of April 23, 1932, disbanding all literary and artistic groups ■ In addition to the larger, relatively longlived associations, there were quite a few others, at times small, which existed briefly before merging completely or in part with other organizations: the New Society of Painters known by its startling acronym, NOZh (which means "knife"). Its members (Samuil Adlivankin, Mikhail Perutsky, and others) strove to achieve an organic fusion of high technical standards, Primitivist traditions, and biting social irony. Their work had an analogue in the satirical prose of the twenties ■ The larger and more durable associations seemed to flow into one another. Thus, the Society of Moscow Artists (OMKh), which came into being as late as 1928, absorbed artists who had made their names in the Jack of Diamonds (Ilia Mashkov, Aristarkh Lentulov, Robert Falk, Alexander Drevin, Alexander Kuprin, Alexander Osmerkin, and others) along with former members of Makovets (Sergei Gerasimov, Arthur Fonvizin, Alexander Shevchenko) and several other associations. The Society proclaimed itself to be an association of artists of refined painterly culture in the tradition of the Jack of Diamonds and the Society of Moscow Painters, whose roots lay primarily in "Russian Cézannism." The Society of Moscow Artists maintained high professional standards: even a cursory examination of the play of colors in Falk's misty, flickering, at times almost aggressively tense paintings, of Mashkov's celebration of powerful color harmonies, of the splendor of Lentulov's now menacing, now lyrical blossoms, shows that the painterly elements still reigned supreme here. These artists perceived and represented the present less through subject than by treatment. Their art was not the "mirror" of events that attracted such crowds to the AKhRR exhibitions. It, like the work to come out of OST, remained a focus of ideas that were more purely artistic than social. Today, half a century later, it is clear that a straightforward depiction of events is not always evidence that they have been deeply and genuinely felt. The Society of Moscow Artists' experiments stand out for their drama, optimism gained through suffering, and their expression of the doubts of the age ■ At the start of the thirties the tone in the struggle between artistic ideas began to be set by the Russian Association of Proletarian Writers (RAPP) and the Russian Association of Proletarian Artists (RAPKh), which aggressively advanced "proletarian" art and declared war on those who asserted their own point of view. The situation became painfully tense, accusations flew back and forth, often contentious but at times even dramatic discussions took place, and not infrequently art took second place to the quarrels. AKhRR attained genuine popularity with the public and gained the upper hand over the other groups, often dictating its will and determining exhibition policy ■ Though in the early thirties there were many associations, as well as many artists who belonged to none, it is nevertheless possible to divide the art world into four basic camps ■ First, there was AKhRR together with a number of artists from other organizations, including OST and the Circle, who had a greater or lesser degree of affinity with the dominant group in terms of the character of their art. In its day this movement was popularly regarded as the most progressive, and all else "less realistic" was expected to coalesce with it ■ Second, there were the artists (OST, the Circle) who tried to depict the times and the events that marked them through painting that was remote from the socially involved Peredvizhniki tradition, and occasionally through fairly complex experiments in form ■ Third, there were the artists who concurred in the principles set forth by the Society of Moscow Artists and regarded the fine arts as a resonator rather than a reflection of the age. They, like many of the Four Arts members, were most vulnerable to attack from RAPKh ■ Finally, there were those who remained committed to the avant-garde. They had practically no contact with the other groups ■ The decree disbanding the independent literary and artistic organizations did not aim merely to bring them together under a single umbrella and to sanction AKhRR's realism to the exclusion of all other styles. It was also intended to confer orderliness and logic on Soviet art, particularly as the system of state commissions—which were to have such a decisive influence on the development of music, literature, the theater, cinema, and fine arts—was then becoming significant ■ But art in the mid-thirties was not an island unto itself. The authoritarianism of the political judgments then being made was paralleled of course in cultural life. A monopoly on the truth and an understanding of Socialist Realism increasingly became the prerogative of a narrow group of people, while AKhRR (though it no longer had a formal existence) acted as standard and judge ■ The approved style had not been foisted on the art world "from above," nor was it fundamentally at variance with the interests of artists or the public. To be sure, authoritarian administration was practiced in the arts but its adherents extended beyond those who stood to gain from it. We should not forget that the fine arts were not the hub of the cultural process. To a large extent the public's tastes were formed by films and the magnificent newsreels in particular (mention should also be made of the high level of photojournalism that created its "aesthetic of triumph" in the highly effective magazine *SSSR na stroike* (*U.S.S.R. in Construction*), published from 1930 on. For all its rich diversity, innovations in montage, and complex depictive methods, the cinema of the thirties continued to paint a recognizable portrait of the physical world and retained an enormous optimism. Moviegoers who saw *Chapaev* (1934), *We Are from the Kronstadt Fortress* (1936), and *The Baltic Deputy* (1937) believed that the theme of heroism and the affirmation of a serene present and future were indispensable to art. For many members of the arts the dramatic thirties were a time of great hopes and even accomplishments ■ Painting that attempted to solve profound, intricate problems, and to find the answers to the age-old philosophical questions inherent in the art form through harmony of space and color, inevitably lost its following, all the more as optimism about specific events was encouraged by those in authority in the art world. Increasingly one style was singled out as the only correct style to avoid disputes and doubts; exhibition policy became more and more rigid. Depictions of ceremonies, renowned leaders, labor achievements, and military victories consistently occupied center stage at exhibitions and were favorably received by the critics. The aesthetic of triumph was all, but it does not mean that every artist submitted under duress ■ Arkady Plastov's *Collective-Farm Celebration* (1937) is a completely sincere depiction of great plenty and unrestrained joy, a pictorial myth peopled by carefully chosen types and executed enthusiastically, boldly, and freely. To suspect the artist of servility or varnishing the truth would be unforgivable. It was a time of astounding labor achievements and genuine zeal. And the artist concentrated his knowledge and notions concerning all the very best that was happening in the country in a specific event so typical that his painting could lay claim to journalistic accuracy. In those days many people believed in miracles, but then miracles were indeed performed ■ It is another matter that the real dramas of the past and present, like artistic experimentation, were not reflected in the major exhibitions any more. The critics savaged those artists they labeled Formalists—now almost everyone who did not advocate realism as understood by AKhRR. But again, it would be unwise to oversimplify. Filonov continued to paint, without hope of showing the works we nevertheless see today. Malevich hesitatingly moved toward figurative painting; splendid landscapes were executed by former Circle members Lapshin and Tyrsa, though the all-embracing optimism did not pass them by. Deineka essentially built on the discoveries made in the OST period. Ermolaev produced strange, astounding, slightly *lubok*-like psychological portraits of sailors. Tatlin turned to lyrical still lifes and did a good deal of work for the theater. Tyshler continued to create his magical world. Today, decades later, the drama of the period can be seen as an inalterable fact to be neither excused nor vilified but rather understood. We must recognize that the twenties and thirties are an integral part of a larger whole, that the experimentation of those decades nevertheless sank into the groundwork, and that art has complex ties with the history of this country.

Mikhail Guerman

PLATES

THE WORLD OF ART
THE UNION OF YOUTH
MASS AND AGIT ART
VASILY KANDINSKY
KAZIMIR MALEVICH

UNOVIS
OBMOKHU
ZORVED
MAKOVETS
THE PATH OF PAINTING
PAVEL FILONOV
THE FILONOV SCHOOL
NOZh
AKhRR/AKhR
THE FOUR ARTS SOCIETY
OST
THE CIRCLE OF ARTISTS
THIRTEEN
OMKh
UNAFFILIATED ARTISTS

Organized in 1898, the World of Art (Mir Iskusstva) grew out of an informal student group whose members included Alexandre Benois, Sergei Diaghilev, Konstantin Somov, Dmitri Filosofov, Walter Nuvel, Léon Bakst, and Evgeny Lanceray. Soon after it was established, the World of Art sponsored an "Exhibition of Russian and Finnish Painters" at St. Petersburg's Stieglitz Museum. The same year the society began publishing a review, also named *The World of Art*, under Diaghilev's editorship. The first issues featured a series of articles by Diaghilev which served as the society's declaration: "Difficult Questions," "Our Current Decline," "Eternal Struggle," "Searching for Beauty," "Fundamental Artistic Appraisals" ■ The years 1898—1904 are considered the "classic" period in the World of Art's history. In that time six exhibitions were mounted: in 1899 (international), 1900 and 1901 (both in St. Petersburg), 1902 (St. Petersburg and Moscow), 1903 and 1906 (both in St. Petersburg). The last was an attempt by Diaghilev to prevent the split that was occurring in the World of Art group (in 1901 the Moscow artists had left the society and organized the "Exhibition of 36 Artists"; in 1903 the Union of Russian Artists was born in Moscow) ■ The year 1907 marked the start of Diaghilev's "Russian seasons" in Paris. Many works by the World of Art members were shown at these exhibitions ■ In 1904 the World of Art disbanded but was revived six years later after an article by Alexandre Benois criticizing the leading painters in the Union of Russian Artists appeared in the newspaper *Rech*. While there was a substantial influx of young artists (among them, Kuzma Petrov-Vodkin, Alexei Karev, Natan Altman, Vladimir Tatlin, Martiros Sarian), this fact also indicated a lack of unity in the World of Art, which in time became purely an exhibiting society. Shows were held in 1911 and 1912 (both in St. Petersburg and Moscow), 1913 (St. Petersburg, Moscow, and Kiev), 1915 (Petrograd and Moscow), 1915: "Exhibition of Drawings and Sketches by Evgeny Lanceray and Mstislav Dobuzhinsky"

Mstislav Dobuzhinsky
The Priazhka Embankment. 1922
Lithograph. 9 11/16×13 7/8"
(24.6×35.1 cm)

Yuri Annenkov
Portrait of the Photographer Sherling. 1918
Oil on canvas. 28 1/8×22 5/8" (71.5×57.5 cm)

Sergei Chekhonin
Book cover. 1924
Lithograph. 7 13/16×9 3/16" (19.8×23.3 cm)

Ю. Анненковъ · 1918 г.

3

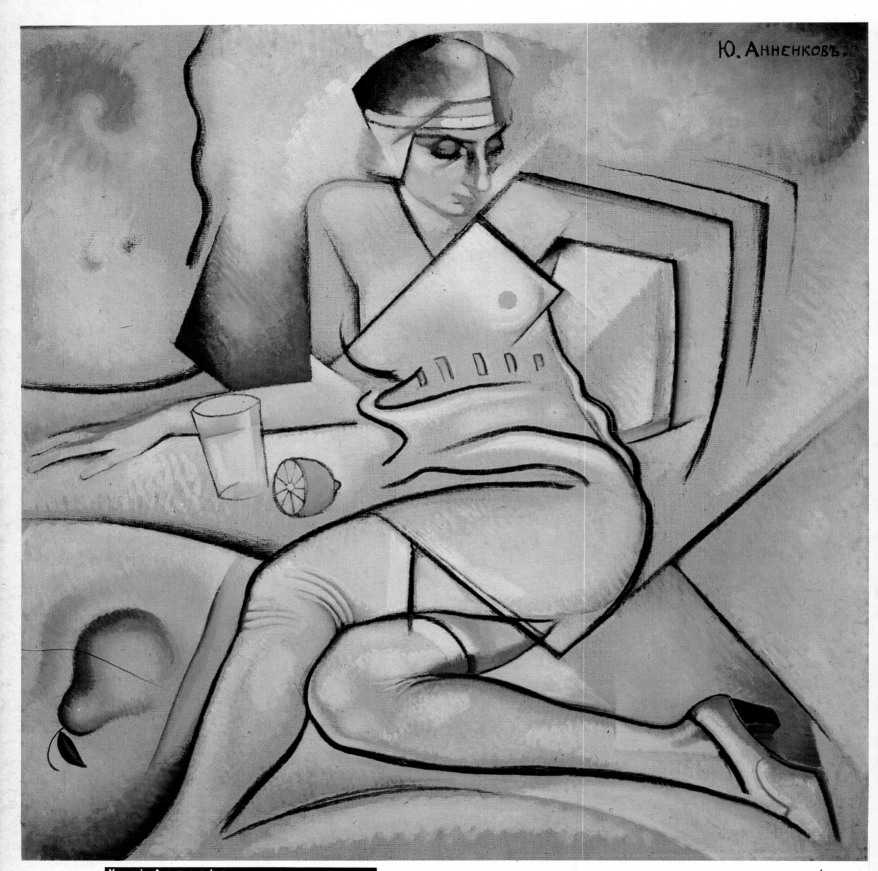

Ю. Анненковъ.

Yuri Annenkov

Portrait of Elena Annenkova. 1917
Oil on canvas. 33 1/8×32 1/4″ (84×82 cm)

Still Life in Black. 1922
Oil on canvas. 30 1/8×39 3/8″ (76.5×100 cm)

5

(Petrograd), 1916 (Petrograd), 1916: "Exhibition of Studies, Sketches, and Drawings" (Petrograd), 1917 (Petrograd and Moscow), 1918 (Petrograd), 1921 (Moscow), 1922: "Exhibition of Painting, Sculpture, and Architecture by the World of Art Group" (Moscow and Petrograd), 1924: "Exhibition of Works by the World of Art Members" (Leningrad). In addition, the World of Art was represented at the "First State Free Exhibition of Works of Art" (1919, Petrograd) and at the "Exhibition of Paintings by Petrograd Artists of Every Trend: 1918—23" (1923, Petrograd). The World of Art held its last exhibition in 1927 in Paris; works by fourteen artists were shown ■ In the 1920s many of the World of Art members joined Zhar-Tsvet (Heat-Color), a Moscow art group organized in 1924, or the Four Arts Society, established in Moscow and Leningrad in 1925.

6

In 1910 a new attempt was made to revive the World of Art exhibitions. . . .

But only the outward appearance was revived!. . . we no longer had among us an individual who wished to shoulder the responsibility of resolving questions that involved an unavoidable risk. On the other hand, not everyone joined us as readily as they had in the days when the World of Art was unquestionably the most progressive group there was. Finally, the idea central to the World of Art—a broad, all-encompassing idea based on a humanitarian utopianism, an idea typical of the social psychology of the late nineteenth century—now proved to be outdated. That was true in the years prior to the World War, during the war itself, and during the prolonged rebuilding that ensued. Reconciliation under the badge of beauty is no longer the motto; rather, it is bitter struggle. . . .

Maybe someday the original idea the World of Art was based on will rise again and take on new forms, but at present it marks a particular historical and cultural phase and is fundamentally anachronistic.

Alexandre Benois: *The Origin of the "World of Art" (Vozniknovenie "Mira iskusstva"),* Leningrad, 1928, p. 56

Boris Kustodiev
Summertime. 1918
Oil on canvas. $25^{3}/_{4} \times 72^{1}/_{4}$" (65.5×183.5 cm)

7

Boris Grigoriev
The Countryside. 1918
From the *Russia* cycle
Oil on canvas. $31^{3}/_{4} \times 38^{3}/_{8}$" (80.5×97.5 cm)

Sviatoslav Voinov

8

Little Houses
Pencil drawing. 8¹/₄×13¹/₂″ (20.8×34.5 cm)

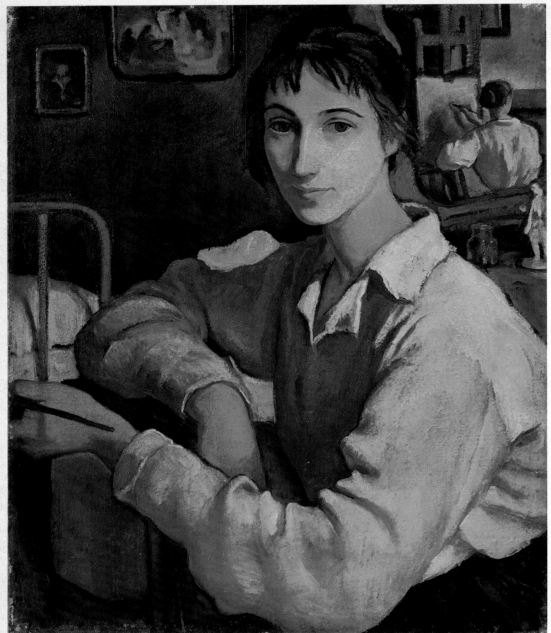

Zinaida Serebriakova
Self-Portrait. 1922
Oil on canvas. 27 1/8×22" (69×56 cm)

Participants in the group:

Yuri Annenkov
Léon Bakst
Vladimir Baranov-Rossiné
Alexandre Benois
Ivan Bilibin
Marc Chagall
Sergei Chekhonin
Vasily Chekrygin
Leonid Chupiatov
Mstislav Dobuzhinsky
Alexander Golovin
Boris Grigoriev
Alexei Karev
Sergei Konionkov
Konstantin Korovin
Elizaveta Kruglikova
Boris Kustodiev
Evgeny Lanceray
Mikhail Larionov
Aristarkh Lentulov
Isaac Levitan
El Lissitzky
Sergei Maliutin
Alexander Matveev
Nikolai Milioti
Vasily Milioti
Dmitri Mitrokhin
Anna Ostroumova-Lebedeva
Leonid Pasternak
Kuzma Petrov-Vodkin

10

Zinaida Serebriakova
House of Cards. 1919
Oil on canvas. 25 5/8×29 3/4" (65×75.5 cm)

Vasily Shukhaev
Still Life with Loaves of Bread: Normandy. 1923
Oil on canvas. 35³/₄×28⁷/₈″ (91×73.5 cm)

Nikolai Roerich
Nikolai Sapunov
Vasily Shukhaev
Konstantin Somov
Apollinarius Vasnetsov
Victor Vasnetsov
Mikhail Vrubel
Alexander Yakovlev
Georgi Yakulov

The Union of Youth

The Union of Youth (Soiuz molodezhi) was formed in 1910 and adopted its charter the same year. At the six independent exhibitions it organized, almost all the major representatives of the Russian avant-garde showed their work. The Union of Youth had over thirty members, but quite a few artists who did not belong took part in its exhibitions. Among the latter were the Moscow painters of the Donkey's Tail group ■ Exhibitions were held in 1910 (St. Petersburg and Riga), 1911 (St. Petersburg), December 4, 1911—January 10, 1912 (St. Petersburg), 1912 (Moscow; together with the Donkey's Tail), 1912 (St. Petersburg), and November 10, 1913—January 10, 1914 (St. Petersburg). A publication, also called *The Union of Youth,* appeared once in 1912 and twice in 1913 ■ In 1913 the Union of Youth merged with the literary section of the Futurist group Gilea (Hylaea), whose members included Vladimir Maiakovsky, Velimir Khlebnikov, Elena Guro, and Alexei Kruchenykh. The group put on theatricals, notably the opera *Victory over the Sun* (score by Mikhail Matiushin, libretto by Alexei Kruchenykh and Velimir Khlebnikov, costumes and sets by Kazimir Malevich). It was first produced at the Luna Park Theatre in St. Petersburg in December 1913 ■ The new literary members collaborated on the final issue of *The Union of Youth* in 1913, in which a manifesto by Olga Rozanova was published ■ The chairman of the society was Levkii Zheverzheev, a collector and patron of the arts ■ After its merger with Gilea and subsequent burst of activity, the Union of Youth broke up. In 1917 an attempt was made to revive it. The new Union of Youth participated in the "First State Free Exhibition of Works of Art" (1919, Petrograd). In 1921 some of the society's former members, led by Vladimir Tatlin, founded the Union of New Trends in Art, which had as its goal to bring together Petrograd's "leftists." It was joined by a number of young artists including Vladimir Lebedev and Nikolai Lapshin. In 1922 the society's first exhibition opened at the Museum of Artistic Culture (IKhK). The core of the Union of New Trends in Art participated in the "Exhibition of Paintings by Petrograd Artists of Every Trend: 1918—23."

13

Natan Altman

Cover design for the journal *Plamia.* 1918
Black chalk on cardboard. 14 3/4×10 5/8″ (37.6×27.1 cm)

Natan Altman

Petrocommune. 1921
Oil and enamel paints on canvas. 41×34 7/8″ (104×88.5 cm)

12

The Union of Youth

Yuri Annenkov
Lev Bruni
Varvara Bubnova
David Burliuk
Vladimir Burliuk
Valentin Bystrenin
Marc Chagall
Alexandra Exter
Pavel Filonov
Alexei Grishchenko
Ivan Kliun
Nadezhda Lermontova
Kazimir Malevich
Waldemars Matvejs
Piotr Miturich
Alexei Morgunov
Ivan Puni
Olga Rozanova
Alexander Shevchenko
Iosif Shkolnik
Eduard Spandikov
Vladimir Tatlin
Nikolai Tyrsa
Nadezhda Udaltsova
Sviatoslav Voinov
Levkii Zheverzheev

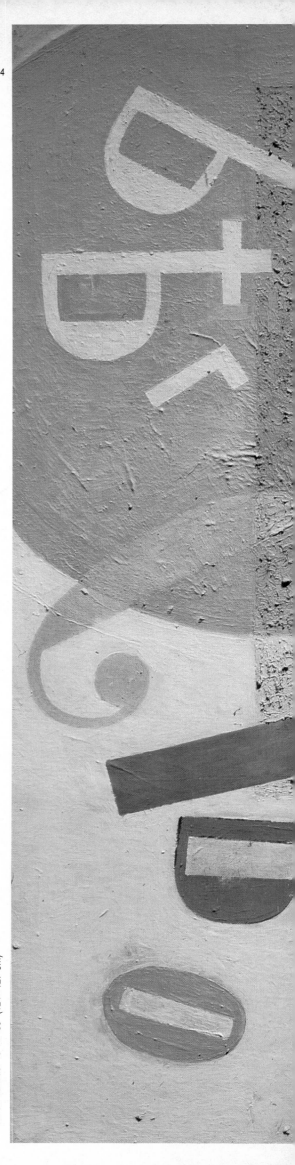

14

Ivan Puni
Still Life with Russian Characters. 1919
Oil on canvas. 48 7/8 × 50" (124 × 127 cm)

Natan Altman

Material Painting (Still Life with a White Jug). 1919
Oil and enamel paints on canvas. $33^{1}/_{4} \times 24^{3}/_{8}$" (84.5×62 cm)

Ivan Puni
Still Life with a Red Violin. 1919
Oil on canvas. 57 1/8×45 1/4″ (145×115 cm)

16

We propose to liberate painting from its subservience to ready-made forms of reality and to make it primarily a creative, not reproductive, art. The aesthetic value of an abstract picture lies in the completeness of its painterly content. The obtrusiveness of reality has hampered the artist and consequently common sense has triumphed over unfettered vision; but fainthearted vision has created unprincipled works of art—the mongrels of today's contradictory world views.

Olga Rozanova: *The Bases of the New Creation, 1913,* from the catalogue of the Tenth State Exhibition: *Nonobjective Creation and Suprematism,* Moscow, 1919, p. 24 (in Russian)

18

Alexandra Exter
Nonobjective Composition. 1917 or 1918
Oil on canvas. $34^{5}/_{8} \times 27^{1}/_{2}''$ (88×70 cm)

Alexandra Exter
City by Night. 1919?
Oil on canvas. $34^{5}/_{8} \times 28''$ (88×71 cm)

Vladimir Lebedev

Still Life with a Palette. 1919
Oil on canvas. 35×25 5/8″ (89×65 cm)

19

Natan Altman
Still Life: Color Volumes and Planes. 1918
Oil on canvas, gypsum powder. 23³/₈×17¹/₈″ (59.5×43.5 cm)

Nadezhda Udaltsova

Model. 1914
Oil on canvas. 41³/₄×28″ (106×71 cm)

Nikolai Lapshin

The River Moika. 1919?
Oil on canvas. 30×37 5/8″ (76×95.5 cm)

Victor Palmov

Composition with a Red Rider. 1920
Oil on canvas, gold leaf. 24 3/4×21″ (63×53.5 cm)

David Burliuk

Portrait of the Futurist Poet Vasily Kamensky. 1917
Oil on canvas. 41×41″ (104×104 cm)

Natan Altman

A Material Arrangement. 1920
Oil and enamel paints on canvas; glue, sawdust
and plaster. 32 5/8×25 3/4″ (83×65.5 cm)

25

Natalia Goncharova
Composition with Trees. Early 1920s
Watercolor and India ink. 10 3/4×11″ (27.5×28 cm)

Ivan Kliun
Suprematist Drawing Within a Circle
Watercolor and pencil. 10 7/8×8 5/8″ (27.7×21.8 cm)

27

Vladimir Tatlin
Stage design for Velimir Khlebnikov's *Zangezi*. 1923
Charcoal. 21³/₄×30″ (55.4×76.1 cm)

28

29

Vladimir Tatlin
Costume design for Richard Wagner's *The Flying Dutchman*. 1915—17
Charcoal. 28¹/₂×20″ (72.2×51 cm)

Nadezhda Udaltsova

Still Life. 1919
Oil on canvas. 36 1/4 × 42 1/8″ (92×108 cm)

Wladislaw Strzeminski

The Tools and Fruits of Production. 1920
Oil on canvas mounted on wood, metal details,
gypsum powder, and cork. 17 1/2×13″ (44.5×33 cm)

32

Kirill Zdanevich
Nude Seen from Behind. Late 1910s
India ink. 8⁵/₈×8¹/₈″ (22×20.5 cm)

33

Pavel Mansurov
Mirage. 1918
Ink drawing. 7¹/₄×5¹/₈″ (18.5×13.1 cm)

Natalia Goncharova

Still Life with Portrait and White Tablecloth. 1910s
Oil on canvas. 31 3/4×40 1/2″ (80.5×103 cm)

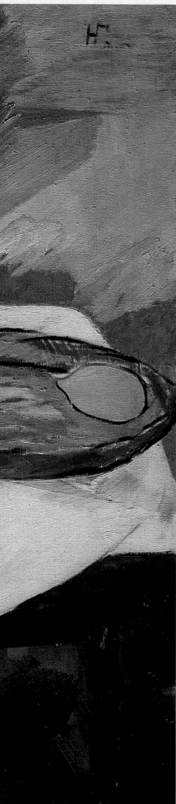

34

35

Ivan Puni

Still Life with Jug, Black Umbrella and Hatbox. 1910s
Oil on canvas. $29^3/_4 \times 25^1/_2''$ (75.5×64.7 cm)

36

Alexei Grishchenko

Portrait of a Woman. 1918
Oil on canvas. $23^3/_4 \times 20^1/_2''$ (60.5×52 cm)

Vladimir Kozlinsky

A Sailor. 1919
Linocut. 13 1/2×8 1/2″ (34.4×21.5 cm)

Vladimir Lebedev

Katka the Prostitute. 1918 (1916?)

Oil on canvas. 49⁵/₈×26″ (126×66 cm)

38

Artist unknown

A Worker
Sketch for a street decoration
Gouache and whitening on cardboard. 16³/₈×11¹³/₁₆″ (41.7×30 cm)

Nikolai Tyrsa

Worker with a Hammer. Sketch for a street decoration
India ink and watercolor. 11×5¹/₄″ (27.9×13.2 cm)

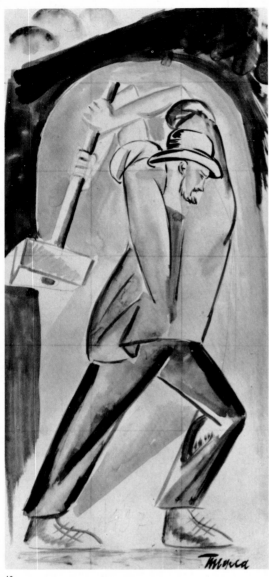

... Many city squares and streets are decked out, sometimes in great taste, which does credit to the artists and designers.
Posters.
Of course, I'm absolutely certain that there will be admonishments against posters.
After all, it's so easy to berate the Futurists. Essentially all that remains of Cubism and Futurism are their precision and power, along with their vivid colors, so vital to outdoor painting intended for an enormous audience numbering hundreds of thousands.
And the enthusiasm with which the young artists threw themselves into the job! Many worked on the huge canvases for fourteen to fifteen hours at a time without stopping once to stretch. And having drawn a giant peasant and a giant worker, they carefully traced out the letters: We won't give up Red Petrograd or All power to the Soviets.
Youth's strivings and the crowd's strivings have definitely merged here.

Anatoli Lunacharsky: *Notes on the Decorations for Petrograd on May 1, 1918*, in: *Soviet Decorative Art. Materials and Documents: 1917—32*, Moscow, 1984, p. 47 (in Russian)

Vladimir Kozlinsky

A Worker. Sketch for a street decoration
Watercolor, gouache, and India ink
10⁷/₈×10″ (27.5×25.5 cm)

41

I v a n   P u n i
Sketch for a street decoration. 1918—20
Watercolor, India ink, and whitening
24 3/8×18 5/8″ (62×47.4 cm)

Ksenia Boguslavskaia

Sketch for a street decoration. 1918—20
Watercolor, India ink, and whitening. 16³/₄×13¹/₈″ (42.7×33.4 cm)

1.

Вот, граждане, разительный пример—
Не первый честный офицер
Несет нам знанье и труды,
Вступая в красные ряды.

Vladimir Kozlinsky
Red Army Commander. 1920—21
Poster design
Gouache and watercolor. 43 1/4×28 1/2″ (109.7×72.3 cm)

Vladimir Lebedev

Worker at the Anvil. 1920—21
Collage on cardboard. 30³/₄×28″ (78.2×71.1 cm)

45

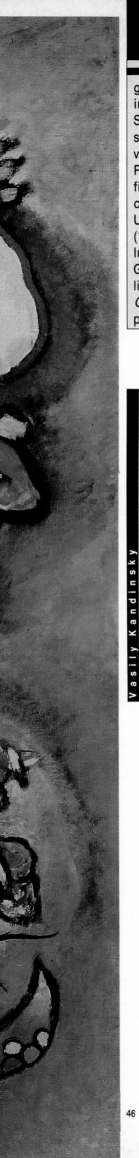

Vasily Kandinsky

Born Moscow, 1866; died Neuilly-sur-Seine, 1944 ■ Painter and graphic artist ■ One of the founders of Abstract art ■ 1897—98: studied in Munich under Anton Ažbé, and at the Academy of Arts under Franz von Stuck ■ 1903—7: traveled in Western Europe and Africa ■ Founded several art societies in Munich: the Phalanx (1901), the Neue Künstlervereinigung together with Alexei von Jawlensky (1909), and the Blaue Reiter group together with Franz Marc (1911) ■ 1910: contributed to the first Jack of Diamonds exhibition ■ 1911: executed his first Abstract compositions ■ 1914: returned to Russia, becoming professor at Moscow University (1920) and founding the Russian Academy of Artistic Sciences (1921) ■ Helped establish the Museum of Artistic Culture (1919) and the Institute of Artistic Culture (Inkhuk) (1920) ■ 1921: emigrated to Germany ■ 1922—33: taught at the Bauhaus ■ 1933: left for France and lived at Neuilly-sur-Seine, near Paris ■ His main theoretical work: *Über das Geistige in der Kunst* (*Concerning the Spiritual in Art*), written in 1910, published in Munich (1912), and translated into many languages.

Painting is art, and art is not, on the whole, the senseless creation of works that diffuse in a void, but a purposeful force; it is intended to serve the development and perfection of the human soul.... Painting is a language, whose forms, unique to it alone, speak to our soul of its daily bread; and in this case that daily bread can only be provided to the soul in this way and this way alone.

Vasily Kandinsky: *On the Spiritual in Art,* Bern, 1967, p. 140 (in German)

Vasily Kandinsky
Composition No. 218. 1919
Oil on canvas. 42 1/8×35 1/4″ (107×89.5 cm)

47

Vasily Kandinsky
An Amazon in the Mountains. 1917—18
Oil and bronze paints on stamped cardboard; gold leaf and glass. 12 1/4×9 3/4″ (31×24.7 cm)

Vasily Kandinsky
Dusky. 1918
Oil on canvas. 36 1/4×27 1/2″ (92×70 cm)

Vasily Kandinsky
Composition No. 223. 1919
Oil on canvas. 49 5/8×37 3/8″ (126×95 cm)

46

48

49

Kazimir Malevich

Born near Kiev, 1878; died Leningrad, 1935 ■ 1903: entered the Moscow School of Painting, Sculpture, and Architecture ■ C. 1910: went through phases of Neo-Impressionist and Fauve influence and was closely linked with Larionov and the Russian avant-garde movement ■ After 1912: one of the most influential Russian Cubists ■ 1913: designed decor for the Kruchenykh-Matiushin opera *Victory over the Sun* ■ Illustrated Futurist booklets ■ 1914: met the Italian Futurist F. T. Marinetti on the latter's arrival in Russia ■ 1915: exhibited his first Suprematist pictures at "The Last Futurist Exhibition of Pictures: 0.10" in Petrograd ■ 1911—17: contributed to the "Union of Youth," "Donkey's Tail," "Target," "Tramway V," "Jack of Diamonds," and other exhibitions ■ 1918: active on various levels with Narkompros ■ 1919—21: at the Vitebsk Art Institute, where he replaced Chagall as head; organized Unovis ■ 1920 to the late 1920s: worked on experimental Suprematist constructions — the so-called *arkhitektony* and *planity* ■ 1922—26: headed the Institute of Artistic Culture in Petrograd ■ 1927: visited Warsaw and Berlin with his one-man show ■ C. 1930: returned to a more representational kind of painting; continued teaching in Leningrad ■ His main theoretical works: *Ot kubizma i futurizma k suprematizmu. Novyi zhivopisnyi realizm* (*From Cubism and Futurism to Suprematism: The New Painterly Realism*) (Petrograd, December 1915), *Die gegenstandslose Welt* (München, 1927).

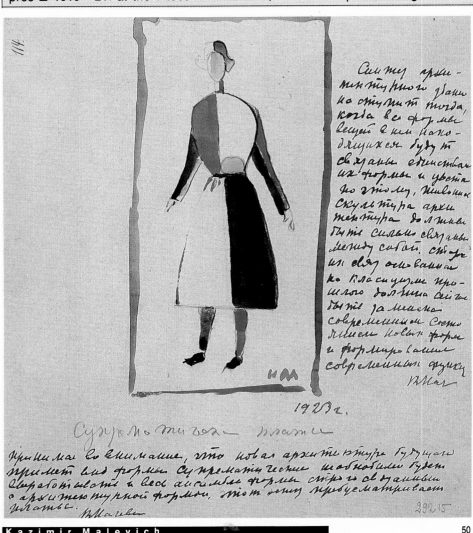

Kazimir Malevich

A Suprematist Dress. 1923
Watercolor and pencil. 7 1/2×6 11/16″ (19×17 cm)

50

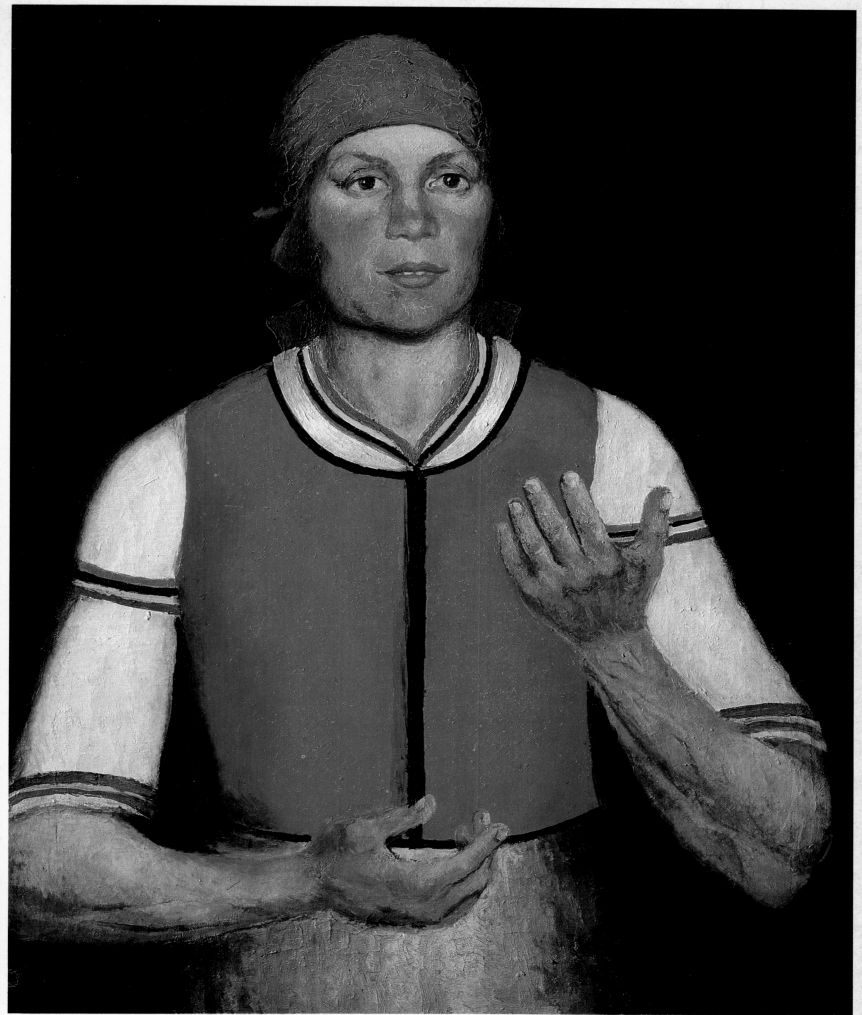

Kazimir Malevich
A Working Woman. 1933
Oil on canvas. 27 1/2×22 7/8″ (70×58 cm)

I have broken through the blue lampshade of color limitations and passed into the white beyond: follow me, comrade aviators, sail on into the depths —I have established the semaphores of Suprematism. I have conquered the line of the colored sky, I have plucked the colors, put them into the bag I have made, and tied it with a knot. Sail on! The white, wide-open depths, eternity, is before you.

Kazimir Malevich ▬▬▬▬▬▬▬**Suprematism**
From the catalogue of the Tenth State Exhibition: *Nonobjective Creation and Suprematism,* Moscow, 1919, p. 20 (in Russian)

Kazimir Malevich
Sportsmen: Suprematism in Sportsmen's Contours. 1928—32
Oil on canvas. 56×64 1/2″ (142×164 cm)

KMalevic

53

Kazimir Malevich
Landscape with Five Houses. 1928—32
Oil on canvas. 32³/₄×24¹/₂″ (83×62 cm)

Kazimir Malevich
Torso in a Yellow Shirt. 1928—32
Oil on canvas. 38³/₄×31″ (98.5×78.5 cm)

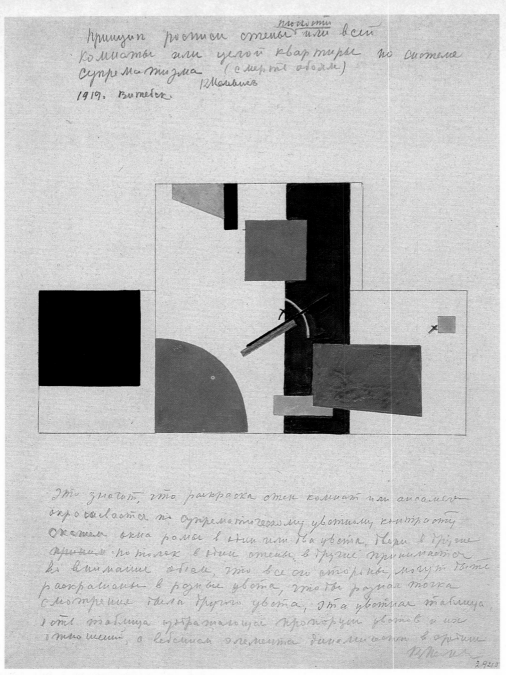

55

Death to Wallpaper: The Suprematist Principle of Painting Walls. 1919
Watercolor, gouache and India ink. 13 ³/₈ × 9 ³/₄″ (34 × 24.8 cm)

■ *Suprematism provides me with the keys to the still unperceived. My new painting does not pertain to the earth alone. The earth has been abandoned like a termite-ridden house. And man really does consciously seek space, he longs to "break loose from the earth."*

From a letter by Kazimir Malevich to Mikhail Matiushin, June 1916, in: *Annual of the Ms. Division of the Pushkin House, 1974,* Leningrad, 1976, p. 192 (in Russian)

56

Organized in late 1919, Unovis (Unia novogo iskusstva/Utverditeli novogo iskusstva—Union of the New Art/Affirmers of the New Art) was an association of Kazimir Malevich's students at the Vitebsk Art School. When Malevich moved to Petrograd in 1922, Unovis followed him and continued to exist within the framework of the Institute of Artistic Culture (IKhK), whose director was Malevich ■ Among the group's members were Vera Ermolaeva, El Lissitzky, Ilia Chashnik, Lev Yudin, and Evgenia Magaril. They adhered to the ideas and principles of Suprematism ■ In late 1921 and early 1922 the group's second exhibition was held in Moscow ■ Similar groups were formed in Smolensk, Orenburg, Saratov, Perm, and other cities.

Nikolai Suetin
Woman with a Saw. 1920s?
Oil on wooden panel. 21 5/8×13 1/8″ (55×33.3 cm)

57

Ilia Chashnik
Poster design
Black and red India ink. 38 5/8×26″ (98×66 cm)

58

Nikolai Suetin
Design for a mural. 1920
Colored India ink. 8×7 1/8″ (20.3×18.2 cm)

Ilia Chashnik
Cigarette case design
India ink and silver paint. 12 7/8×18 3/4″ (32.8×47.6 cm)

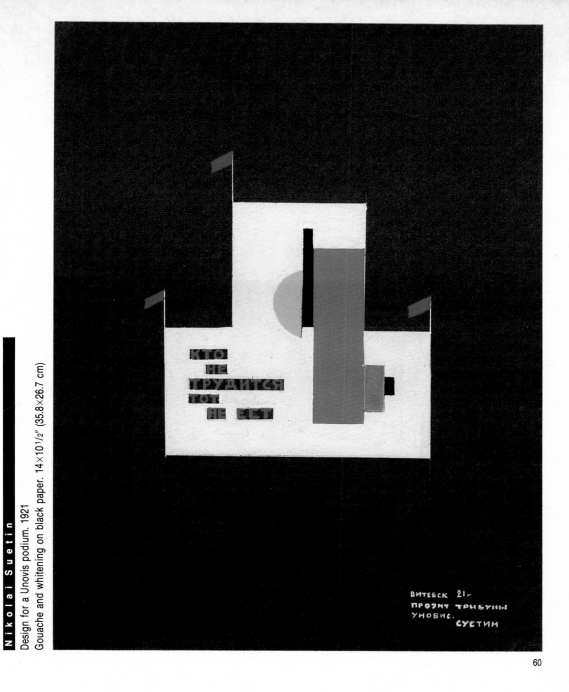

Nikolai Suetin
Design for a Unovis podium. 1921
Gouache and whitening on black paper. 14×10½" (35.8×26.7 cm)

60

61

Lev Yudin
Still Life with Orange Creamer and Bottle. 1930s
Oil on canvas. 18×13 1/4" (45.5×33.5 cm)

63

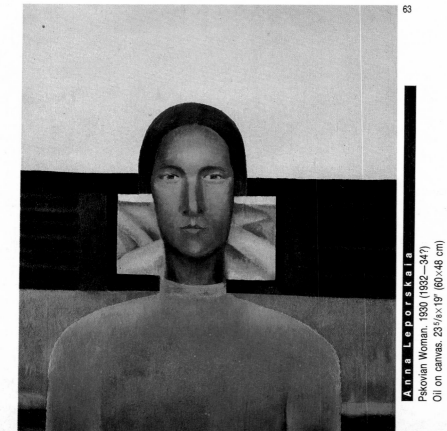

Anna Leporskaia
Pskovian Woman. 1930 (1932—34?)
Oil on canvas. 23 5/8×19" (60×48 cm)

El Lissitzky

Illustration for a Yiddish children's book. 1919
Color lithograph. 6 11/16 × 7 7/8″ (17 × 20 cm)

Obmokhu

Participants in the group:

Nikolai Denisovsky
Boris Ioganson
Vasily Komardenkov
Sergei Kostin
Aristarkh Lentulov
Konstantin Medunetsky
Leonid Naumov
Alexander Rodchenko
Georgi Stenberg
Vladimir Stenberg
Sergei Svetlov
Georgi Yakulov
Alexander Zamoshkin

Alexander Rodchenko
Nonobjective Composition. 1918
Oil on wooden panel. 20⁷/₈×8¹/₄″ (53×21 cm)

Obmokhu (Obshchestvo molodykh khudozhnikov) was organized in 1919 by students of Vkhutemas (Higher Art-Technical Studios). Most were pupils of Aristarkh Lentulov, Georgi Yakulov, and Alexander Rodchenko. The young members of the society combined easel painting and sculpture with applied art; they designed and produced stencils for postcards and badges, decorated streets and squares, worked on theater sets, constructed traveling libraries, and organized exhibitions to tour rural areas. As early as 1919 they had been provided with a studio with machines to cut and stamp metal and welding equipment ■ The group's first exhibition was held in 1919. The creators of the individual pieces were not identified; everything was presented to the public as the result of collective effort. The society subsequently organized three more exhibitions, one in 1920 and two in 1921. September 1921 saw the sensational "5×5=25" exhibition organized in Moscow under the auspices of the Institute of Artistic Culture (Inkhuk). The "five," each with five contributions, were Alexandra Exter, Liubov Popova, Alexander Rodchenko, Varvara Stepanova, and Alexander Vesnin. Works by members of the Society of Young Artists were also displayed at the "First Russian Art Exhibition" in Berlin (Van Diemen Gallery, 1922).

V a r v a r a   S t e p a n o v a

66

Sheet from the artist's album *VARST.* 1919?
Linocut on red paper. 6¹/₂×4¹/₂″ (16.7×11.5 cm)

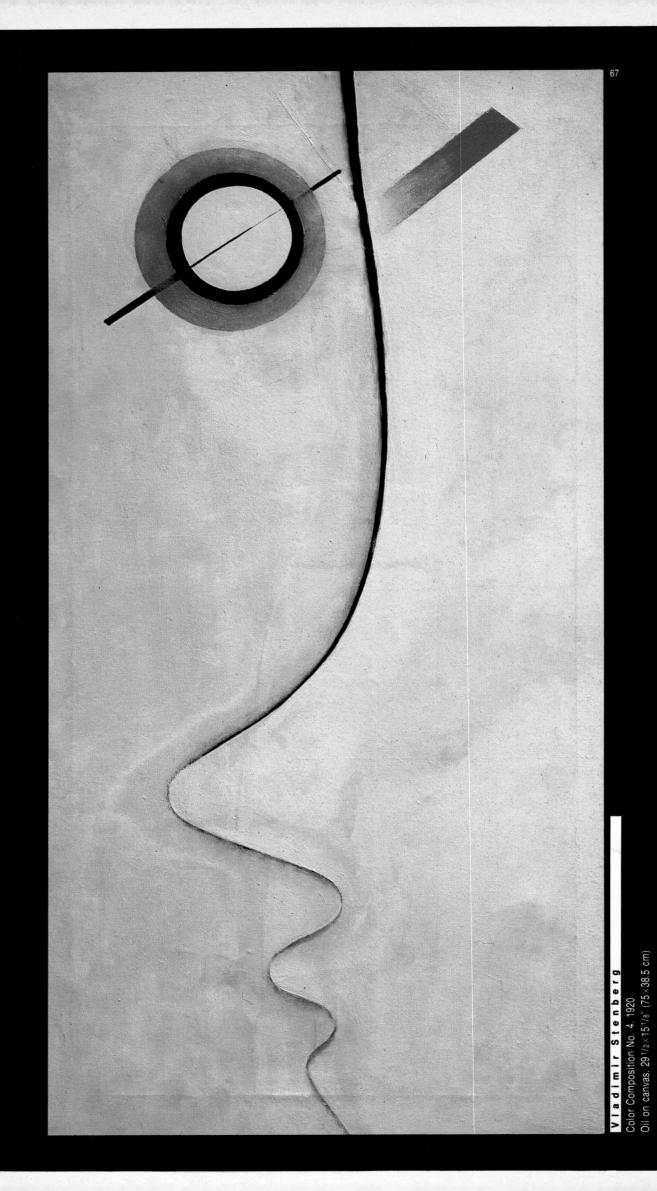

Vladimir Stenberg

Color Composition No. 4. 1920

Oil on canvas. 29 1/2 × 15 1/8″ (75 × 38.5 cm)

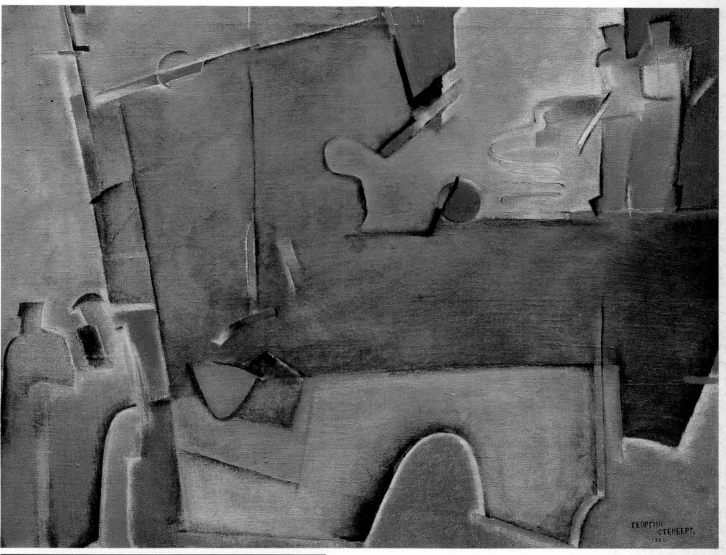

Georgi Stenberg

68

A Hoisting Crane. 1920
Oil on canvas. 27 15/16×35″ (71×89 cm)

Alexander Rodchenko
Black on Black. 1918
Oil on canvas. $33 1/8 \times 26 1/8''$ (84×66.5 cm)

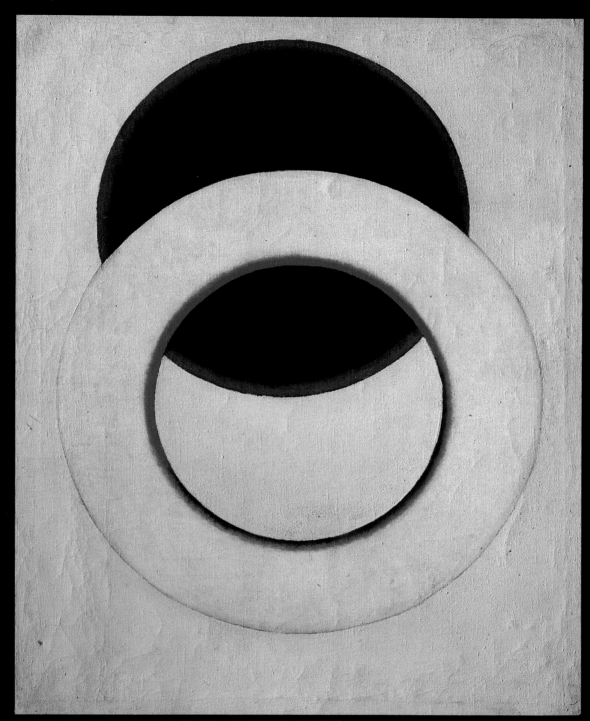

Alexander Rodchenko
White Circle. 1918
Oil on canvas. 35 1/8×28 1/8″ (89.2×71.5 cm)

As the funeral bells of color painting toll, the last "ism" [of painting] goes to its eternal rest, the last love and hope collapse, and I leave the house of dead truths. The moving force is invention (analysis), not synthesis. Painting is the body, creativity the spirit. My job is to create something new out of painting, so I examine what I do practically. Literature and philosophy are for the experts in those fields, but I am making new discoveries in painting. Christopher Columbus was neither a writer nor a philosopher; he merely discovered new lands.

Alexander Rodchenko: *Rodchenko's System, 1919,* from the catalogue of the Tenth State Exhibition: *Nonobjective Creation and Suprematism,* Moscow, 1919 (in Russian)

Zorved

Zorved [an abbreviation of the Russian *zor* (look) and *ved* (*vedenie*, knowledge)] was formed by pupils of Mikhail Matiushin in Petrograd in 1923. Its establishment coincided with the publication of an article by Matiushin entitled "Not Art but Life" ■ The Zorved members included painters and printmakers, among them Irina Valter, Olga Vaulina, Maria Ender. Evgenia Magaril and Nikolai Kostrov were also among Matiushin's pupils ■ The society studied the theory of color and the applications of that theory. The most significant work to result was a guidebook to color, *Zakonomernost izmeniaemosti tsvetovykh sochetanii* (*The Rules of the Variability of Color Combinations*, published in 1932 in an edition of 400). It was used extensively not only by individual artists but by organizations involved in major civic projects (restoration, construction).

72

71

Mikhail Matiushin
A Haystack, Lakhta. 1921
Watercolor. 20⁷/₈×16³/₈" (53×41.5 cm)

Mikhail Matiushin
Movement in Space. 1922?
Oil on canvas. 48 3/4×66 1/8″ (124×168 cm)

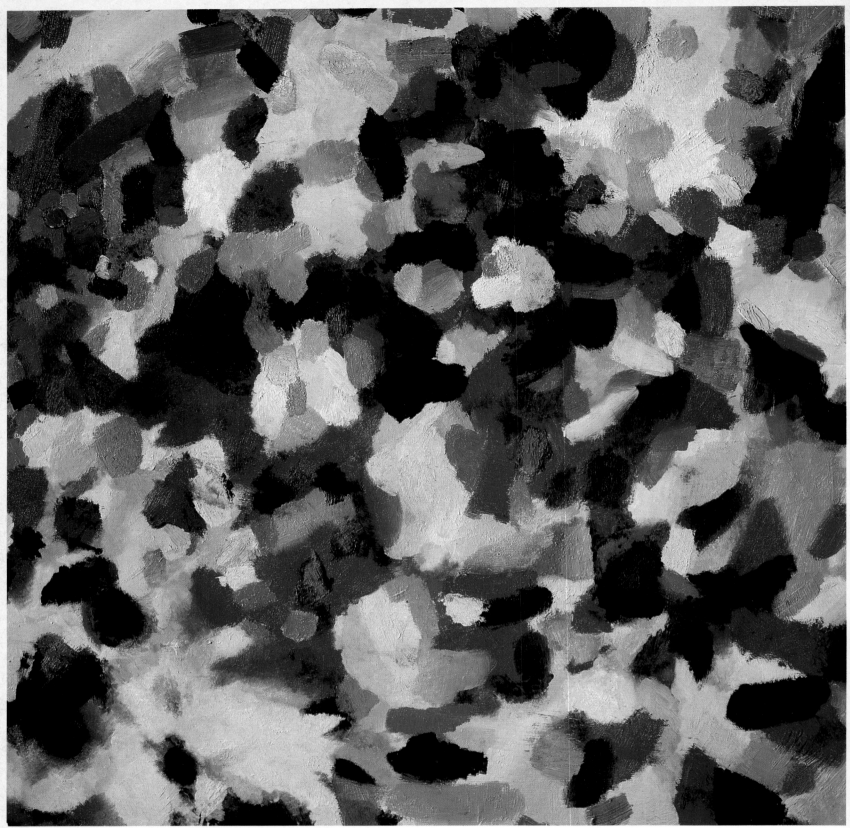

Maria Ender
Experiment in a New Spatial Measurement. 1920
Oil on canvas. 26 3/8×26 3/8″ (67×67 cm)

Mikhail Matiushin

One Landscape from Every Angle. Siverskaia. 1924
Watercolor. 8³/₄×13¹/₂″ (22.2×34.3 cm)

74

75

Evgenia Magaril

Portrait of a Boy. 1920s
Oil on cardboard. 12⁵/₈×10⁷/₁₆″ (32×26.5 cm)

Organized in 1921, the Makovets* society held its first show the following year: "Exhibition of Pictures by the 'Art-Life' [Makovets] Union of Artists and Poets." Subsequent exhibitions took place in Moscow in 1924, 1925 ("Exhibition of Drawings by Artists of the Makovets Group"), and in 1925—26 ■ The society also published a journal, which came out twice in 1922 and a third time in 1923. Among the contributors were Nikolai Aseev, Konstantin Bolshakov, Alexander Reshetov, Boris Pasternak, and Velimir Khlebnikov ■ Makovets had over twenty members. Some had formerly belonged to the Jack of Diamonds (Bubnovy valet), others were up-and-coming young artists ■ After the demise of Makovets some of its members formed an organization, The Path of Painting (1927—30), while others joined such associations as the Four Arts and the Society of Moscow Artists. The manifesto was issued in the journal *Makovets*.

The Makovets society was named after the hill on which Sergius of Radonezh built the Trinity-Sergius Monastery (now the Zagorsk Monastery and museum complex) in the fourteenth century, a gesture that expressed its members' emphasis on the spiritual quality of art.

76

Vladimir Favorsky
Cover design for the journal *Makovets*. 1923
Wood engraving. 7 1/8×6 7/8″ (18.2×17.5 cm)

Alexander Shevchenko

A Woman Ironing. 1920
Oil on canvas. 37×32 1/8″ (94×82.5 cm)

Nikolai Sinezubov

A Street, Early Spring. 1920
Oil on cardboard. 24×19 7/8″ (61×50.5 cm)

The Path of Painting

Formally organized in 1927 by Lev Zhegin, the group that was to become the Path of Painting (Put zhivopisi), former pupils of Zhegin, Nikolai Chernyshev, and Nikolai Rodionov, had coalesced the previous year. The group held two exhibitions in Moscow in 1927 and 1930, along with a third in Paris in 1928 ■ Among the members of the society were Tatiana Alexandrova, Piotr Babichev, Vasily Gubin, Lev Zhegin, Vera Pestel, Ivan Nikolaevtsev, and Vladimir Dmitriev.

Vera Pestel

Interior. Family at the Table. 1920—21
Oil on canvas. 34 1/4 × 33 7/8″ (87 × 86 cm)

Ekaterina Beliakova

80

Figures and a Horse Cart. Early 1920s
Watercolor, gouache, and India ink
10⁹/₁₆×14″ (26.8×34.5 cm)

81

Sergei Gerasimov

A Peasant. 1921
Lithograph. 8⁵/₁₆×7″ (21.1×17.8 cm)

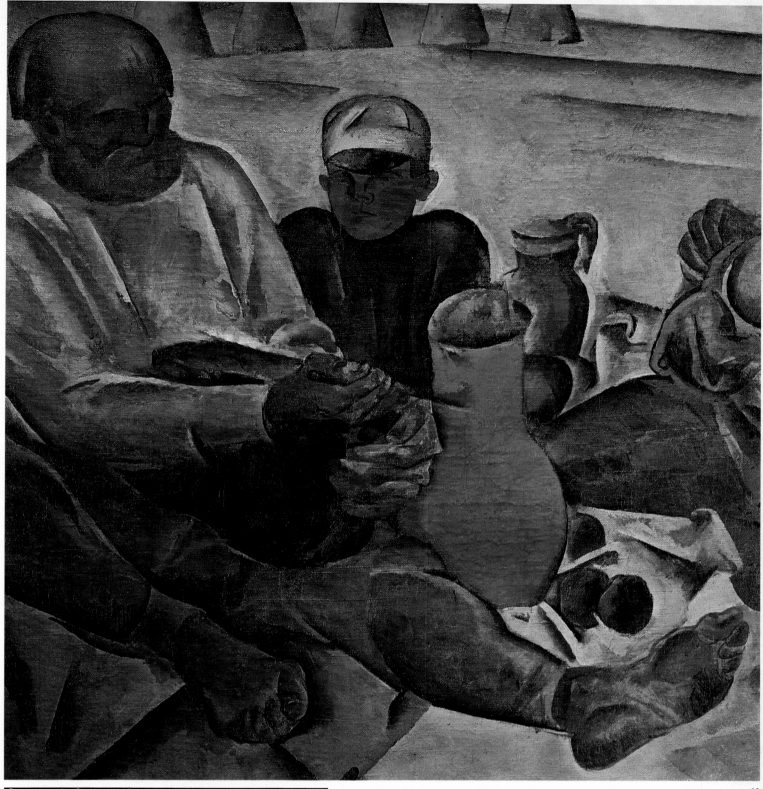

Sergei Gerasimov

Our Daily Bread. 1921
Oil on canvas. $32\,7/8 \times 32\,5/8''$ (83.5 × 83 cm)

82

Nikolai Sinezubov
Mother and Child. 1919
Oil on canvas. 25 1/4×18 1/8" (64×46 cm)

We presume that art can be revived only if the continuity with the artists of the past is strictly maintained and the sources of what is vital and eternal are resurrected without exception. . . .

We are not in contention with anyone, we are not the creators of the latest "ism."

The time of radiant creativity is coming. Unshakable values will be needed. Art, ever-changing, will be revived and requires only the simple wisdom of the inspired.

"Our Prologue," *Makovets* (Moscow), 1922, no. 1, p. 4 (in Russian)

Vasily Chekrygin
Composition. 1922
Charcoal and lead pencil. 9 1/8×12 5/8″ (23.2×32 cm)

85

Makovets

Participants in the group:

Tatiana Alexandrova
Piotr Babichev
Victor Bart
Piotr Bromirsky
Vasily Chekrygin
Nikolai Chernyshev
Vladimir Favorsky
Arthur Fonvizin
Sergei Gerasimov
Nikolai Grigoriev
Konstantin Istomin
Yuri Pavilionov
Vera Pestel
Nikolai Rodionov
Sergei Romanovich
Vadim Ryndin
Alexander Shevchenko
Nikolai Sinezubov
Sviatoslav Yastrzhemsky
Konstantin Zefirov
Lev Zhegin

Piotr Bromirsky
Design for a monument to the painter Surikov. 1919
Charcoal. 11 3/8×6 7/8″ (29×17.4 cm)

Nikolai Grigoriev

Turks. 1921
Lithograph. 8 13/16×7 1/2″ (22.4×19.1 cm)

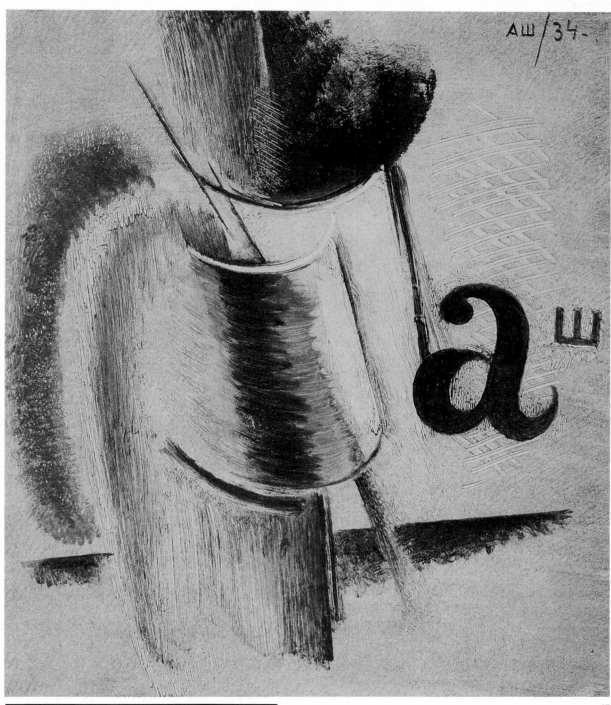

Alexander Shevchenko

87

Composition with the Artist's Initials. 1934
Color monotype. 9 1/2×8 1/16″ (24.2×20.5 cm)

Vladimir Favorsky 88

1919—1920—1921
From the *Revolutionary Years* series. 1928
Wood engraving. 5 1/2×9 7/16" (14×24 cm)

89

Tatiana Alexandrova
Portrait of a Young Girl. 1927
Oil on canvas. 40×28 1/8" (101.5×71.5 cm)

Vasily Chekrygin

Fate. 1922
Oil on canvas. 56³/₈×42¹/₄″ (143×107.5 cm)

90

Pavel Filonov

Born Moscow, 1883; died Leningrad, 1941 ■ 1897: moved to St. Petersburg ■ 1901—3: engaged in house painting, decorating, and restoration work ■ 1903—8: at the private studio of the academician Lev Dmitriev-Kavkazsky ■ 1908—10: attended the St. Petersburg Academy of

Arts ■ 1910 and thereafter: close to the Union of Youth, contributing to three of its exhibitions ■ 1912: traveled to Italy and France ■ 1913: with Iosif Shkolnik designed decor for Maiakovsky's production of *Vladimir Maiakovsky: A Tragedy* ■ 1914—15: illustrated Futurist booklets and published a neologistic poem with his own illustrations; propounded the first ideas of his theory of analytical art and his system called *Universal Flowering (Mirovoi rastsvet)* ■ 1916—18: military service ■ 1923: professor at the Petrograd Academy of Arts and associate of the Petrograd Institute of Artistic Culture; wrote the second draft of his theory of analytical art (published as *The Declaration of Universal Flowering)* ■ 1925: established the Collective of Masters of Analytical Art (Filonov School); the group held several exhibitions in the late 1920s and early 1930s ■ 1929—30: one-man show planned at the Russian Museum, Leningrad; the exhibition catalogue was printed in 1929 and issued in 1930, and although the preparations for the exhibition reached their final stage, ultimately it did not open ■ 1930s: continued to paint according to his theories ■ The artist willed all his work "to the State, so that it will form the basis of a museum of analytical art" ■ Filonov's main theoretical work: *The Ideology of Analytical Art (Ideologia analiticheskogo iskusstva),* was published in: *Pavel Filonov. Catalogue of Works in the Russian Museum,* Leningrad, 1930, pp. 41—52.

92

Pavel Filonov

The Painter: Self-Portrait. 1925
India ink and pencil. $4 \times 2^{15}/_{16}''$ (10.2×7.5 cm)

Pavel Filonov

War with Germany. 1915
Oil on canvas. $69^{1}/_{4} \times 61^{1}/_{2}''$ (176×156.3 cm)

Pavel Filonov

93

Houses. 1920s
Watercolor and pencil. 5³/₄×6¹/₂″ (14.6×16.5 cm)

Pavel Filonov

Untitled (Heads, Boots, and a Fish). 1920s
Ink and wash, watercolor. $8\,5/8 \times 9\,3/16''$ (22×23.3 cm)

Do not start with the general, with a construction—that is charlatanism—but rather with the particular, and work toward the general, in keeping with the formula "the general is the product of details developed to the highest degree."...

Send all the existing trends to hell and act as a research naturalist would (as in the exact sciences). . . .

Know that a work of art is any piece of work made with the maximum tension of analytical madeness.* That is the only professional criterion for evaluating it.

From a letter from Filonov to the young artist Vera Sholpo, June 1928, in: *Annual of the Ms. Division of the Pushkin House, 1977*, Leningrad, 1979, pp. 228, 229, 231 (in Russian)

* The Russian is *sdelannost*, a noun that Filonov formed from the verb *sdelat*—"to make/do."

Pavel Filonov
The Principle of Spring. 1928—29
Oil on canvas. 98 1/2 × 112 1/4" (250×285 cm)

Pavel Filonov
The Narva Gates. 1929
Oil on paper. 34 5/8 × 24 3/8″ (88 × 62 cm)

97

Pavel Filonov
A Collective Farmer. 1931
Oil on canvas. 27 1/8 × 20 7/8″ (69 × 53 cm)

Pavel Filonov

Red Apple. 1925
India ink, watercolor, and pencil
5⁷/₈×7″ (14.9×17.7 cm)

98

99

Pavel Filonov

Two Horses. 1923—24
Ink, watercolor, and pencil
3¹/₈×3³/₈″ (8×8.7 cm)

Pavel Filonov

Rowdies. 1925—26
Ink and pencil. 11³/₈×8⁵/₈″ (29×22 cm)

100

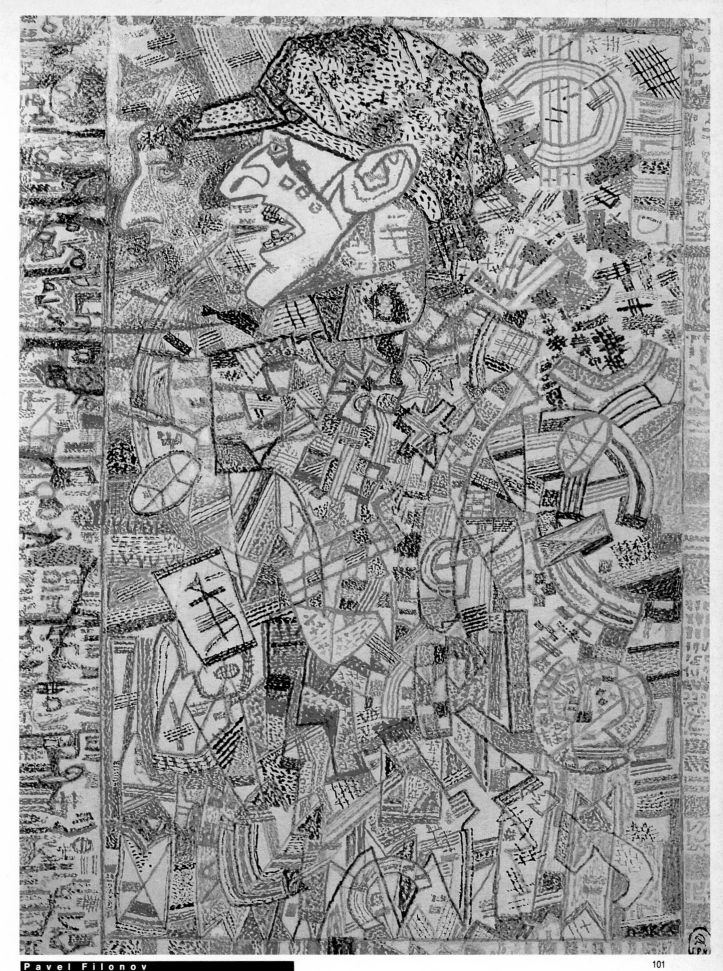

Pavel Filonov

A Burglar. 1926—28
Watercolor, ink, and pencil. 8^{7}/$_{8}$×6^{1}/$_{4}$″ (22.6×15.8 cm)

Pavel Filonov
Visages. 1940
Oil on paper. 25×22″ (63.5×56 cm)

Pavel Filonov
Portrait of the Singer Eudokiya Glebova,
the Artist's Sister. 1915
Oil on canvas. 38³/₈×30¹/₂″ (97.5×77.5 cm)

103

An association of Pavel Filonov's students, or the Collective of Masters of Analytical Art, it was established in 1925 and officially existed until 1932, although Filonov continued to hold classes in his studio until his death in the Leningrad blockade in 1941. The membership changed over the years; about seventy painters belonged at some time. The most popular artists to come out of the Filonov School were Tatiana Glebova, Alisa Poret, Yulia Arapova, Mikhail Tsybasov, Pavel Zaltsman, Evgeny Kibrik, Boris

Gurvich, Sofia Zaklikovskaia, Pavel Kondratiev, and Vsevolod Sulimo-Samuillo ■ The fundamental principles of analytical art as well as the methods to be used in applying and teaching the theory were laid out by Filonov in a letter to the young artist Vera Sholpo and in his unpublished manuscript *The Ideology of Analytical Art* ■ The Filonov School continued to exist during the early 1930s, contributing, among other activities, to an exhibition of painted panels and sculpture in 1927, the decor for a production of Gogol's *The Inspector General* performed the same year, and illustrations for the remarkable edition of the Finnish *Kalevala* (1933).

Pavel Kondratiev

Summer Crèche. 1930
Watercolor. 7 1/2×15 1/4″ (19×38.9 cm)

Andrei Sashin

Costume design for Gogol's *The Inspector General*. 1927
Watercolor and India ink. 20³/₄×12¹/₂″ (52.7×31.9 cm)

Vasily Kuptsov

"The Maxim Gorky." 1934
Oil on canvas. 43 1/4×47 5/8" (110×121 cm)

Nikolai Evgrafov

Carnival. 1938—40

107   Oil on canvas. 34 5/8×46 1/8″ (88×117 cm)

Sofia Zaklikovskaia

Old and New Life Styles. 1927
Oil on canvas. 47 5/8×111 1/4″ (121×282 cm)

Vsevolod Sulimo-Samuillo

Self-Portrait
Pencil and watercolor. 9 3/4×7″ (24.6×17.6 cm)

109

Vsevolod Sulimo-Samuillo
A Skating Rink
Ink. 8 1/2×6″ (21.8×15.1 cm)

Sofia Zaklikovskaia
Composition: In the Countryside. Early 1930s
India ink and pencil. 12 1/2×7 7/8″ (31.7×20 cm)

Pavel Kondratiev. 1928

In the Harbor. 1928
India ink and pencil. 9 1/4 × 6 3/4" (23.5 × 17.3 cm)

112

NOZh: The New Society of Painters

■ Formally organized in 1922, NOZh (Novoe obshchestvo zhivopis-tsev) had, in fact, come together the previous year. Many of its members were former pupils of Vladimir Tatlin, Kazimir Malevich, and Alexandra Exter. One exhibition was held in Moscow in 1922 featuring works by six artists: Samuil Adlivankin, Alexander Gluskin, Amshei Niurenberg, Mikhail Perutsky, Georgi Riazhsky, and Nikolai Popov. The exhibition catalogue contained the society's declaration, "Our Path." In 1924 the majority of its members went over to the Bytie (Objective Reality) society.

To fight for real art, for real painting.

To fight, in order to **find real art** and get a glimpse of its long awaited, joyful, and sanguine face **through suffering and struggle**, in defiance of the inventions of theoreticians and the predictions of "sage" professors (the hardest, thorniest path).

. . . such should be the art we have turned our gaze to. **Painting that is objective and realistic**.

We regard realism not as an impersonal and literal representation of life, but as its creative reappraisal, a profoundly personal attitude. We have not started out from an artistic or socio-economic theory; emotions have led us here. Artistic feeling lies at the core of our work. . . .

We are pioneering an unprecedented **revival** of Russian painting.

Our Path. Declaration, 1922, from the catalogue of the "First New Society of Painters Exhibition," Moscow, 1922 (in Russian)

113

Samuil Adlivankin

Tram B. 1922
Oil on plywood. 18 1/2 × 23 5/8″ (47 × 60 cm)

AKhRR/AKhR

AKhRR—Association of Artists of Revolutionary Russia. AKhR—Association of Artists of the Revolution.

The impetus to the founding of AKhRR was the forty-seventh exhibition of the Peredvizhniki (Society of Traveling Art Exhibitions), which opened in January 1922 in Moscow. The exhibition catalogue contained the Peredvizhniki declaration. At the time, this society attracted the interest of a number of young artists who decided to form their own association. Among the founders of what was to become AKhRR (Assotsiatsia khudozhnikov revoliutsionnoi Rossii) were Alexander Grigoriev, Pavel Radimov, Evgeny Katsman, Nikolai Kotov, Vasily Zhuravlev, Piotr Kiselis, Sergei Maliutin, Piotr Shukhmin, and Boris Yakovlev ■ The "Exhibition of Pictures by Realist Artists in Aid of the Starving," which opened May 1, 1922, in Moscow, is regarded as the first AKhRR show. It was quickly followed by two more in Moscow, in June and July: the "Exhibition of Studies, Sketches, Drawings, and Graphic Works from the Life of the Workers' and Peasants' Red Army" (with the AKhRR declaration in the catalogue), and the "Exhibition of Pictures, Studies, Sketches, Graphic Works, and Sculptures from the Life of Workers." Subsequent exhibitions were "The Red Army: 1918—23" (1923, Moscow), "The Lenin Room" (Moscow), "Revolution, Life and Labor" (Moscow; two exhibitions, one immediately following the other, had this title), "The Life of the Peoples of the U.S.S.R." (Moscow and a smaller show in Leningrad), the "Exhibition of Studies, Sketches, and Sculptures by Members of the Moscow AKhRR Organization" (held in honor of the tenth anniversary of the Revolution; the AKhRR declaration was published in the catalogue), and the "AKhRR Tenth Exhibition in Honor of the Red Army's Tenth Anniversary" (artists from other associations took part in this Moscow exhibition; a declaration by AKhRR was published in the catalogue). In 1928 the first exhibition of the Association of AKhRR Youth opened in Moscow. In the same year AKhRR held its First All-Union Convention, which approved a new declaration and changed the organization's name to AKhR (Assotsiatsia khudozhnikov revoliutsii); the last of AKhR's periodic exhibitions was the eleventh, "Art to the Masses" (Moscow). A wide-ranging show, it encompassed the decorative arts, typography, and textile design as well as painting, sculpture, and graphic work. The catalogue contained declarations by AKhR and the Society of Easel Painters. The Leningrad branch of AKhRR/AKhR had its own declaration, and the works of its members were shown in Leningrad in 1924 and 1928—29 ("Exhibition of Contemporary Leningrad Art Groups"), as well as at the regular exhibitions organized by the association. In 1928 AKhR arranged two traveling exhibitions for workers' clubs in Moscow; a German affiliation was established in Berlin. A special young artists' section called the Association of AKhR Youth (OMAKhR) put on two shows in 1929. AKhR works were also displayed in Cologne in 1929 at an art and industry exhibition. Subsequently the association members took part in various thematic exhibitions including "Paintings, Drawings, Photo- and Cinematography, Typography, and Sculpture on the Theme: The Life of Children in the Soviet Union" (1929—30), "The First Traveling Exhibition" (1929), "The Red Army in Soviet Art" (Moscow), and the "Exhibition of Works on Revolutionary and Soviet Themes" (1930) ■ The membership was not stable, fluctuating between eighty and three hundred. The organization's first elected officers were Pavel Radimov (chairman), Alexander Grigoriev (vice-chairman), and Evgeny Katsman (secretary). In 1923 the chairmanship passed to Grigoriev. The following year a publishing house was set up under Victor Perelman, and Alexei Volter was placed in charge of the Production Bureau. In 1925 the AKhR Information Office and the Central Bureau of AKhR affiliations were created. In 1929 the association established its own journal, *Art to the Masses (Iskusstvo v massy)* ■ In 1932, together with all other formal art and literary groups, AKhR was dissolved by the decree *On the Reconstruction of Literary and Artistic Organizations.*

Semion Pavlov
A Vasilievsky Island Landscape. 1923
Oil on canvas. 35³/₄×30³/₄" (91×78 cm)

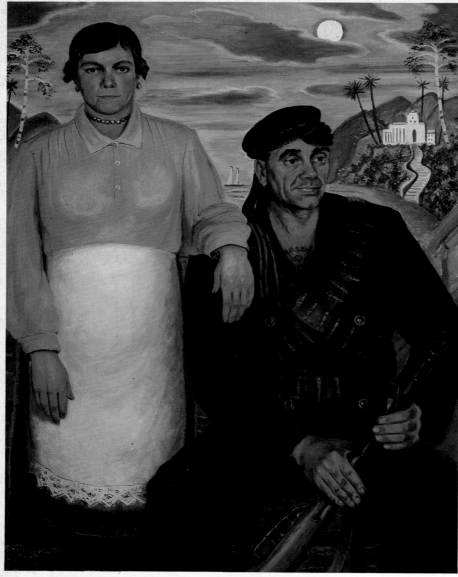

115

116

Fiodor Bogorodsky
At a Photographer's. 1932
Oil on canvas. 43 1/4×32 5/8″ (110×83 cm)

As artists of the Proletarian Revolution, we have the duty of

transforming the authentic revolutionary reality into realistic forms comprehensible to the broad masses of the workers and of participating actively in Socialist construction by our socioartistic work ■ The tasks of artistically designing everyday life (architecture, clubs, leisure, mass celebrations) and also of artistically finishing articles of mass consumption (duplicating designs, textiles, ceramics, the processing of wood, metal, etc.) confront the artists of the Proletarian Revolution as urgent, present-day tasks ■ The heroic class struggle, the great workdays of construction, should be the mainsprings of the content of our art. The subjects of our immediate work are not only the past and present of the struggle, but also the prospects created by the Proletarian Revolution. We consider this profound content—invested in an artistically perfect, realistic form organically engendered by it—a sign of truth in a contemporary work of visual art ■ In actively realizing the slogans of the cultural revolution on the visual-arts front, in organizing the feelings, thoughts, and will of the toiling masses by our artistic and social work, we set as our primary objective: to assist the proletariat in the realization of its class objectives ■ Art—to the masses.

AKhR Declaration, 1928, from the Bulletin of the AKhR Information
Office dedicated to the First All-Union Convention of AKhR, in: *Soviet Art of the
Last 15 Years,* ed. Ivan Matsa et al., Moscow—Leningrad, 1933, p. 356 (in Russian)

Nikolai Dormidontov

The Steelworks. 1932
Oil on canvas. 24 5/8×38 5/8″ (62.5×98 cm)

Ivan Vladimirov

The Photographer's Visit. 1921
Oil on canvas. 15 1/4×22" (39×56 cm)

118

Vasily Yakovlev

A Courtyard. 1918
Oil on canvas. 31 7/8×25 1/4" (81×64 cm)

Participants in the group:

Nikolai Andreev
Abram Arkhipov
Mikhail Avilov
Vasily Baksheev
Georgi Bibikov
Fiodor Bogorodsky
Isaac Brodsky
Vitold Bialynitsky-Birulia
Efim Cheptsov
Vladimir Domogatsky
Nikolai Dormidontov
Alexander Gerasimov
Ilia Gintsburg
Mitrofan Grekov
Alexander Grigoriev
Vladimir Grinberg
Boris Ioganson
Nikolai Ionin
Nikolai Kasatkin
Evgeny Katsman
Nikolai Kotov
Piotr Kotov
Boris Kustodiev
Sergei Luppov
Sergei Maliutin
Matvei Manizer
Sergei Merkurov
Vasily Meshkov
Fiodor Modorov
Semion Pavlov
Victor Perelman
Pavel Radimov
Georgi Riazhsky
Arkady Rylov
Sofia Riangina
Georgi Savitsky
Ivan Shadr
Piotr Shukhmin
Pavel Sokolov-Skalia
Vasily Svarog
Nikolai Terpsikhorov
Ivan Vladimirov
Boris Yakovlev
Vasily Yakovlev
Konstantin Yuon

Vasily Svarog   119

Self-Portrait. 1923
Oil on cardboard. 34 5/8×20 7/8″ (88×53 cm)

120

Nikolai Dormidontov

Street Musicians. 1931—34

Oil on canvas. 29⁷/₈×23⁵/₈" (76×60 cm)

Isaac Brodsky 121

Winter. 1917
Oil on cardboard. 15 3/8×23 5/8″ (39×60 cm)

The Four Arts Society

■ Founded in 1925, the group spanned generations and artistic interests, counting among its number former members of the Symbolist group Blue Rose and the World of Art at one extreme and "leftists" on another. It took its name from the fact that it included architects, painters, graphic artists, and sculptors—whose diverse arts it hoped to synthesize. Over the years more than seventy artists belonged to the society, with Konstantin Istomin as secretary and Pavel Kuznetsov as chairman. Exhibitions were held in 1925, 1926, and 1929 in Moscow, and in 1928 in Leningrad. In addition, the group was represented in 1929—30 at the exhibition "Paintings, Drawings, Photo- and Cinematography, Typography, and Sculpture on the Theme: The Life of Children in the Soviet Union," as well as two traveling exhibitions organized by IZO Narkompros (the Visual Arts Section of the People's Commissariat for Education). The Leningrad section of the society showed its works at the "Exhibition of Contemporary Leningrad Art Groups" in 1929. That year also saw the publication of the society's declaration.

Declaration, 1929

What the artist shows the public first and foremost is the artistic quality of his work. Only in this quality does the artist express his attitude toward the world around him. . . .

Within the conventions of the Russian tradition, we regard painterly realism to be the style most appropriate to the artistic culture of our time. We regard the French school as having the most value for us, as it is developing the basic qualities of painterly art most fully and comprehensively.

From the *Annual of Literature and Art,* Moscow, October 1929, pp. 551—552 (in Russian)

122

Kuzma Petrov-Vodkin
Still Life with a Herring. 1918
Oil on oilcloth. 22⁷/₈×34⁷/₈" (58×88.5 cm)

Kuzma Petrov-Vodkin

Death of the Commissar. 1928
Oil on canvas. 77 1/8×97 5/8″ (196×248 cm)

124

Kuzma Petrov-Vodkin
Nocturnal Fantasy (2:30 a.m.). 1921
Pencil and watercolor. 15¹/₈×12³/₈″ (38.4×31.5 cm)

Kuzma Petrov-Vodkin

Sketch for the panel *Stepan Razin.* 1918
Watercolor. 14¹/₂×25″ (36.8×63.5 cm)

125

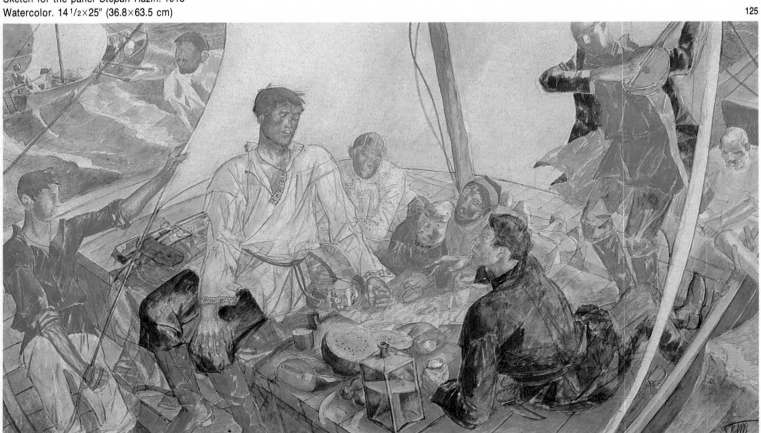

Kuzma Petrov-Vodkin

Portrait of the Poet Anna Akhmatova. 1922
Oil on canvas. 21 1/2×17 1/8″ (54.5×43.5 cm)

127

Vladimir Lebedev
Still Life with Red Guitar and Palette. 1930
Oil on canvas. 17 1/2×31 1/4″ (44.5×79.5 cm)

The Four Arts Society

Vladimir Lebedev
A Woman Ironing. 1925
Gouache, charcoal, and pencil on cardboard; collage.
26 3/4 × 17 1/2″ (68 × 44.5 cm)

128

129

Alexei Karev
A Townscape. The Andreevsky Market. 1927
Oil on canvas. 35×53 1/2″ (89×136 cm)

Konstantin Istomin
In the Artist's Studio. 1929
Oil on canvas. 48 7/8×34 3/8″ (124×88.5 cm)

Vladimir Bekhteev

Sketch for a poster for the Moscow Circus. 1921
Watercolor, pencil, gouache, and charcoal. 26×17⁷/₁₆″ (66×44.3 cm)

Alexei Kravchenko   132

Head of a Girl. 1925
Wood engraving. 10×7 1/16″ (25.3×17.9 cm)

Nikolai Kupreianov   133

Portrait of Anatoli Lunacharsky,
People's Commissar for Education
Wood engraving. 10 1/2×9 1/2″ (26.8×24 cm)

Vladimir Bekhteev

The Blast Furnace. 1930
Watercolor. 16 3/8×17″ (40.5×43.3 cm)

134

135

Elena Bebutova
Still Life with Glassware. 1923
Oil on canvas. 22 7/8×19 3/8″ (58×49 cm)

136

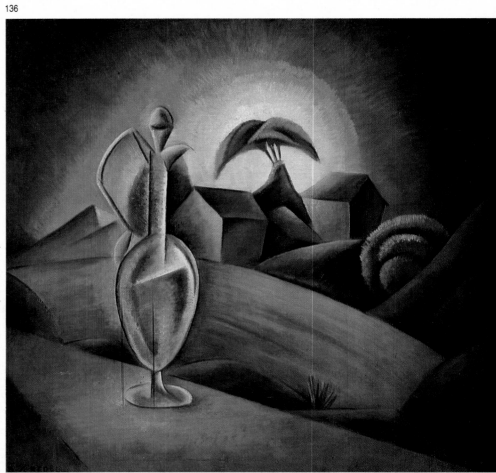

Elena Bebutova
A Lake (Switzerland). Not later than 1927
Oil on canvas. 17 1/2×20 7/8″ (44.5×53 cm)

Piotr Utkin
Flowers in a White Jug. 1923
Oil on canvas. 19³/₄×18″ (50×45.5 cm)

Nikolai Tyrsa
Portrait of the Artist's Daughter. 1929
Watercolor. 14³/₄×13¹/₂″ (37.5×34.2 cm)

139

Nikolai Tyrsa
Portrait of the Poet Anna Akhmatova. 1928
Lampblack. 14³/₈×8⁷/₈″ (36.5×22.7 cm)

Ivan Kliun

Still Life with Flowers and a Jug. 1929
Oil on canvas. 42 1/8×39″ (107×99 cm)

141

Nikolai Kupreianov
Still Life with an Oil Lamp. 1920
Wood engraving. 7×6 1/2″ (17.7×16.4 cm)

Rudolf Frenz

The Merry-Go-Round. 1922
Oil on plywood. 22×31 1/8″ (56×79 cm)

142

143

Georgi Vereisky

A Young Painter. 1928
Black chalk. 23 1/2×16 3/4″ (60×42.6 cm)

Zoia Matveeva-Mostova
Girl with a Bowl. 1923/5?
Oil on canvas. 33 7/8×26 3/4" (86×68 cm)

145

146

P a v e l   K u z n e t s o v

Sart Woman with a Lamb. 1923
Color lithograph. 12×8⁵/₈″ (30.4×22.6 cm)

P a v e l   K u z n e t s o v

Red Grapes. 1930—31
Oil on canvas. 38×27¹/₄″ (96.5×69 cm)

P a v e l   K u z n e t s o v

Portrait. 1923
Lithograph. 11¹/₄×9″ (28.5×22.7 cm)

Pavel Kuznetsov

Tobacco Workers. 1925—26
Tempera on canvas. 38 1/4×41 3/4" (97×106 cm)

150

Pavel Kuznetsov

Portrait of Alexander Matveev. 1928
Oil on canvas. 38¼×25″ (97×63.5 cm)

Martiros Sarian

A Bright Landscape. 1924
Oil on canvas. $55^{1}/_{8} \times 41''$ (140×104 cm)

Martiros Sarian

Yerevan. 1924
Oil on canvas. 27 1/8×26 3/4″ (69×68 cm)

Vladimir Lebedev
Young Girl in a Jersey, Holding a Bouquet. 1933
Watercolor, gouache, and whitening
25 1/4×17 1/2″ (64.2×44.6 cm)

154

Vladimir Lebedev

Nude with a Guitar. 1930
Oil on canvas. 31 1/2×25 1/2″ (80×65 cm)

Established formally in 1925, OST (Obshchestvo khudozhnikov-stankovistov) arose as an informal group in late 1924, just after the "First Discussional Exhibition of Associations of Active Revolutionary Art," in which the eventual OST members participated as the Projectionists (Sergei Luchishkin, Solomon Nikritin, Kliment Redko, Nikolai Triaskin, Alexander Tyshler), the Concretists (Piotr Williams, Konstantin Vialov, Vladimir Liushin, Yuri Merkulov), and the Association of Three (Andrei Goncharov, Alexander Deineka, Yuri Pimenov). Most of the OST members were former Vkhutemas students who had studied under David Shterenberg and Vladimir Favorsky. The founding members were Yuri Annenkov, Shterenberg (chairman), Lazar Vainer, Vladimir Vasiliev, Williams, Vialov, Deineka, Nikolai Denisovsky, Sergei Kostin, Alexander Labas, Merkulov, and Pimenov. The elected officers for 1925—26 were Vainer, Williams, Denisovsky, and Pimenov. In 1927 Nison Shifrin replaced Denisovsky ■ OST ultimately had over thirty members and organized four exhibitions in Moscow from 1925 to 1928. In addition, the group contributed to two traveling exhibitions (1929 and 1930), to the exhibition "Paintings, Drawings, Photo- and Cinematography, Typography, and Sculpture on the Theme: The Life of Children in the Soviet Union" (1929, Moscow), and to a number of other thematic exhibitions. In 1931 almost half the membership of OST left to form a new group, the Art Brigade (Izobrigada), while the others joined October—Association of Artistic Labor. Subsequently the elected officers of OST were Shterenberg (chairman), Alexander Labas, Tyshler, and Alexander Kozlov. The OST Platform was registered in 1929.

Platform, 1929

On the basis of the following program, the Society of Easel Artists aims to unite artists who are doing practical work in the field of the visual arts: ...

Bearing in mind that only high-quality art can envisage such tasks, we consider it essential, given the current state of art, to proclaim the basic lines that our work in the visual arts must follow. These lines are:

a/ The rejection of abstraction and the Peredvizhniki approach as regards subject matter;

b/ The rejection of sketchiness as a phenomenon of latent dilettantism;

c/ The rejection of pseudo Cézannism as a disintegrating force in the discipline of form, drawing, color;

d/ Revolutionary contemporaneity and clarity of subject matter;

e/ Aspiration to absolute technical mastery in the field of thematic easel painting, drawing, and sculpture as the formal attainments of the last few years are developed further;

f/ Aspiration to make a picture a finished article;

g/ Orientation toward young artists.

From *Soviet Art of the Last 15 Years,* ed. Ivan Matsa et al., Moscow—Leningrad, 1933, p. 575 (in Russian)

156

Alexander Deineka
Textile Workers. 1927
Oil on canvas. 67 1/4 × 76 3/4" (171 × 195 cm)

David Shterenberg

157

Table with a Roll. 1919
Oil on canvas. 35×21″ (89×53.5 cm)

Sergei Luchishkin

Skiers (Amid Trees). 1926
Oil on canvas. 41 3/4×37 3/8″ (106×95 cm)

Participants in the group:

Yuri Annenkov
Alexander Barshch
Georgi Berendgof
Alexander Deineka
Nikolai Denisovsky
Mecheslav Dobrokovsky
Victor Ellonen
Andrei Goncharov
Ivan Ivanovsky
Ivan Kliun
Alexander Kozlov
Ivan Kudriashov
Nikolai Kupreianov
Alexander Labas
Sergei Luchishkin
Vladimir Liushin
Elena Melnikova
Yuri Merkulov
Yuri Pimenov
Nison Shifrin
David Shterenberg
Nikolai Triaskin
Lazar Vainer
Vladimir Vasiliev
Konstantin Vialov
Piotr Williams

Andrei Goncharov
Portrait of Sen Katayama. 1927
Oil on canvas. 56×31 3/4″ (142.5×80.5 cm)

David Shterenberg

Portrait of Nadezhda Shterenberg, the Artist's Wife. 1925
Oil on canvas. 55 7/8 × 34 5/8″ (142 × 88 cm)

David Shterenberg

Still Life with Oil Lamp and Herring. 1920
Oil on plywood. 35 1/4×24 5/8″ (89.5×62.5 cm)

Kliment Redko

Midnight Sun over the Sea. 1925
Oil on canvas. 66 9/10×31 3/4″ (170×80.5 cm)

162

163

Ivan Ivanovsky

The Washerwomen. Late 1920s
Oil on canvas. 31 1/4×26 1/4″ (79.5×66.5 cm)

Yuri Pimenov

Disabled Veterans. 1926
Oil on canvas. 104 1/2×70″ (265.6×177.7 cm)

164

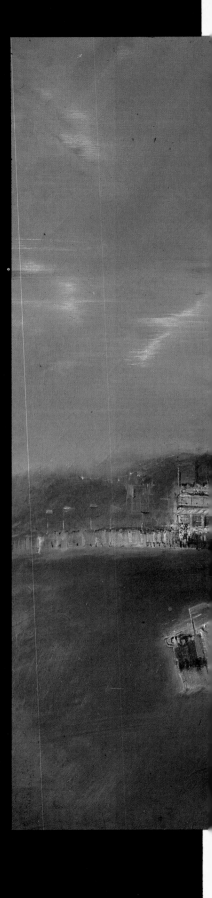

Alexander Labas

The Airship. 1931
Oil on canvas. 61 1/4×78 1/4″ (155.5×199 cm)

Alexander Labas

Airship and Children from the Orphanage. 1930
Oil on canvas. 63×31 1/2″ (160×80 cm)

Solomon Nikritin

Composition. 1930
Oil on canvas. 26³/₄×22³/₄" (68×58 cm)

167

Alexander Kozlov

Moscow's Central Recreation Park. 1933
Oil on canvas. 35 1/2×39 1/8″ (90×99.5 cm)

168

169

Alexander Tyshler

Portrait of a Woman. 1934
Oil on canvas. 25 3/4×21 3/4″ (65.5×55.5 cm)

Alexandèr Tyshler

Young Red Army Men Reading a Newspaper. 1936
Oil on canvas. 22×25 1/2″ (56×65 cm)

171

Piotr Williams

Portrait of Konstantin Stanislavsky. 1933
Oil on canvas. 51 1/4×69 1/2″ (130×175.5 cm)

Alexander Labas

The Train Is Coming. 1929
Oil on canvas. 38 1/4×29 3/8″ (97×74.5 cm)

Organized in 1926, the group had come together the previous year when its first members—pupils of Alexei Karev, Kuzma Petrov-Vodkin, and Alexander Matveev—graduated from Vkhutein (Higher Art-Technical Institute) in Leningrad. It soon attracted other young Leningrad artists. During its brief existence the Circle of Artists acquired over forty members. Viacheslav Pakulin was its chairman ■ The Circle of Artists held four exhibitions, in 1927, 1928, 1929 in Leningrad, and in 1930 in Kiev. They displayed their works at the Education Center (1927) and at the Red Triangle Factory Club (1929), and contributed to the "Exhibition of Contemporary Leningrad Art Groups" (1929, Moscow). The society's declaration was published in the catalogue of its second exhibition; a revised version appeared in the journal *Art to the Masses* in 1930. In 1929 a number of artists left the Circle. Some joined AKhR, while others went over to October.

Alexander Vedernikov

173

Nude on a Sofa. 1935
Watercolor and India ink
16 1/4 × 11 1/2″ (41.5 × 29.5 cm)

Viacheslav Pakulin

Sailors (In a Tavern). 1929?
Oil on canvas. 35×22⁷/₈" (89×58 cm)

Viacheslav Pakulin

A Woman Reaping. 1926—27
Oil on canvas. 59 3/4×73 5/8″ (152×187 cm)

The Circle of Artists
Declaration, 1926

This Society aspires to:

unite and coordinate the works of all artists (painters and sculptors) who wish to work on
developing professional qualities and tasks
as against dilettantism and hack work. . . .

This Society aspires:

. . . on the basis of collective leadership
as against individuals and subjectivism—
through the picture of a concrete painterly expression (representation), one of the means of
organizing life (the same is true of sculpture)
as against philistinism and the prevailing fascination with literary effects and styles of the
past—
to create (in painting and sculpture) a style of the era
as against petty trendiness, "isms," etc.

From *Art to the Masses* (Leningrad), 1930, no. 3 (in Russian)

Viacheslav Pakulin

Woman Carrying Water. 1928?
Oil on canvas. 73 5/8×59 5/8" (187×151.5 cm)

176

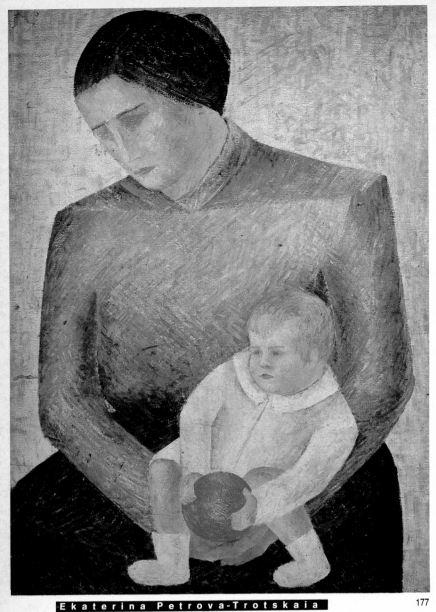

Ekaterina Petrova-Trotskaia

177

Child Holding an Orange. 1928?
Oil on canvas. 55 1/2×39 3/8″ (141×100 cm)

178

Ivan Orekhov

A Little Girl. 1927
Oil on canvas. 43 1/4×39 1/4″ (110×101 cm)

A l e x a n d e r   R u s a k o v

The Electrician. 1928?
Oil on canvas. 64 1/2×26 3/4″ (164×68 cm)

Vladimir Malagis

A Tractor Driver. 1932
Oil on canvas. 32 1/2×19 3/8" (82.5×49 cm)

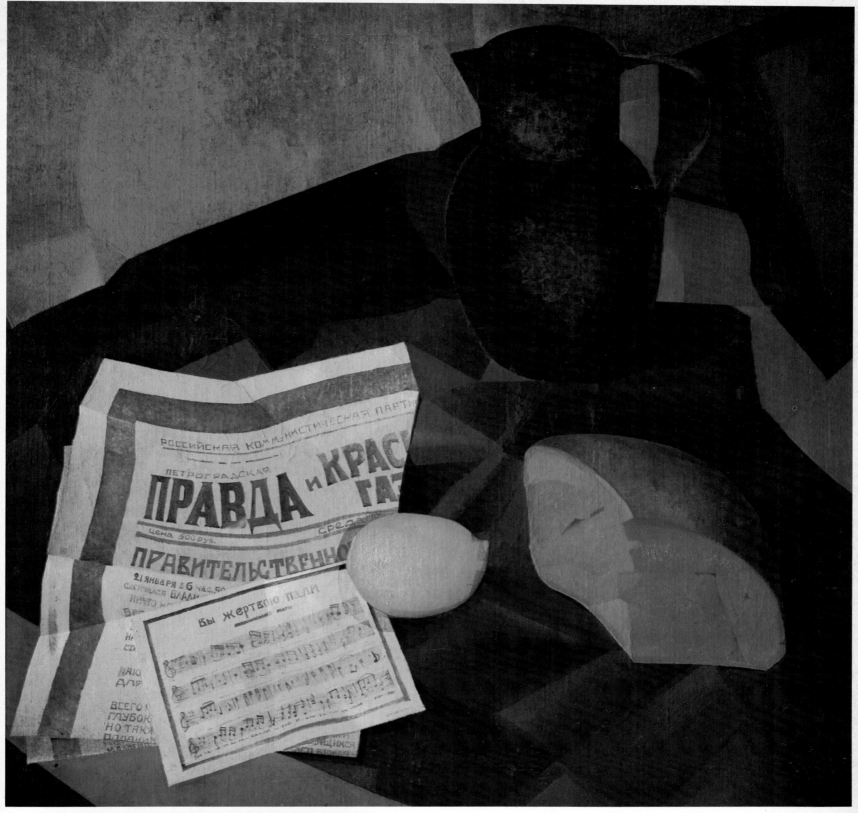

Vladimir Malagis

Funereal Still Life. 1924
Oil on canvas. 29 1/8 × 29 1/8" (74×74 cm)

Piotr Osolodkov

Sailors in October 1917. 1928
India ink. 18³/₄×21³/₄" (47.5×55 cm)

182

Piotr Osolodkov

A Gas Mask. Early 1930s
Oil on canvas. 34⁵/₈×26⁵/₈" (88×67.5 cm)

183

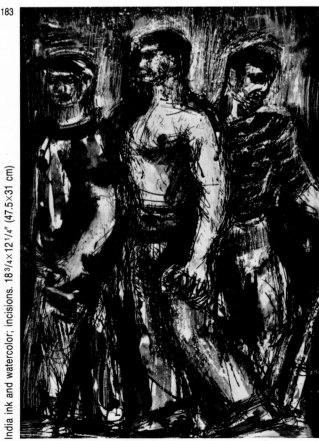

Piotr Osolodkov

Metalworkers. 1929
India ink and watercolor; incisions. 18³/₄×12¹/₄" (47.5×31 cm)

Piotr Osolodkov

185

A Miner. 1933—34
Oil on canvas. 46³/₄×33³/₄" (119×85.6 cm)

Alexei Pochtenny

Athletic Meet. Early 1930s
Oil on canvas. 37 1/8×49 1/4″ (145×125 cm)

187

David Zagoskin

Sewing. 1929
Oil on canvas mounted on plywood
46 1/4×39 3/8″ (117.5×100 cm)

188

Alexander Vedernikov

Leningrad: View from a Window
of the Sculptor Kapliansky's Studio. 1930
Oil on canvas. 27×22″ (68.5×56 cm)

189

Alexei Pakhomov

Young Girl in Blue. 1929
Oil on canvas. 31 1/4×20 1/2″ (79.5×52 cm)

190

Alexei Pakhomov

Young Archers. 1930
Oil on canvas. 42 1/8×24 5/8″ (107×62.5 cm)

Alexei Pakhomov 191

A Woman Reaping (Harvest Time). 1928
Oil on canvas. 33 1/2×41 3/4″ (85×106 cm)

192

Alexei Pakhomov

Portrait of a Milkmaid, Molodtsova. 1931
Oil on canvas mounted on cardboard. 21 5/8×13″ (55×33 cm)

Alexander Samokhvalov

A Tram Conductor. 1928
Tempera on canvas. 51 1/4×50″ (130×127 cm)

Alexander Samokhvalov

A Camel. 1921
Watercolor and pencil. 17³/₄×14″ (45.1×35.6 cm)

Thirteen

This association took its name from the number of artists who participated in its first exhibition in 1929. Other artists showed their work at a subsequent exhibition, bringing the total number of participants to twenty-one. Three catalogues, for exhibitions in 1929, 1930, and 1931, were published; however, the 1930 exhibition never took place. In contrast to other groups, this association's founding was not accompanied by manifestoes or declarations—an omnipresent feature of artistic life at the time ■ Thirteen was composed primarily of artists who concentrated on drawing and pursued specific aesthetic aims. It was a heterogeneous group with a well-defined and active core. In exhibition matters the key figures were Nikolai Kuzmin and Vladimir Milashevsky.

Thirteen

Participants in the 1929 exhibition:

Daniil Daran
Olga Gildenbrandt
Nadezhda Kashina
Nina Kashina
Nikolai Kuzmin
Tatiana Lebedeva
Vladimir Milashevsky
Mikhail Nedbailo
Sergei Rastorguev
Boris Rybchenkov
Yuri Yurkun
Valentin Yustitsky
Lev Zevin

Thirteen

Participants in the 1931 exhibition:

David Burliuk
Daniil Daran
Alexander Drevin
Olga Gildenbrandt
Sergei Izhevsky
Tatiana Mavrina-Lebedeva
Vladimir Milashevsky
Boris Rybchenkov
Roman Semashkevich
Antonina Sofronova
Cheslav Stefansky
Nadezhda Udaltsova

195

Nina Kashina

At a Holiday Home. 1934
Gouache and whitening. 17 1/4×18″ (43.7×45.8 cm)

L e v   Z e v i n

Poultry House of a Jewish Commune. 1930
Watercolor, gouache, and whitening
13³/₄×20³/₈″ (35×51.7 cm)

N a d e z h d a   K a s h i n a

Oriental Women, Samarkand. 1929
Watercolor and whitening
17¹/₂×14¹/₄″ (44.3×36 cm)

198

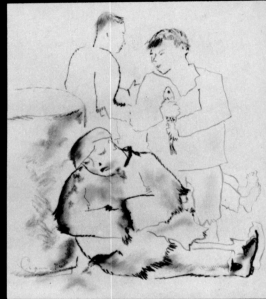

Antonina Sofronova

Street Urchins by an Asphalt Boiler. 1924
Charcoal. 14×12″ (35.7×30.7 cm)

199

200

Antonina Sofronova

A Constructivist Composition. 1922
Black India ink and gouache on colored paper
8 7/8×7 1/8″ (22.5×18.1 cm)

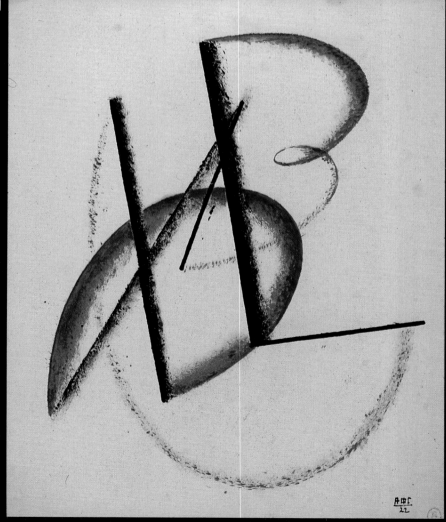

Antonina Sofronova

A Constructivist Composition. 1922
Black India ink and gouache on colored paper
8 7/8×7 1/8″ (22.5×18.1 cm)

Antonina Sofronova

After the Bathhouse. 1933?
Oil on canvas. $23^{5}/_{8} \times 19^{5}/_{8}''$ (60×50 cm)

This group brings together the most energetic and healthy trends in Russian drawing. It primarily aspires to a healthy and joyful perception of life, free of Gothic arrangement and mental unbalance. The group is distinguished by the active work it is doing on language, on means of expressing its thoughts.

From a letter from the Thirteen members to Anatoli Lunacharsky, in: M. Nemirovskaia: *The Artists of Thirteen: From the History of the Art of the 1920s and 1930s*, Moscow, 1986, p. 131 (in Russian)

The Society of Moscow Painters (OMZh—Obshchestvo moskovskikh zhivopistsev) was organized in 1924. Most of its members had formerly belonged to the Jack of Diamonds. The following year the group held an exhibition in Moscow. Thirty-seven artists took part, including Mikhail Avetov, Alexander Drevin, Igor Grabar, Alexander Kuprin, Piotr Konchalovsky, Boris Korolev, Aristarkh Lentulov, Ilia Mashkov, Vasily Rozhdestvensky, Nadezhda Udaltsova, Alexander Osmerkin, Robert Falk, and Vera Favorskaia. The exhibition catalogue contained the group's declaration ■ In 1926 the Society of Moscow Painters merged with AKhRR, and a number of its members participated in AKhRR's eighth exhibition, "The Life of the Peoples of the U.S.S.R.," held in Moscow and Leningrad ■ Unity did not last long, though. The following year most of the artists who had belonged to the Moscow Painters left AKhRR and joined forces with former members of Makovets, The Wing (organized in 1927 by pupils of Osmerkin), and Bytie (Objective Reality; organized in 1921), to create the Society of Moscow Artists (OMKh—Obshchestvo moskovskikh khudozhnikov). It had approximately seventy members and candidate members headed by Lentulov (chairman), Sergei Gerasimov (vice-chairman), and Osmerkin (secretary) ■ The society published statements of purpose in the journals *Art to the Masses* (*Iskusstvo v massy*, 1929, no. 7: "An Address of the Society of Moscow Artists to the Artistic Societies") and *For Proletarian Art* (*Za proletarskoe iskusstvo*, 1931, no. 5: "A Statement of the Society of Moscow Artists to the Fourth Plenary Session of the AKhR Central Council") ■ Three of the society's exhibitions were held in Moscow: one in 1928 and two in 1929. The society also took part in the exhibition "Paintings, Drawings, Photo- and Cinematography, Typography, and Sculpture on the Theme: The Life of Children in the Soviet Union" (1929) and two traveling exhibitions organized by IZO Narkompros (1929, 1930).

202

Valentina Khodasevich

A Village Couple
Black lead. 8 3/4 × 14 1/8″ (22.3 × 35.8 cm)

OMKh

Participants in the group:

Nikolai Chernyshev
Alexander Drevin
Robert Falk
Guerman Fiodorov
Arthur Fonvizin
Sergei Gerasimov
Igor Grabar
Nikolai Grigoriev
Piotr Konchalovsky
Nikolai Krymov
Alexander Kuprin
Aristarkh Lentulov
Ilia Mashkov
Alexei Morgunov
Alexander Osmerkin
Vasily Rozhdestvensky
Georgi Rubliov
Antonina Sofronova
Olga Sokolova
Nadezhda Udaltsova
Konstantin Zefirov

Arthur Fonvizin

The Circus. 1931
Watercolor. 16 3/4×13 3/4″ (42.4×35 cm)

Declaration, 1925

... We, the artists of the Society of Moscow Artists, firmly reject the prior view of painting and sculpture as "chamber" art.... Likewise, we consider the hasty judgments some theoreticians and groups have made on the "death of painting" and its irrelevance in our age dead and buried.

... painting can and should exist and evolve as a mass art. ...

... painting is not contemplation, not the static replication of everyday life, not a passive naturalistic depiction of reality, and not a means that can be applied only to perceiving that reality, but a powerful tool for exerting a creative influence on the world, a tool for the active reconstruction of life.

... we therefore reject naturalistic genre painting together with superficial and static literalism because they are incapable of helping art do the enormous job that faces it today.

From *The Struggle for Realism in the Art of the 1920s (Borba za realizm v iskusstve dvadtsatykh godov),* Moscow, 1962, p. 224

204

Igor Grabar
A Moscow Courtyard. 1930
Oil on canvas. 26³/₄×31⁷/₈" (68×81 cm)

Ilia Mashkov

Still Life with Mirror and Equine Skull. 1919
Oil on canvas. 43×53 1/4″ (109×135.5 cm)

206

Robert Falk

Still Life with Books. 1921
Oil on canvas. 27 3/8×36 3/8″ (69.5×92.5 cm)

Robert Falk

An Old Bridge, Paris. 1930
Gouache. 14 3/8×19 5/8″ (36.5×50 cm)

207

Robert Falk

A French Landscape, Aix. 1932/4?
Oil on canvas. 28 1/2×35 5/8″ (72.5×90.5 cm)

208

Robert Falk

Self-Portrait in Yellow. 1924
Oil on canvas. 39 3/8×32 5/8″ (100×83 cm)

Piotr Konchalovsky

Novgorodians. 1925
Oil on canvas. 55×71³/₄″ (139.5×182.5 cm)

211

Piotr Konchalovsky

A Window, Balaklava, the Crimea. 1929
Oil on canvas. 37×44″ (94×112 cm)

V a s i l y R o z h d e s t v e n s k y

Still Life with a Red Pitcher. 1918
Oil on canvas. 35×33¹/₈″ (89×84 cm)

212

213

V a s i l y R o z h d e s t v e n s k y

Wood Grouse. 1921
Oil on canvas. 28×28¹/₈″ (71×71.5 cm)

Konstantin Zefirov

Portrait of a Girl (The Artist's Daughter Lena). 1920s
Oil on canvas. 27 3/4×22 3/4″ (70.5×58 cm)

215

Konstantin Zefirov

Woman at Work. 1920s
Oil on canvas. $29^{3}/_{4} \times 24^{1}/_{4}''$ (75.7×61.5 cm)

216

Olga Sokolova

Women's Bazaar at Urgut. 1932
Oil on canvas
$49^{1}/_{4} \times 49^{3}/_{8}''$ (125×125.5 cm)

A r i s t a r k h L e n t u l o v.

Monastery Landscape
(Landscape with Withered Trees and Tall Houses). 1920
Oil on canvas. 41×55 1/8" (104×140 cm)

Alexander Drevin

Steppe Landscape with a Horse. 1933
Oil on canvas. 29 1/2×36 1/4″ (75×92 cm)

Alexander Drevin

Barges. 1932
Oil on canvas. 22 7/8×25 3/8″ (58×64.5 cm)

219

Sergei Gerasimov

A Townswoman. 1923
Oil on canvas. 35 1/2×26 3/4″ (90×68 cm)

221

Portrait of the Producer Alexander Tairov. 1919—20
Oil on canvas. 41 1/8×39″ (104.7×99 cm)

222

Alexander Osmerkin

Portrait of Ekaterina Barkova. 1921
Oil on canvas. 49 1/4×38″ (125×96.5 cm)

Alexander Osmerkin

Still Life with a White Bowl. 1921
Oil on canvas. 33 1/8×24 5/8″ (84×62.5 cm)

Alexander Osmerkin

Still Life with a Skull. 1921
Oil on canvas. 32 1/4 × 25 3/8" (82 × 64.5 cm)

225

Samuil Adlivankin
Clearing Up a Crisis
at the Collective Farm. 1931
Oil on canvas. 37 3/8×47 1/4″ (95×120 cm)

Natan Altman
Illustration for Gogol's
Nevsky Prospekt. 1937
Gouache and black chalk on cardboard;
incisions. 12 7/8×9 7/8″ (32.6×25 cm)

226

227

Leonid Akishin
Family Portrait. 1931
Oil on canvas. 34 1/2×27 3/4″ (87.5×70.5 cm)

Vasily Baksheev
The Last Snow. 1936
Oil on canvas. 31 1/8×39 1/8″ (79×99.5 cm)

228

Rostislav Barto
Derbent. 1932
Oil on canvas. 34 7/8 × 48 7/8" (88.5 × 124 cm)

229

Pavel Basmanov
Landscape with Figures. 1935
Watercolor. 8 × 8 7/8" (20.3 × 22.5 cm)

230

Georgi Bibikov
"Osoaviakhim—1" Stratospheric Balloon. 1935
Oil on canvas. 93 3/4×61 3/8" (238×156 cm)

Konstantin Chebotarev
Breakfast at Suuk-Su. 1918
Oil on cardboard. 20 1/8 × 28 3/8″ (51 × 72 cm)

Konstantin Chebotarev
In the Canteen. 1932
Gouache and whitening. 32 1/2×25 1/8″ (82.5×63.8 cm)

Nikolai Chernyshev
A Young Pioneer. 1930
Oil on canvas. 41 3/8×25 1/4" (105×64 cm)

Leonid Chupiatov
Costume design. 1927
Watercolor and gouache. 10 5/8×7 1/8" (27.1×18.1 cm)

235

234

Leonid Chupiatov
Still Life in White. 1936
Oil on canvas
23 3/8×29 5/8" (59.5×75.3 cm)

236

Alexander Deineka
A Collective-Farm Work Team. 1934
Oil on canvas. 50³/₈×69¹/₄″ (128×176 cm)

238

Evgenia Evenbakh
Two Students. 1923
Oil on canvas. 63×52″ (160×132 cm)

239

Boris Ermolaev
Red Navy Officers. 1934 (1933?)
Oil on canvas mounted on cardboard
13⁵/₈×20¹/₂″ (34.5×52 cm)

Boris Ermolaev
Red Navy Men. 1934
Oil on canvas mounted on cardboard
15 1/2 × 13 3/4″ (39.5 × 35 cm)

Boris Ermolaev
Family Portrait. 1930s
Oil on canvas mounted on cardboard
16 3/8 × 12 3/4″ (40.5 × 32.5 cm)

Boris Ermolaev
A Family Around the Samovar. 1930s
Oil on canvas mounted on cardboard
15 3/4 × 19 7/8″ (40 × 50.5 cm)

Boris Ermolaev
Street in the Volodarsky District. 1935
Oil on canvas mounted on cardboard
14×16″ (35.5×40.5 cm)

243

244

Boris Ermolaev
A Horse Cart. 1937
Oil on canvas mounted on cardboard
13³/₈×14¹/₈″ (34×36 cm)

Vera Ermolaeva
Don Quixote and Sancho Panza. 1933—34
Tempera. 17×12 1/2″ (43.3×31.8 cm)

245

Vera Ermolaeva
Composition based on Lucretius's *De rerum natura*. 1934
Tempera and pencil. 12 1/2×8 1/2″ (31.9×21.5 cm)

246

247

Vera Ermolaeva
Fisherman with a Basket. 1933
Gouache and whitening
11 1/2×8 1/4″ (29.3×22.1 cm)

Sergei Gerasimov
Lenin with Peasant Delegates to the 2nd Congress of the Soviets. 1935—36
Oil on canvas. 93 1/8×73 3/8″ (236.5×186.5 cm)

248

Alexander Gerasimov
Summer Rain at Noon. 1939
Oil on canvas. 50×39″ (127×99 cm)

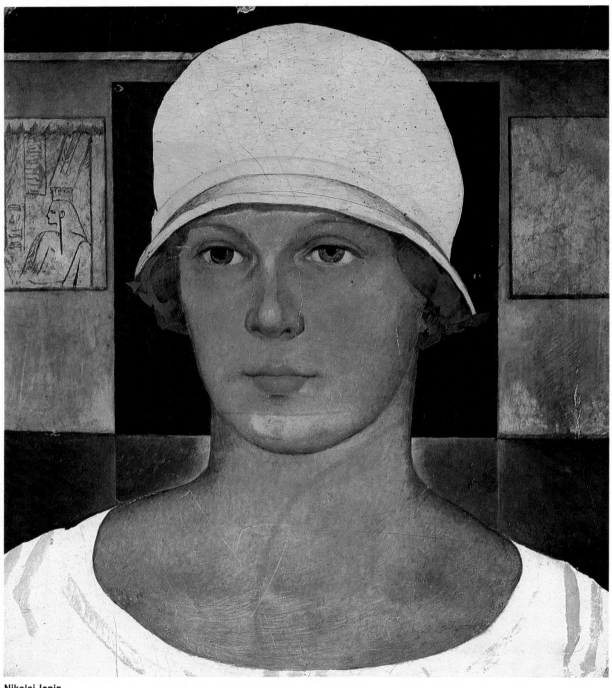

Nikolai Ionin
Portrait of Ekaterina Ionina, the Artist's Wife. 1920s
Oil on panel surfaced with gesso. 14 1/8×12 1/4″ (36×31 cm)

Evgeny Kibrik
Illustration for Rolland's *Colas Breugnon.* 1935
Color lithograph. 8 1/4×6″ (21×15.3 cm)   251

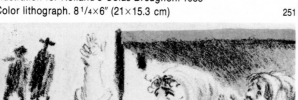

Nikolai Kostrov
A Fresh Coat of Paint. 1928
Watercolor. 14×9 7/8″ (35.5×25 cm)

253

Vladimir Konashevich
Winter at Pavlovsk. 1932
Ink and brush. 31×21 1/2″ (79×54.5 cm)

Eduard Krimmer
Stage design
Watercolor. 12³/₁₆×12″ (31×30.5 cm)

Valentin Kurdov
A Pie Vendor. From the *Street Vendors* series. 1925
Ink. 6 1/2×4 1/2″ (16.5×11.3 cm)

Valentin Kurdov
A Samovar. 1926—27
Oil on canvas. 30×22″ (76×56 cm)

255

257

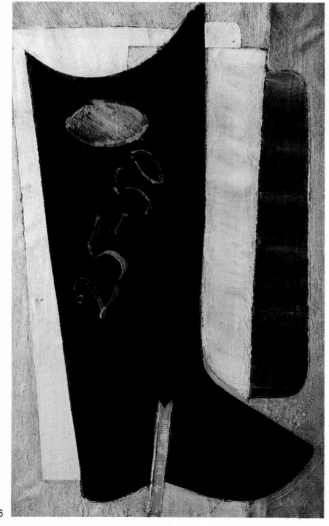

256

Valentin Kurdov
A Felt Boot. 1926—27
Oil on canvas. 36×21 3/4″ (91.5×55.5 cm)

Alexander Lappo-Danilevsky
Grinding an Ax. 1919
Ink. 11 3/16×12″ (28.4×30.5 cm)

258

Nikolai Lapshin
Leningrad: The Admiralty. 1938
Watercolor. 12 3/4×17 1/8″ (32.5×43.5 cm)

Nikolai Lapshin
Self-Portrait. 1935
Oil on canvas. 20×13 3/4″
(51×35 cm)

Valentina Markova
Self-Portrait. 1930?
Oil on canvas. 41 1/8×26 3/4″
(104.5×68 cm)

259

Nikolai Lapshin
Blue Bridge. 1937
Oil on cardboard. 23 1/4×31 3/4″ (59×80.5 cm)

Alexander Morozov
Marketplace at Kineshma. 1930s
Oil on canvas. 52³/₄×78″ (134×198 cm)

263

Arkady Plastov
Collective-Farm Celebration. 1937
Oil on canvas. 74×120 3/4″ (188×307 cm)

264

Victor Proshkin
Near the Birzhevoi Bridge. 1935
Oil on canvas. 26×32⁷/₈″ (66×83.5 cm)

265

Igor Popov
Interior. 1937
Oil on canvas. 27¹/₂×33¹/₄″ (70×84.5 cm)

266

Kliment Redko
A Parisienne. 1931
Oil on canvas. 77 9/16×38 3/8″ (197×97.5 cm)

Georgi Riazhsky
The Letter. 1939
Oil on canvas. 39 3/8×31 1/8″ (100×79 cm)

267

268

Alexander Samokhvalov
A Member of Osoaviakhim. 1932
Oil and tempera on canvas. 47 1/4×45 3/4″ (120×116 cm)

269

270

Alexander Shevchenko
Still Life with a Guitar. 1933
Oil on canvas. 25 5/8×31 3/8″ (65.2×79.8 cm)

Alexander Shchipitsyn
Springtime. 1933
Oil on canvas. 39 3/8×51 1/8″ (100×130 cm)

Tatiana Shishmareva
Horses. At Noon. 1939
Watercolor and whitening. 11 7/8×15 1/4″ (30.3×38.8 cm)   272

Yuri Shchukin
An Airship over the Town. 1933
Oil on canvas. 39 9/16×43 5/16″ (100.5×110 cm)
                                                                          273

Mikhail Sokolov
Still Life with Fish. 1930s
Oil on canvas. 20 3/4×27 3/4″ (52.7×70.5 cm)

Piotr Stroev
At a State Poultry Farm. 1934
Oil on canvas. 31 1/8×38 3/4″ (79×98.5 cm)

Vladimir Tambi
Tanks. 1930
Gouache on colored paper. $10^{5}/_{8} \times 15^{1}/_{2}''$ (27×39.5 cm)

Vladimir Tatlin
Flowers. 1940
Oil on wooden panel. $29^3/_4 \times 26^1/_2''$ (75.5 $\times$ 67.5 cm)

Boris Tsvetkov
Heated Reservoir and Log Conveyer. 1932
Oil on canvas. 41×27″ (104×68.5 cm)

Nikolai Tyrsa
Interior in Pink. 1935
Oil on canvas. 21 3/4×26″ (55×66 cm)

279

278

Alexei Uspensky
Girl in a Rocking Chair
Watercolor and whitening. 12 7/8×8 3/4″ (32.8×22.3 cm)

280

Yuri Vasnetsov
Still Life with a Chess Board. 1926—28
Oil on plywood, wooden cane
42¹/₂×22″ (108×56 cm)

Yuri Vasnetsov
A Storehouse. 1925
Colored crayons and pencil. 12 1/2×17 1/4″ (31.7×43.8 cm)

283

Yuri Vasnetsov
Vyatka: A Courtyard. 1925
Pencil. 12×14 1/2″ (30.7×36.7 cm)

282

Yuri Vasnetsov
Composition with Artificial Fishes. 1928—31
Oil on canvas. 46 1/2×37″ (118×94 cm)

284

Alexander Volkov
Cotton Hilling. 1930s
Oil on canvas. 46¹/₂×81³/₄″ (118×208 cm)

Alexander Volkov
Tea. 1926
Tempera, India ink, and watercolor; varnish
11³/₄×11⁷/₈″ (30×30.3 cm)

Alexander Volkov
Black Woman. 1921
Oil on canvas
39³/₈×39³/₈″ (100×100 cm)

Piotr Williams
Woman in a Window. 1930s
Oil on canvas. 62³/₄×51¹/₄″ (159.5×130 cm)

Annotated Catalogue/Index to Names

Dimensions are given in inches and centimeters, with height preceding width.

The place names, dates, signatures, etc., appearing on the works are given in Russian; English translation, if any, is put in brackets [   ].

Numbers refer to illustrations between pp. 16 and 242.

Adlivankin, Samuil Yakovlevich
1897—1966
113
Tram B. 1922
Oil on plywood. 18 1/2×23 5/8″ (47×60 cm)
Lower right: *С. Адливанкин Москва. 1922*
Inscribed on the picture: *Сам. Адливанкин. Москва 1922 г.*
1967 Acquired from the artist's daughter
E. Strakhova (Moscow). Inv.no. Ж-8388
225
Clearing Up a Crisis at the Collective Farm
1931
Oil on canvas. 37 3/8×47 1/4″ (95×120 cm)
The artist's inscription on a label on the reverse: *С. Адливанкин. В штабе колхоза перед штурмом прорыва 1931 г.*
1967 Acquired from the artist's daughter
E. Strakhova (Moscow). Inv.no. Ж-8389

Akishin, Leonid Ilich
1893—1966
227
Family Portrait. 1931
Oil on canvas. 34 1/2×27 3/4″ (87.5×70.5 cm)
Lower right: *Л. Акишин 31 г.*
1968 Acquired from the artist's widow,
M. Akishina (Leningrad). Inv.no. Ж-8498

Alexandrova, Tatiana Borisovna
1907—87
89
Portrait of a Young Girl. 1927
Oil on canvas. 40×28 1/8″ (101.5×71.5 cm)
The artist's inscription on the reverse:
Т. Александрова. 1927. Портрет девушки
1980 Acquired from the artist (Moscow)
Inv.no. Ж-10185

Altman, Natan Isaevich
1889—1970
12
Petrocommune [*Petrokommuna* *]. 1921
Oil and enamel paints on canvas
41×34 7/8″ (104×88.5 cm)
Lower left: *Нат. Альтман 921*
On the reverse: *Nat Altman 921*
1972 Acquired from the artist's widow,
I. Shchegoleva (Leningrad). Inv.no. Ж-8837
13
Cover design for the journal *Plamia* [The Flame]
1918
Black chalk on cardboard. 14 3/4×10 5/8″
(37.6×27.1 cm)
Lower right: *Нат. Альтман*
1920 Acquired from the Committee of the All-Russian Society for the Encouragement of the Arts
Inv.no. СрБ-484

*
During the Civil War period Petrograd was also called
Petro[grad] Commune. In the picture, upper left: the Russian
characters for R.S.F.S.R.—Russian Soviet Federated Socialist
Republic.

15
Material Painting (Still Life with a White Jug)
1919
Oil and enamel paints on canvas
33 1/4×24 3/8″ (84.5×62 cm)
Lower right: *Нат. Альтман 19.*
1926 Acquired from the Museum of Artistic Culture
Inv.no. ЖБ-1538
20
Still Life: Color Volumes and Planes. * 1918
Oil on canvas; gypsum powder
23 3/8×17 1/8″ (59.5×43.5 cm)
Lower right: *Нат Альтманъ 18 г.*
1926 Acquired from the Museum of Artistic Culture
Inv.no. ЖБ-1570
25
A Material Arrangement. 1920
Oil and enamel paints on canvas; glue, sawdust, and plaster. 32 5/8×25 3/4″ (83×65.5 cm) (oval)
Lower left: *Нат. Альтман 920*
1972 Acquired from the artist's widow,
I. Shchegoleva (Leningrad). Inv.no. Ж-8838
226
Illustration for Gogol's *Nevsky Prospekt*
In: N. V. Gogol, *St. Petersburg Stories*
(Peterburgskie povesti), Moscow, 1937
Gouache and black chalk on cardboard; incisions
12 7/8×9 7/8″ (32.6×25 cm)
Lower right in India ink: *Nathan Altman*
1969 Acquired from the artist (Leningrad)
Inv.no. Pc-7834

Annenkov, Yuri Pavlovich
1889—1974
3
Portrait of the Photographer Sherling. 1918
Oil on canvas. 28 1/8×22 5/8″ (71.5×57.5 cm)
Lower left: *Ю. Анненковъ. 1918 г.*
1924 Acquired from the State Museum Reserve
(Leningrad). Inv.no. ЖБ-1226
4
Portrait of Elena Annenkova, the Artist's Wife
1917
Oil on canvas. 33 1/8×32 1/4″ (84×82 cm)
Upper right: *Ю. Анненковъ*
1920 Acquired from the A. Korovin Collection
Inv.no. ЖБ-1227

Artist unknown
39
A Worker. Sketch for a street decoration
Gouache and whitening on cardboard
16 3/8×11 13/16″ (41.7×30 cm)
1939 Acquired from the Hermitage Museum Reserve
(Leningrad). Inv.no. СрБ-1085

Baksheev, Vasily Nikolaevich
1862—1958
228
The Last Snow. 1936
Oil on canvas. 31 1/8×39 1/8″ (79×99.5 cm)
Lower right: *Бакшеев В. 1936 г.*
1937 Acquired from the State Purchasing
Commission. Inv.no. Ж-5850

*
The picture was shown at the "First State Free Exhibition of
Works of Art" (Petrograd, 1919).

Barto, Rostislav Nikolaevich
1902—73
229
Derbent. 1932
Oil on canvas. 34 7/8×48 7/8″ (88.5×124 cm)
Lower right: *RB 32 Derbent*
On the reverse: *Р. Барто 1932 холст масло 88×124 (Дербент)*
1933 Acquired from the artist (?) at the exhibition "Artists of the Russian Federation: Fifteen Years." Inv.no. ЖБ-1487

Basmanov, Pavel Ivanovich
Born 1906
230
Landscape with Figures. 1935
Watercolor. 8×8 7/8″ (20.3×22.5 cm)
1939 Acquired from the artist (Leningrad)
Inv.no. Pc-206

Bebutova (Bebutova-Kuznetsova), Elena Mikhailovna
1892—1970
135
Still Life with Glassware. 1923
Oil on canvas. 22 7/8×19 3/8″ (58×49 cm)
Lower left: *H. Beboutoff*
On the reverse: *Helene Beboutoff*
1933 Acquired from the artist (Moscow)
Inv.no. ЖБ-1560
136
A Lake (Switzerland). Not later than 1927
Oil on canvas. 17 1/2×20 7/8″ (44.5×53 cm)
1933 Acquired from the artist (Moscow)
Inv.no. ЖБ-1561

Beliakova, Ekaterina Mikhailovna
Born 1892
80
Figures and a Horse Cart. Early 1920s
Watercolor, gouache, and India ink
10 9/16×14″ (26.8×34.5 cm)
1984 Acquired from the artist (Moscow)
Inv.no. Pc-12401

Bekhteev, Vladimir Georgievich
1878—1971
131
Sketch for a poster for the Moscow Circus. 1921
Watercolor, pencil, gouache, and charcoal
26×17 7/16″ (66×44.3 cm)
Lower left in pencil: *W. B. 21 г.*
1973 Acquired from the artist's widow,
N. Bekhteeva (Moscow). Inv.no. Pc-8793
134
The Blast Furnace. 1930
From the *Sartana* series. 1930—32
Watercolor. 16 3/8×17″ (40.5×43.3 cm)
Lower right: *W. B.*
1973 Acquired from the artist's widow,
N. Bekhteeva (Moscow). Inv.no. Pc-8798

Bibikov, Georgi Nikolaevich
1903—76
231
"Osoaviakhim—1" Stratospheric Balloon. 1935
Oil on canvas. 93 3/4×61 3/8″ (238×156 cm)
Lower left: *Бибиков 35 г.*
1940 Acquired from Lensovet. Inv.no. ЖБ-1887

1982 Acquired from the artist (Leningrad)
Inv.no. Ж-10639

Kustodiev, Boris Mikhailovich
1878—1927
6
Summertime. 1918
Oil on canvas. 25 3/4×72 1/4" (65.5×183.5 cm)
Lower left: *Б. Кустодiев 1918*
Acquired in 1919; gift of the Committee of the
All-Russian Society for the Encouragement
of the Arts. Inv.no. ЖБ-1867

Kuznetsov, Pavel Varfolomeevich
1878—1968
147
Red Grapes. 1930—31
Oil on canvas. 38×27 1/4" (96.5×69 cm)
Lower right: *П. К. 30—31*
1933 Acquired from the artist (Moscow)
Inv.no. ЖБ-1904

148
Sart Woman with a Lamb. 1923
Sheet 1 from the *Mountainous Bukhara* album
Color lithograph. 12×8 5/8" (30.4×22.6 cm)
Lower right: *Павел Кузнецов*
Acquired in 1923. Inv.no. Crp-2615

149
Portrait. 1923
Sheet from the *Turkistan* album, 2nd series
Lithograph. 11 1/4×9" (28.5×22.7 cm)
Acquired in 1923. Inv.no. Crp-2613

150
Tobacco Workers. 1925—26
Tempera on canvas. 38 1/4×41 3/4" (97×106 cm)
Lower right: *Павел Кузнецов 1925—6*
The artist's (?) inscription on a label on the
stretcher: *Кузнецов Сбор табака 96× 106*
1927 Acquired from the State Museum Reserve
Inv.no. ЖБ-1182

151
Portrait of the Sculptor Alexander Matveev
1928
Oil on canvas. 38 1/4×25" (97×63.5 cm)
1974 Acquired from O. Durylina (Moscow)
Inv.no. Ж-9072

Labas, Alexander Arkadievich
1900—83
165
Airship and Children from the Orphanage. 1930
Oil on canvas. 63×31 1/2" (160×80 cm)
Lower right: *Александр Лабас 30 г*
1931 Acquired from the artist (Moscow)
Inv.no. ЖБ-1702

166
The Airship. 1931
Oil on canvas. 61 1/4×78 1/4" (155.5×199 cm)
Lower right: *Александр Лабас 31*
1933 Acquired from the artist at the exhibition
"Artists of the Russian Federation: Fifteen
Years." Inv.no. ЖБ-992

171
The Train Is Coming. 1929
Oil on canvas. 38 1/4×29 3/8" (97×74.5 cm)
Lower right: *Александр Лабас 29*
On the reverse: *«Поезд идет» Александр Лабас
1929 г.*

1967 Acquired from the artist (Moscow). Inv.no.
Ж-8391

Lappo-Danilevsky, Alexander Alexandrovich
1898—1920
258
Grinding an Ax. 1919
Ink. 11 3/16×12" (28.4×30.5 cm)
1984 Acquired from E. Baikova (Leningrad)
Inv.no. Pc-12513

Lapshin, Nikolai Fiodorovich
1888—1942
22
The River Moika. 1919?
Oil on canvas. 30×37 5/8" (76×95.5 cm)
On the reverse: the artist's painting entitled
Landscape (1910s)
1926 Acquired from the Museum of Artistic
Culture. Inv.no. ЖБ-1417

259
Leningrad: The Admiralty. 1938
Watercolor. 12 3/4×17 1/8" (32.5×43.5 cm)
Lower right: *27 XII 38*
Acquired in 1958; gift of V. Vlasov (Leningrad)
Inv.no. Pc-4137

260
Blue Bridge. 1937
Oil on canvas. 23 1/4×31 3/4" (59×80.5 cm)
Lower left: *22 X 37*
On the reverse: the artist's painting entitled
Landscape. The River Moika (1930s)
1982 Acquired from the artist's son M. Lapshin
(Vladivostok). Inv.no. Ж-10717

261
Self-Portrait. 1935
Oil on canvas. 20×13 3/4" (51×35 cm)
Lower left: *15 IX 35*
1979 Acquired from the artist's son M. Lapshin
(Vladivostok). Inv.no. Ж-10098

Lebedev, Vladimir Vasilievich
1891—1967
19
Still Life with a Palette. 1919
Oil on canvas. 35×25 5/8" (89×65 cm)
Upper left: *В. Лебедев 1919*
1926 Acquired from the Museum of Artistic
Culture. Inv.no. ЖБ-1435

38
Katka the Prostitute. 1918 (1916?)
Oil on canvas. 49 5/8×26" (126×66 cm)
Inscribed by the artist Boris Grigoriev (?)
on the stretcher: *Борис Григорьев*
1985 Acquired from B. Okunev's estate (Leningrad)
Inv.no. Ж-11273

45
Worker at the Anvil. 1920—21
Collage on cardboard
30 3/4×28" (78.2×71.1 cm)
1928 Acquired from the artist (Leningrad)
Inv.no. СрБ-477

127
Still Life with Red Guitar and Palette. 1930
Oil on canvas. 17 1/2×31 1/4" (44.5×79.5 cm)
Lower left: *ВЛ 30*
1981 Acquired from the artist's widow, A. Lazo
(Leningrad). Inv.no. Ж-10346

128
A Woman Ironing. 1925
Gouache, charcoal, and pencil on cardboard;
collage. 26 3/4×17 1/2" (68×44.5 cm)
Lower left in pencil: *В Л 1925.*
1981 Acquired from the artist's widow, A. Lazo
(Leningrad). Inv.no. Ж-10347

154
Young Girl in a Jersey, Holding a Bouquet. 1933
Watercolor, gouache, and whitening
25 1/4×17 1/2" (64.2×44.6 cm)
Lower left: *В Л 33*
1973 Acquired from the artist's widow, A. Lazo
(Leningrad). Inv.no. Pc-8792

155
Nude with a Guitar. 1930
Oil on canvas. 31 1/2×25 1/2" (80×65 cm)
Lower left: *В. Л. 30*
1933 Acquired from the artist at the exhibition
"Artists of the Russian Federation: Fifteen
Years." Inv.no. Ж-4484

Lentulov, Aristarkh Vasilievich
1882—1943
217
*Monastery Landscape (Landscape with Withered
Trees and Tall Houses)*. 1920
Oil on canvas. 41×55 1/8" (104×140 cm)
1967 Acquired from the artist's daughter
M. Lentulova (Moscow). Inv.no. Ж-8280

221
Portrait of the Producer Alexander Tairov
1919—20
Oil on canvas. 41 1/8×39" (104.7×99 cm)
1929 Acquired from the Tretiakov Gallery
(Moscow). Inv.no. ЖБ-1699

Leporskaia, Anna Alexandrovna
1900—82
63
Pskovian Woman. 1930 (1932—34?)
Oil on canvas. 23 5/8×19" (60×48 cm)
1981 Acquired from the artist (Leningrad)
Inv.no. Ж-10498

El Lissitzky (Lissitsky, Lazar Markovich)
1890—1941
64
Illustration for a Yiddish children's book. 1919
Color lithograph. 6 11/16×7 7/8" (17×20 cm)
Acquired in 1935; gift of K. Kostenko
(Leningrad). Inv.no. СрБ-1197

Luchishkin, Sergei Alexeevich
Born 1902
158
Skiers (Amid Trees). 1926
Oil on canvas. 41 3/4×37 3/8" (106×95 cm)
On the reverse: *Сергей Лучишкин 1926 г.*
1930 Acquired from the Tretiakov Gallery (Moscow)
Inv.no. ЖБ-1495

Lvov, Piotr Ivanovich
1882—1944
145
An April Day. 1917
Oil on canvas. 31 1/8×21 1/4" (79×54 cm)
1982 Acquired from the artist's daughter
L. Danilovskaia (Leningrad). Inv.no. Ж-10646

Magaril, Evgenia Markovna
Born 1902
75
Portrait of a Boy. 1920s
Oil on cardboard. 12 5/8×10 7/16″ (32×26.5 cm)
1983 Acquired from the artist (Leningrad)
Inv.no. Ж-10985

Malagis, Vladimir Ilich
1902—74
180
A Tractor Driver. 1932
Oil on canvas. 32 1/2×19 3/8″ (82.5×49 cm)
On the reverse: *Малагис В. И. "Трактористка" х/м
82,5× 49 1932 г.*
1979 Acquired from the artist's widow,
E. Baikova (Leningrad). Inv.no. Ж-9987

181
Funereal Still Life. 1924
Oil on canvas. 29 1/8×29 1/8″ (74×74 cm)
On the reverse: the inscription *Малагис В. И.
н/м "траурный" х/м 74× 74 1924 г.* and the
artist's painting entitled *Composition:
The Crucifixion*
1978 Acquired from the artist's widow, E. Baikova
(Leningrad). Inv.no. Ж-9998

Malevich, Kazimir Severinovich
1878—1935
50
A Suprematist Dress. 1923
Watercolor and pencil. 7 1/2×6 11/16″ (19×17 cm)
(size of the entire sheet)
To the right in watercolor: *К М 1923 г.*;
lower in pencil: *супрематическое платье*
The drawing is surrounded by the artist's text
in ink
1930 Acquired from the artist (Moscow)
Inv.no. СрБ-33

51
A Working Woman. 1933
Oil on canvas. 27 1/2×22 7/8″ (70×58 cm)
Lower left: Malevich's square as his signature
On the reverse: *"Работница" № 10 1933 К. Малевич*
1978 Acquired from the U.S.S.R. Ministry
of Culture. Inv.no. Ж-9494

52
Sportsmen: Suprematism in Sportsmen's Contours
1928—32
Oil on canvas. 56×64 1/2″ (142×164 cm)
Lower left: *К. Малевич*; incised lower right: *К. М.*
On the reverse: *Супрематизмъ в контуре
"Спортсменов" 1915 го К Мал*
1978 Acquired from the U.S.S.R. Ministry
of Culture. Inv.no. Ж-9439

53
Landscape with Five Houses. 1928—32
Oil on canvas. 32 3/4×24 1/2″ (83×62 cm)
1978 Acquired from the U.S.S.R. Ministry
of Culture. Inv.no. Ж-9496

54
Torso in a Yellow Shirt. 1928—32
Oil on canvas. 38 3/4×31″ (98.5×78.5 cm)
On the reverse: *К. Malewicz*
On the reverse: *Сложное предчувствие 1928—32 г.
Композиция сложилась из элементов ощущения
пуст<оты>, одиночест<ва>, безысходност<и>
жизни 1913 г. Ку<нцево>.* [Complicated prescience
of 1928—32. The composition originated from

the feeling of a void, loneliness, and the hope-
lessness of life. 1913. Kuntsevo.]
1978 Acquired from the U.S.S.R. Ministry
of Culture. Inv.no. Ж-9477

55
*Death to Wallpaper: The Suprematist Principle of
Painting Walls.* 1919
Watercolor, gouache, and India ink. 13 3/8×9 3/4″
(34×24.8 cm) (size of the entire sheet)
Above the picture the artist's text in pencil:
*Принцип росписи стены плоскости или всей
комнаты или целой квартиры по системе
супрематизма (смерть обоям) К. Малевич 1919
Витебск* [The principle of painting a planar
wall or entire room or apartment according to
the Suprematist system (Death to wallpaper).
K. Malevich. 1919. Vitebsk.]
1930 Acquired from the artist (Moscow)
Inv. no. Pc-978

56
Portrait of Natalia Malevich, the Artist's Wife. 1933
Oil on canvas. 39 1/4×29 1/3″ (99.5×74.5 cm)
Lower left: Malevich's square
Lower right: *33* [1933]
1978 Acquired from the U.S.S.R. Ministry
of Culture. Inv.no. Ж-9389

Mansurov, Pavel Andreevich
1896—1983
33
Mirage. 1918
Ink drawing. 7 1/4×5 1/8″ (18.5×13.1 cm)
Upper right: *Мираж*
1935 Acquired from the Section of Drawings of the
Russian Museum. Inv.no. Pc-3037

Markova, Valentina Petrovna
1906—41/42?
262
Self-Portrait. 1930?
Oil on canvas. 41 1/8×26 3/4″ (104.5×68 cm)
1974 Acquired from D. Kaufman (Moscow)
Inv.no. Ж-9002

Mashkov, Ilia Ivanovich
1881—1958
205
Still Life with Mirror and Equine Skull. 1919
Oil on canvas. 43×53 1/4″ (109×135.5 cm)
Lower right: *Илья Машков*
1926 Acquired from the Museum of Artistic
Culture. Inv.no. ЖБ-1730

Matiushin, Mikhail Vasilievich
1861—1934
71
A Haystack. Lakhta. 1921
Watercolor. 20 7/8×16 3/8″ (53×41.5 cm)
Acquired in 1967; gift of the artist's widow,
O. Matiushina (Leningrad). Inv.no. Pc-6591

72
Movement in Space. 1922?
Oil on canvas. 48 3/4×66 1/8″ (124×168 cm)
Lower left: *М. М.*
1926 Acquired from the Museum of Artistic
Culture. Inv.no. ЖБ-996

74
One Landscape from Every Angle. Siverskaia. 1924

From the *Peasant Cottages* series
Watercolor. 8 3/4×13 1/2″ (22.2×34.3 cm)
Acquired in 1967; gift of the artist's widow,
O. Matiushina (Leningrad). Inv.no. Pc-6590

Matveeva-Mostova, Zoia Yakovlevna
1884—1972
144
Girl with a Bowl. 1923/25?
Oil on canvas. 33 7/8×26 3/4″ (86×68 cm)
1974 Acquired from the artist (Leningrad)
Inv.no. Ж-9112

Morozov, Alexander Ivanovich
Born 1902
263
Marketplace at Kineshma. 1930s
Oil on canvas. 52 3/4×78″ (134×198 cm)
1986 Acquired from the artist (Moscow)
Without inventory number

Nikritin, Solomon Borisovich
1898—1965
167
Composition. 1930
Oil on canvas. 26 3/4×22 3/4″ (68×58 cm)
Lower left in pencil: *Никритин*
On the reverse in black paint: *240 Эксп. 1930 г.
С. Никритин "Композиция" х/м 70× 59*; signed
in pencil: *С. Никритин*
1977 Acquired from Y. Kadzhan (Moscow)
Inv.no. Ж-9252

Orekhov, Ivan Vasilievich
1888—1940?
178
A Little Girl. 1927
Oil on canvas. 43 1/4×39 1/4″ (110×101 cm)
Lower left: *И Орехов*
On the reverse: *И. Орехов 1927 г.*
1930 Acquired from the artist's collection
(Leningrad). Inv.no. ЖБ-1490

Osmerkin, Alexander Alexandrovich
1892—1953
222
Portrait of Ekaterina Barkova, the Artist's Wife. 1921
Oil on canvas. 49 1/4×38″ (125×96.5 cm)
Lower right: *А. Осмеркин 1921*
On the reverse: *А. Осмеркин*
1961 Acquired from the artist's widow,
N. Osmerkina (Moscow). Inv.no. Ж-7547

223
Still Life with a White Bowl. 1921
Oil on canvas. 33 1/8×24 5/8″ (84×62.5 cm)
Upper right: *А. Осмеркин 921 VI*
On the reverse: *Осмеркин "Natur Mort" 1921*
1959 Acquired from the artist's widow,
N. Osmerkina (Moscow). Inv.no. Ж-7007

224
Still Life with a Skull. 1921
Oil on canvas. 32 1/4×25 3/8″ (82×64.5 cm)
Lower left: *А. Осмеркин 921/VI*
The artist's (?) inscription on the stretcher:
А. Осмеркин 1921 г. Натюрморт с черепом
1964 Acquired from the artist's widow,
N. Osmerkina (Moscow). Inv.no. Ж-7999

Osolodkov, Piotr Alexeevich
1898—1942
182
Sailors in October 1917. 1928
India ink. 18³/₄×21³/₄″ (47.5×55 cm)
1971 Acquired from the Zagorsk Art Reserve
Inv.no. Pc-8170

183
Metalworkers. 1929
India ink and watercolor; incisions. 18³/₄×12¹/₄″
(47.5×31 cm)
1971 Acquired from the Zagorsk Art Reserve
Inv.no. Pc-1871

184
A Gas Mask. Early 1930s
Oil on canvas. 34⁵/₈×26⁵/₈″ (88×67.5 cm)
1967 Acquired from the sculptor Boris
Kapliansky (Leningrad). Inv.no. Ж-8394

185
A Miner. 1933—34
Oil on canvas. 46³/₄×33³/₄″ (119×85.6 cm)
On the reverse: *Петр Осолодков 1933—34*
1934 Acquired from the artist (Leningrad)
Inv.no. ЖБ-1797

Pakhomov, Alexei Fiodorovich
1900—73
189
Young Girl in Blue. 1929
Oil on canvas. 31¹/₄×20¹/₂″ (79.5×52 cm)
Lower left: the artist's monogram *АП* and
the date *III 1929*
1929 Acquired from the artist (Leningrad)
Inv.no. Ж-8604

190
Young Archers. 1930
Oil on canvas. 42¹/₈×24⁵/₈″ (107×62.5 cm)
Lower right: the artist's monogram *АП* and
the date *II 30*
1970 Acquired from the artist (Leningrad)
Inv.no. Ж-8607

191
A Woman Reaping (Harvest Time). 1928
Oil on canvas. 33¹/₂×41³/₄″ (85×106 cm)
1970 Acquired from the artist (Leningrad)
Inv.no. Ж-8603

192
Portrait of a Milkmaid, Molodtsova. 1931
From the *Krasivaia Mech Commune* series
Oil on canvas mounted on cardboard. 21⁵/₈×13″
(55×33 cm)
Lower left: the artist's monogram *АП* and
the date *IX 31*
1933 Acquired from the artist (Leningrad)
Inv.no. ЖБ-1671

Pakulin, Viacheslav Vladimirovich
1900—51
174
Sailors (In a Tavern). 1929?
Oil on canvas. 35×22⁷/₈″ (89×58 cm)
1973 Acquired from the Leningrad branch
of the Russian Federation Artists Union
Inv.no. Ж-9207

175
A Woman Reaping. 1926—27
Oil on canvas. 59³/₄×73⁵/₈″ (152×187 cm)
Acquired in 1975; gift of the artist's daughter

L. Pakulina (Leningrad)
Inv.no. Ж-9441

176
Woman Carrying Water. 1928?
Oil on canvas. 73⁵/₈×59⁵/₈″ (187×151.5 cm)
Acquired in 1980; gift of the artist's daughter
L. Pakulina (Leningrad). Inv.no. Ж-10265

Palmov, Victor Nikandrovich
1888—1929
23
Composition with a Red Rider. 1920
Oil on canvas; gold leaf. 24³/₄×21″ (63×53.5 cm)
Lower right, in capitals: *Palmof*
On the reverse: *PALMOF 1920 г 200 р.*
1929 Acquired from the Tretiakov Gallery (Moscow)
Inv.no. ЖБ-1384

Pavlov, Semion Andreevich
1893—1941
114
A Vasilievsky Island Landscape. 1923
Oil on canvas. 35³/₄×30³/₄″ (91×78 cm)
Lower left: the artist's monogram *ПС* and *1923*
1977 Acquired from the artist's widow,
E. Pavlova (Leningrad). Inv.no. Ж-9302

Pestel, Vera Efremovna
1887—1952
79
Interior. Family at the Table. 1920—21
Oil on canvas. 34¹/₄×33⁷/₈″ (87×86 cm)
1974 Acquired from the artist's daughter
S. Pestel (Moscow). Inv.no. Ж-9016

Petrov-Vodkin, Kuzma Sergeevich
1878—1939
122
Still Life with a Herring. 1918
Oil on oilcloth. 22⁷/₈×34⁷/₈″ (58×88.5 cm)
Upper left: *1918 КПВ*
1933 Acquired from the artist (Leningrad)
Inv.no. ЖБ-1254

123
Death of the Commissar. 1928
Oil on canvas. 77¹/₈×97⁵/₈″ (196×248 cm)
Lower left: *КПВ 28*
1962 Acquired from the U.S.S.R. Central Museum
of Armed Forces (Moscow). Inv.no. Ж-7685

124
Nocturnal Fantasy (2:30 a.m.). 1921
Pencil and watercolor. 15¹/₈×12³/₈″ (38.4×31.5 cm)
To the left, in pencil: *2¹/₂ du matin;* lower:
23—24/XII—1921 года; lower left: *КПВ*
1969 Acquired from K. Guiterman (Leningrad)
Inv.no. Pc-7001

125
Sketch for the panel *Stepan Razin.* 1918
Watercolor. 14¹/₂×25″ (36.8×63.5 cm)
Lower right in pencil: *КПВ*
Acquired in 1920; gift of the Committee of the
All-Russian Society for the Encouragement
of the Arts. Inv.no. Pc-1437

126
Portrait of the Poet Anna Akhmatova. 1922
Oil on canvas. 21¹/₂×17¹/₈″ (54.5×43.5 cm)
Lower right: *КПВ 1922*
1933 Acquired from the artist (Leningrad)
Inv.no. Ж-2407

**Petrova-Trotskaia (Troitskaia),
Ekaterina Mikhailovna**
1900—32
177
Child Holding an Orange. 1928?
Oil on canvas. 55¹/₂×39³/₈″ (141×100 cm)
1987 Acquired from S. Shuster (Leningrad)
Inv.no. Ж-11623

Pimenov, Yuri Ivanovich
1903—77
164
Disabled Veterans. 1926
From the *War to War* cycle
Oil on canvas. 104¹/₂×70″ (265.6×177.7 cm)
Lower left: the artist's monogram *ПЮ, 1926,*
and *Москва*
1929 Acquired from the Tretiakov Gallery
(Moscow). Inv.no. ЖБ-994

Plastov, Arkady Alexandrovich
1893—1972
264
Collective-Farm Celebration. 1937
Oil on canvas. 74×120³/₄″ (188×307 cm)
Lower left: *А. П. 37.*
1953 Acquired from the Committee for Art Affairs
Attached to the Council of U.S.S.R. Ministers
Inv.no. Ж-5958

Pochtenny, Alexei Petrovich
1898—1942
186
Athletic Meet. Early 1930s
Oil on canvas. 37¹/₈×49¹/₄″ (145×125 cm)
On the reverse: *А. П. Почтенный. Ленинград В.О.
11 лин. д. 56 А кв. 24 "Легкоатлетические
соревнования"*
1979 Acquired from the artist's son O. Pochtenny
(Leningrad). Inv.no. Ж-9811

Popov, Igor Nikolaevich
Born 1905
266
Interior. 1937
Oil on canvas. 27¹/₂×33¹/₄″ (70×84.5 cm)
On the reverse: *Попов Иг. Ник. "В комнатах" 1937 г.*
1980 Acquired from the artist (Moscow)
Inv.no. Ж-10181

Proshkin, Victor Nikolaevich
1906—83
265
Near the Birzhevoi Bridge. 1935
Oil on canvas. 26×32⁷/₈″ (66×83.5 cm)
Lower right: *В. Прошкин 1935 г*
On the reverse: *В. Н. Прошкин у Биржевого моста
1935 г. х.м. 66× 83.5 (из окн дома 10
по наб. Макарова)*
Acquired from the artist's son V. Proshkin
(Leningrad). Inv.no. Ж-10953

Puni, Ivan Albertovich (later Jean Pougny)
1894—1956
14
Still Life with Russian Characters. 1919
Oil on canvas. 48⁷/₈×50″ (124×127 cm)
Lower right: *Ив. Пуни 1919 г.*
In the picture are individual Russian characters
and the words *spektr/begstvo*

1926 Acquired from the Museum of Artistic
Culture. Inv.no. ЖБ-2074

16
Still Life with a Red Violin. 1919
Oil on canvas. 57^1/$_8$×45^1/$_4$″ (145×115 cm)
1926 Acquired from the Museum of Artistic
Culture. Inv.no. ЖБ-1339

35
Still Life with Jug, Black Umbrella, and Hatbox
1910s
Oil on canvas. 29^3/$_4$×25^1/$_2$″ (75.5×64.7 cm)
Lower right: *Ив. Пуни*
In bottom right corner: *1913*
1920 Acquired from the artist
Inv.no. ЖБ-1354

42
Sketch for decoration for Liteiny Prospekt,
Petrograd. 1918—20
Watercolor, India ink, and whitening
24^3/$_8$×18^5/$_8$″ (62×47.4 cm)
Lower left in pencil: *Пуни. Литейный*
Acquired in 1939. Inv.no. СрБ-906

Redko, Kliment Nikolaevich
1897—1956
162
Midnight Sun over the Sea. 1925
Oil on canvas. 66^9/$_{10}$×31^3/$_4$″ (170×80.5 cm)
Lower right: *C. Redko 25*
1969 Acquired from the artist's widow, G. Redko
(Moscow). Inv.no. Ж-8542

267
A Parisienne. 1931
Oil on canvas. 77^9/$_{16}$×38^3/$_8$″ (197×97.5 cm)
Lower right: *Redko 1931*
1979 Acquired from the artist's widow, G. Redko
(Moscow). Inv.no. Ж-9959

Riazhsky, Georgi Georgievich
1895—1952
268
The Letter. 1939
Oil on canvas. 39^3/$_8$×31^1/$_8$″ (100×79 cm)
Lower right: *Г. Ряжский 1939*
1940 Acquired from the Purchasing Commission
(Moscow). Inv.no. Ж-5676

Rodchenko, Alexander Nikolaevich
1891—1956
65
Nonobjective Composition. 1918
Oil on wooden panel. 20^7/$_8$×8^1/$_4$″ (53×21 cm)
Lower right: *P. 18*
On the reverse: *Родченко 1918 г.*
1926 Acquired from the Museum of Artistic
Culture. Inv.no. ЖБ-1649

69
Black on Black. 1918
Oil on canvas. 33^1/$_8$×26^1/$_8$″ (84×66.5 cm)
1926 Acquired from the Museum of Artistic
Culture. Inv.no. ЖБ-1438

70
White Circle. 1918
Oil on canvas. 35^1/$_8$×28^1/$_8$″ (89.2×71.5 cm)
Lower right: *P. 18*
On the reverse: *Родченко 1918*
1926 Acquired from the Museum of Artistic
Culture. Inv.no. ЖБ-1439

Rozhdestvensky, Vasily Vasilievich
1884—1963
212
Still Life with a Red Pitcher. 1918
Oil on canvas. 35×33^1/$_8$″ (89×84 cm)
Lower right: *Рождественский 1918*
1929 Acquired from the Tretiakov Gallery (Moscow)
Inv.no. ЖБ-1703

213
Wood Grouse. 1921
Oil on canvas. 28×28^1/$_8$″ (71×71.5 cm)
Lower left: *Рождественский 21*
1964 Acquired from the artist's widow,
N. Rozhdestvenskaia (Moscow). Inv.no. Ж-8071

Rusakov, Alexander Isaakovich
1898—1952
179
The Electrician. 1928?
Oil on canvas. 64^1/$_2$×26^3/$_4$″ (164×68 cm)
1978 Acquired from the artist's son Y. Rusakov
(Leningrad). Inv.no. Ж-9771

Samokhvalov, Alexander Nikolaevich
1894—1971
193
A Tram Conductor. 1928
Tempera on canvas. 51^1/$_4$×50″ (130×127 cm)
Left-border center: the artist's monogram
AC and *28* [1928]
1976 Acquired from the artist's daughter
M. Samokhvalova (Leningrad). Inv.no. Ж-9186

194
A Camel. 1921
Watercolor and pencil. 17^3/$_4$×14″ (45.1×35.6 cm)
Lower right: *A. Самох*
1976 Acquired from the artist's daughter,
M. Samokhvalova (Leningrad). Inv.no. Pc-10166

269
A Member of Osoaviakhim. 1932
Study for the painting *Militarized Komsomol*
(1932—33), also in the Russian Museum
Oil and tempera on canvas
47^1/$_4$×45^3/$_4$″ (120×116 cm)
Lower left: *A C. 34—5* (a later inscription)
1940 Acquired from Lensovet. Inv.no. ЖБ-1787

Sarian, Martiros
1880—1972
152
A Bright Landscape. 1924
From the *Armenia* cycle
Oil on canvas. 55^1/$_8$×41″ (140×104 cm)
Lower right: *M. Сарьянъ 1924*
1925 Acquired from the Armenian Picture Gallery
(Yerevan). Inv.no. Ж-1999

153
Yerevan. 1924
Second version of a painting of the same title
and year in a private collection (Venice?)
Oil on canvas. 27^1/$_8$×26^3/$_4$″ (69×68 cm)
Lower right: *M. Сарьянъ, 1924*
On the reverse: *"Эривань" 2-й вариант.*
M. Сарьянъ 1924 г.
1927 Acquired from the State Museum Reserve
Inv.no. Ж-1998

Sashin, Andrei Timofeevich
1896—1965
105
Costume design for the Police Officer in Gogol's
The Inspector General. 1927
Watercolor and India ink
20^3/$_4$×12^1/$_2$″ (52.7×31.9 cm)
Lower left in pencil: *A. Сашин 27 г.*
1930 Acquired from the artist (Leningrad)
Inv.no. СрБ-123

Serebriakova, Zinaida Evgenievna
1884—1967
9
Self-Portrait. 1922
Oil on canvas. 27^1/$_8$×22″ (69×56 cm)
1957 Acquired from the artist's son
E. Serebriakov (Leningrad). Inv.no. Ж-6708

10
House of Cards. 1919
Oil on canvas. 25^5/$_8$×29^3/$_4$″ (65×75.5 cm)
1957 Acquired from the artist's son
E. Serebriakov (Leningrad). Inv.no. Ж-6634

Shchipitsyn, Alexander Vasilievich
1896—1943
270
Springtime. 1933
Oil on canvas. 39^3/$_8$×51^1/$_8$″ (100×130 cm)
Lower left: *A. Щипицын*
1982 Acquired from L. Zelenskaia (Moscow)
Inv.no. Ж-10551

Shchukin, Yuri Prokopievich
1904—35
273
An Airship over the Town. 1933
Oil on canvas. 39^9/$_{16}$×43^5/$_{16}$″ (100.5×110 cm)
Lower right: *Ю. Щ. 33 г.*
On the reverse: *120×150 Юр. Щукин 1933 г.*
"Аттракцион" Москва Юр. Щукин 1933 г.
1967 Acquired from the artist's widow,
A. Magidson (Moscow). Inv.no. Ж-8269

Shevchenko, Alexander Vasilievich
1883—1948
77
A Woman Ironing. 1920
Oil on canvas. 37×32^1/$_8$″ (94×82.5 cm)
Lower left: *АШ/20*
On the reverse: *A. Шевченко Гладильщица 1920*
84,5×94
1966 Acquired from the artist's daughter
T. Shevchenko (Moscow). Inv.no. Ж-8225

87
Composition with the Artist's Initials. 1934
Color monotype. 9^1/$_2$×8^1/$_{16}$″ (24.2×20.5 cm)
Upper right: *АШ/34*; lower: *аш*
Under the picture in pencil: *A. Шевченко 34*
[1934]
1966 Acquired from the artist's daughter
T. Shevchenko (Moscow). Inv.no. Crp-10325

271
Still Life with a Guitar. 1933
Oil on canvas. 25^5/$_8$×31^3/$_8$″ (65.2×79.8 cm)
Upper right: *АШ/33*
1973 Acquired from the artist's daughter
T. Shevchenko (Moscow). Inv.no. Ж-8925

Shishmareva, Tatiana Vladimirovna
Born 1905
272
Horses. At Noon. 1939
Watercolor and whitening
11$^{7}/_{8}$×15$^{1}/_{4}$" (30.3×38.8 cm)
Lower right: *Т. Шишмарева*
1965 Acquired from the artist (Leningrad)
Inv.no. Pc-6114

Shterenberg, David Petrovich
1881—1948
157
Table with a Roll. 1919
Oil on canvas. 35×21" (89×53.5 cm)
Lower left: *Д. Ш.*
On the reverse: *Д. Штеренберг 1919 г Москва*
1920 Acquired from the artist (Moscow)
Inv.no. ЖБ-1379

160
Portrait of Nadezhda Shterenberg, the Artist's Wife
1925
Oil on canvas. 55$^{7}/_{8}$×34$^{5}/_{8}$" (142×88 cm)
Lower left: *D. Sterenberg*
On the stretcher: *Портрет Н. Штеренберг жены
художника 1925 г 142× 88 Д Штеренберг*
1981 Acquired from the artist's daughter
V. Shterenberg (Moscow). Inv.no. Ж-10339

161
Still Life with Oil Lamp and Herring. 1920
Oil on plywood. 35$^{1}/_{4}$×24$^{5}/_{8}$" (89.5×62.5 cm)
Lower left: *Д Штеренберг*
1920 Acquired from IZO Narkompros
Inv.no. ЖБ-1359

Shukhaev, Vasily Ivanovich
1887—1974
11
Still Life with Loaves of Bread: Normandy. 1923
Oil on canvas. 35$^{3}/_{4}$×28$^{7}/_{8}$" (91×73.5 cm)
Lower right: *В. Шухаев 1923 V. I. Choukhaeff
19[23]*
1977 Acquired from the artist's widow,
V. Shukhaeva (Moscow). Inv.no. Ж-9765

Sinezubov, Nikolai Vladimirovich
1891—1948
78
A Street. Early Spring. 1920
Oil on cardboard. 24×19$^{7}/_{8}$" (61×50.5 cm)
Lower left: *Н. Синезубов 1920 г.*
1926 Acquired from the Museum of Artistic
Culture. Inv.no. ЖБ-1353

83
Mother and Child. 1919
Oil on canvas. 25$^{1}/_{4}$×18$^{1}/_{8}$" (64×46 cm)
Lower left: *Н. Синезубов 19*
1920 Acquired from IZO Narkompros
Inv.no. ЖБ-1356

Sofronova, Antonina Fiodorovna
1892—1966
198, 200
Constructivist Compositions (2). 1922
Black India ink and gouache on colored paper
8$^{7}/_{8}$×7$^{1}/_{8}$" (22.5×18.1 cm) (each piece)
Signed lower right on both sheets: *АФС*
1984 Acquired from the artist's daughter
I. Evstafieva (Moscow). Inv.nos. Pc-12412, Pc-12414

199
Street Urchins by an Asphalt Boiler. 1924
From the *Street Scenes: The NEP Period* series
Charcoal. 14×12" (35.7×30.7 cm)
Lower left: *А. Софрон 24*
1974 Acquired from the artist's daughter
I. Evstafieva (Moscow). Inv.no. Pc-8973

201
After the Bathhouse. 1933?
Oil on canvas. 23$^{5}/_{8}$×19$^{5}/_{8}$" (60×50 cm)
Upper right: *А. Софронова 1933 (1939?)*
On the stretcher: *А. Софронова*
1983 Acquired from the artist's daughter
I. Evstafieva (Moscow). Inv.no. Ж-10689

Sokolov, Mikhail Ksenofontovich
1885—1947
274
Still Life with Fish. 1930s
Oil on canvas. 20$^{3}/_{4}$×27$^{3}/_{4}$" (52.7×70.5 cm)
Lower left: *M. Sokolov*
1967 Acquired from E. Tannenberg (Moscow)
Inv.no. Ж-8397

Sokolova, Olga Alexandrovna
Born 1899
216
Women's Bazaar at Urgut. 1932
Oil on canvas. 49$^{1}/_{4}$×49$^{3}/_{8}$" (125×125.5 cm)
On the reverse: *Соколова Ольга Александровна
"Женский базар в Ургуте", 1932 г., Х., М.,
125×125,5*
1980 Acquired from the U.S.S.R. Artists Union
Inv.no. Ж-10248

Stenberg, Georgi Avgustovich
1900—33
68
A Hoisting Crane. 1920
Oil on canvas. 27$^{15}/_{16}$×35" (71×89 cm)
Lower right: *Георгий Стенберг 1920 г.*
On the reverse: *Георгий Стенберг "Подъемный
кран" 1920 г. 1 ар×1 ар. 4 в*
1926 Acquired from the Museum of Artistic
Culture. Inv.no. ЖБ-1440

Stenberg, Vladimir Avgustovich
1889—1982
67
Color Composition No. 4. 1920
Oil on canvas. 29$^{1}/_{2}$×15$^{1}/_{8}$" (75×38.5 cm)
On the reverse: *В. Стенберг 1920 г. Цвето-
конструкция № 4 17×9*
1926 Acquired from the Museum of Artistic
Culture. Inv.no. ЖБ-1645

Stepanova, Varvara Fiodorovna
1894—1958
66
Sheet from the artist's album VARST. 1919?
Linocut on red paper
6$^{1}/_{2}$×4$^{1}/_{2}$" (16.7×11.5 cm)
Acquired from the Section of Graphic Works
of the Russian Museum. Inv.no. Crp-6855

Stroev, Piotr Feonovich
1898—1942
275
At a State Poultry Farm. 1934
Oil on canvas. 31$^{1}/_{8}$×38$^{3}/_{4}$" (79×98.5 cm)

Lower right: *Строев П. Ф. 1934 г.*
1940 Acquired from Lensovet. Inv.no. ЖБ-1863

Strzeminski, Wladyslaw
1893—1953
31
The Tools and Fruits of Production. 1920
Oil on canvas mounted on wood, metal details,
gypsum powder, and cork
17$^{1}/_{2}$×13" (44.5×33 cm)
On the reverse: *Стржеминский*
1926 Acquired from the Museum of Artistic
Culture. Inv.no. ЖБ-1665

Suetin, Nikolai Mikhailovich
1897—1954
57
Woman with a Saw. 1920s?
Oil on wooden panel
21$^{5}/_{8}$×13$^{1}/_{8}$" (55×33.3 cm)
Acquired in 1956. Inv.no. Ж-11545

59
Design for a mural. 1920
Colored India ink. 8×7$^{1}/_{8}$" (20.3×18.2 cm)
Lower left in pencil: *Витебск Суетин 20 г.;*
lower right: *эскиз росписи стены*
1932 Acquired from the artist (Leningrad)
Inv.no. Pc-3053

60
Design for a Unovis podium. 1921
Gouache and whitening on black paper
14×10$^{1}/_{2}$" (35.8×26.7 cm)
Lower right in white: *Витебск 21 г. проект
трибуны УНОВИС. Суетин*
1932 Acquired from the artist (Leningrad)
Inv.no. Pc-3051

Sulimo-Samuillo, Vsevolod Angelovich
1903—65
109
Self-Portrait
Pencil and watercolor. 9$^{3}/_{4}$×7" (24.6×17.6 cm)
1969 Acquired from the artist's widow,
N. Neratova (Leningrad). Inv.no. Pc-7425

110
A Skating Rink
Ink. 8$^{1}/_{2}$×6" (21.8×15.1 cm)
1969 Acquired from the artist's widow,
N. Neratova (Leningrad). Inv.no. Pc-7434

Svarog (Korochkin), Vasily Semionovich
1883—1946
119
Self-Portrait. 1923
Oil on cardboard. 34$^{5}/_{8}$×20$^{7}/_{8}$" (88×53 cm)
Lower left: *В. Сварог 1923*
1954 Acquired from the Tretiakov Gallery (Moscow)
Inv.no. Ж-6053

Tambi, Vladimir Alexandrovich
1906—55
276
Tanks. From the Tanks series. 1930
Gouache on colored paper
10$^{5}/_{8}$×15$^{1}/_{2}$" (27×39.5 cm)
Lower right: *Tambi 1930 г.*
1985 Acquired from the artist's widow, L. Tambi
(Leningrad). Inv.no. Pc-13283

Tatlin, Vladimir Evgrafovich
1885—1953
28
Stage design for Velimir Khlebnikov's *Zangezi*
produced by the Museum of Artistic Culture in
Petrograd. 1923
Charcoal drawing. 21³/₄×30″ (55.4×76.1 cm)
Lower left in pencil: *Тат 23 г.*
1928 Acquired from the artist (Leningrad)
Inv.no. СрБ-416

29
Costume design for Richard Wagner's *The Flying
Dutchman*. 1915—17
Charcoal drawing. 28¹/₂×20″ (72.2×51 cm)
Lower left: *Тат*
Acquired in 1930. Inv.no. СрБ-418

277
Flowers. 1940
Oil on wooden panel. 29³/₄×26¹/₂″ (75.5×67.5 cm)
1967 Acquired from the Shchusev Scientific-
Research Museum of Architecture (Moscow)
Inv.no. Ж-8350

Tsvetkov, Boris Ivanovich
1893/95?—1942/45?
278
Heated Reservoir and Log Conveyer. 1932
From the *Timber Industry* series
Oil on canvas. 41×27″ (104×68.5 cm)
Lower left: *Б. Цветков 1932*
On the stretcher: *"Отепленный бассейн
и бревнотаска" Б. Цветков*
1933 Acquired from the artist (?) at the
exhibition "Artists of the Russian Federation:
Fifteen Years." Inv.no. ЖБ-1394

Tyrsa, Nikolai Andreevich
1887—1942
40
Worker with a Hammer. 1918
Sketch of decoration on Nevsky Prospekt, corner
of Liteiny Prospekt, in Petrograd
Watercolor and India ink. 11×5¹/₄″ (27.9×13.2 cm)
Lower right in India ink: *Тырса*
1939 Acquired from the Hermitage Museum Reserve
Inv.no. СрБ-956

138
*Portrait of the Artist's Daughter (A Sleeping
Girl)*. 1929
Watercolor. 14³/₄×13¹/₂″ (37.5×34.2 cm)
1935 Acquired from the artist (Leningrad)
Inv.no. Рс-1664

139
Portrait of the Poet Anna Akhmatova. 1928
Lampblack. 14³/₈×8⁷/₈″ (36.5×22.7 cm)
1967 Acquired from the artist's daughter
A.Tyrsa (Leningrad). Inv.no. Рс-6681

279
Interior in Pink. 1935
Oil on canvas. 21³/₄×26″ (55×66 cm)
1967 Acquired from the Leningrad branch of the
U.S.S.R. Artists Union. Without inventory number

Tyshler, Alexander Grigorievich
1898—1980
169
Portrait of a Woman. 1934
Oil on canvas. 25³/₄×21³/₄″ (65.5×55.5 cm)

Lower right: *А. Тышлер 1934*
Acquired in 1984; gift of M. Milshtein (together
with G. Levitin's estate) (Leningrad)
Inv.no. Ж-10969

170
Young Red Army Men Reading a Newspaper. 1936
Oil on canvas. 22×25¹/₂″ (56×65 cm)
Lower left: *А. Тышлер*
On the stretcher: *юные красноармейцы читают
газету*
1967 Acquired from the artist (Moscow)
Inv.no. Ж-8292

Udaltsova, Nadezhda Andreevna
1886—1961
21
Model. 1914
Oil on canvas. 41³/₄×28″ (106×71 cm)
1926 Acquired from the Museum of Artistic
Culture. Inv.no. ЖБ-1712

30
Still Life. 1919
Oil on canvas. 36¹/₄×42¹/₈″ (92×108 cm)
Lower right: *Н. Удальц 1919 г.*
On the reverse: *N. Oudaltzowa Nature-morte 1919
Moscou*
1929 Acquired from the Tretiakov Gallery (Moscow)
Inv.no. ЖБ-1697

Ulianov, Nikolai Pavlovich
1885—1949
146
Portrait of the Symbolist Poet Viacheslav Ivanov
1920
Oil on canvas. 31³/₄×29¹/₈″ (80.5×74 cm)
Lower right: *Н. Ульянов 1920*
1947 Acquired from the Tretiakov Gallery (Moscow)
Inv.no. Ж-5622

Uspensky, Alexei Alexandrovich
1892—1941
280
Girl in a Rocking Chair
Watercolor and whitening
12⁷/₈×8³/₄″ (32.8×22.3 cm)
Inv.no. СрБ-279

Utkin, Piotr Savvich
1877—1934
137
Flowers in a White Jug. 1923
Oil on canvas. 19³/₄×18″ (50×45.5 cm)
Lower right: *П. Уткин 923 г*
1933 Acquired from the artist (Leningrad)
Inv.no. ЖБ-1666

Vasnetsov, Yuri Alexeevich
1900—73
281
Still Life with a Chess Board. 1926—28
Oil on plywood, wooden cane. 42¹/₂×22″
(108×56 cm)
On the reverse: *Ю. Васнецов Композиц с шахматн
доской. НИЗ!* Upper center: *ВЕРХ!*
1981 Acquired from the artist's widow,
G. Vasnetsova (Leningrad). Inv.no. Ж-10409

282
Vyatka: A Courtyard. 1925
Pencil. 12×14¹/₂″ (30.7×36.7 cm)

Lower right: *Вятка 1925 Ю. Васн*
1986 Acquired from the artist's widow,
G. Vasnetsova (Leningrad). Inv.no. Рс-13168

283
A Storehouse. 1925
Colored crayons and pencil
12¹/₂×17¹/₄″ (31.7×43.8 cm)
Lower right in pencil: *Вятка 1925 Ю. Васн*
1986 Acquired from the artist's widow,
G. Vasnetsova (Leningrad). Inv.no. Рс-13170

284
Composition with Artificial Fishes. 1928—31
Oil on canvas. 46¹/₂×37″ (118×94 cm)
1981 Acquired from the artist's widow,
G. Vasnetsova (Leningrad). Inv.no. Ж-10412

Vedernikov, Alexander Semionovich
1898—1975
173
Nude on a Sofa. 1935
Watercolor and India ink. 16¹/₄×11¹/₂″
(41.5×29.5 cm)
Lower left in pencil: *А. Ведерников*; lower right:
А. Ведерников 1935
1980 Acquired from the artist's widow, N. Mazais
(Leningrad). Inv.no. Рс-11131

188
*Leningrad. View from a Window of the Sculptor
Kapliansky's Studio*. 1930
Oil on canvas. 27×22″ (68.5×56 cm)
Lower left: *А. Ведерников*
On the reverse: the artist's painting entitled
Landscape: The Volga (1930s)
1978 Acquired from the artist's widow, N. Mazais
(Leningrad). Inv.no. Ж-9704

Vereisky, Georgi Semionovich
1886—1962
143
A Young Painter. 1928
Black chalk. 23¹/₂×16³/₄″ (60×42.6 cm)
Lower left: *Г. В. 1928*
1965 Acquired from the artist's widow,
R. Vereiskaia (Leningrad). Inv.no. Рс-5973

Vladimirov, Ivan Alexeevich
1869—1947
117
The Photographer's Visit. 1921
Oil on canvas. 15¹/₄×22″ (39×56 cm)
Lower right: *И. Владимиров 1921*
1986 Acquired from T. Dioletova (Leningrad)
Inv.no. Ж-11575

Voinov, Sviatoslav Vladimirovich
1890—1920
8
Little Houses
Pencil drawing. 8¹/₄×13¹/₂″ (20.8×34.5 cm)
Acquired in 1972; gift of O. Lavrova (Leningrad)
Inv.no. Рс-8535

Volkov, Alexander Nikolaevich
1886—1957
285
Cotton Hilling. 1930s
Oil on canvas. 46¹/₂×81³/₄″ (118×208 cm)
Upper left: *А. Волков*
1981 Acquired from the artist's son V. Volkov
(Moscow). Inv.no. Ж-10400

286
Tea. 1926
Tempera, India ink, and watercolor; varnish
11 3/4×11 7/8″ (30×30.3 cm)
Lower right in India ink: *А. Волков*
1983 Acquired from the artist's son V. Volkov
(Moscow). Inv.no. Рс-12066

287
Black Woman. 1921
Oil on canvas. 39 3/8×39 3/8″ (100×100 cm)
Lower left: *А. Волков.*
The artist's (?) inscription on the reverse:
А. Волков Черная женщина 1921 г
1983 Acquired from the artist's son V. Volkov
(Moscow). Inv.no. Ж-10585

Williams, Piotr Vladimirovich
1902—47
172
Portrait of Konstantin Stanislavsky. 1933
Oil on canvas. 51 1/4×69 1/2″ (130×175.5 cm)
Lower right: *Петр Вильямс 33*
1934 Acquired from Vsekokhudozhnik. Inv.no. ЖБ-1309

288
Woman in a Window. 1930s
Oil on canvas. 62 3/4×51 1/4″ (159.5×130 cm)
Acquired from Vsekokhudozhnik (?)
Without inventory number

Yakovlev, Vasily Nikolaevich
1893—1956
118
A Courtyard. 1918
Oil on canvas. 31 7/8×25 1/4″ (81×64 cm)
Lower right: *Jakovleff W. fecit <...> 1918.*
1984 Acquired from M. Bogatyreva (Leningrad)
Without inventory number

Yudin, Lev Alexandrovich
1903—41
62
Still Life with Orange Creamer and Bottle. 1930s
Oil on canvas. 18×13 1/4″ (45.5×33.5 cm)
On the reverse: the artist's painting entitled
Still Life with Apple and Fork
1979 Acquired from the artist's widow,
M. Gorokhova (Leningrad). Inv.no. Ж-10094

Zagoskin, David Efimovich
1900—42
187
Sewing. 1929
Oil on canvas mounted on plywood
46 1/4×39 3/8″ (117.5×100 cm)
Lower right: *Д. Загоскйн. 1929 г.*
On the reverse: *Д. Загоскин*
1930 Acquired from the artist (Leningrad)
Inv.no. ЖБ-1476

Zaklikovskaia, Sofia Liudvigovna
1899—1975
108
Old and New Life Styles. 1927
Oil on canvas. 47 5/8×111 1/4″ (121×282 cm)
On the reverse: *Закликовская С. Л. 1927 г.*
1979 Acquired from the artist's daughter
K. Suvorova (Leningrad). Inv.no. Ж-9777

...osition: In the Countryside. Early 1930s

India ink and pencil. 12 1/2×7 7/8″ (31.7×20 cm)
1984 Acquired from the artist's daughter
K. Suvorova (Leningrad). Inv.no. Рс-12461

Zdanevich, Kirill Mikhailovich
1892—1969
32
Nude Seen from Behind. Late 1910s
India ink. 8 5/8×8 1/8″ (22×20.5 cm)
1985 Acquired from the artist's daughter
V. Zdanevich (Tbilisi). Inv.no. Рс-13066

Zefirov, Konstantin Klavdievich
1879—1960
214
Portrait of a Girl (The Artist's Daughter Lena)
1920s
Oil on canvas. 27 3/4×22 3/4″ (70.5×58 cm)
On the reverse: *К. К. Зефиров. Портрет девочки
(дочь Лена) Первая половина 1920х гг*
1980 Acquired from the artist's son A. Zefirov
(Moscow). Inv.no. Ж-10169

215
Woman at Work. 1920s
Oil on canvas. 29 3/4×24 1/4″ (75.7×61.5 cm)
On the reverse: *Работница К. К. Зефиров
"Работница" Вторая половина 1920х гг*
1980 Acquired from the artist's son A. Zefirov
(Moscow). Inv.no. Ж-10171

Zevin, Lev Yakovlevich
1903—42
196
Poultry House of a Jewish Commune. 1930
Watercolor, gouache, and whitening
13 3/4×20 3/8″ (35×51.7 cm)
Lower right in pencil: *Лев Зевин 1930 г.*
1932 Acquired from the artist (Moscow)
Inv.no. СрБ-1173

Abbreviations

AKhR	Association of Artists of the Revolution
AKhRR	Association of Artists of Revolutionary Russia
IKhK	Institute of Artistic Culture, Leningrad
Inkhuk	Institute of Artistic Culture, Moscow
IZO Narkompros	Visual Arts Section of the People's Commissariat for Education
Lef	Left Front of the Arts
Lensovet	Leningrad Soviet of People's Deputies
Mossovet	Moscow Soviet of People's Deputies
NOZh	The New Society of Painters
Obmokhu	The Society of Young Artists
OMAKhR	Association of AKhR Youth
OMKh	The Society of Moscow Artists
OMZh	The Society of Moscow Painters
OST	The Society of Easel Artists
RAPKh	Russian Association of Proletarian Artists
Sovnarkom	The Council of People's Commissars
Unovis	Union of the New Art/Affirmers of the New Art
Vkhutemas/Vkhutein	Higher Art-Technical Studios/Institute
Vsekokhudozhnik	All-Russian Cooperative of Artists

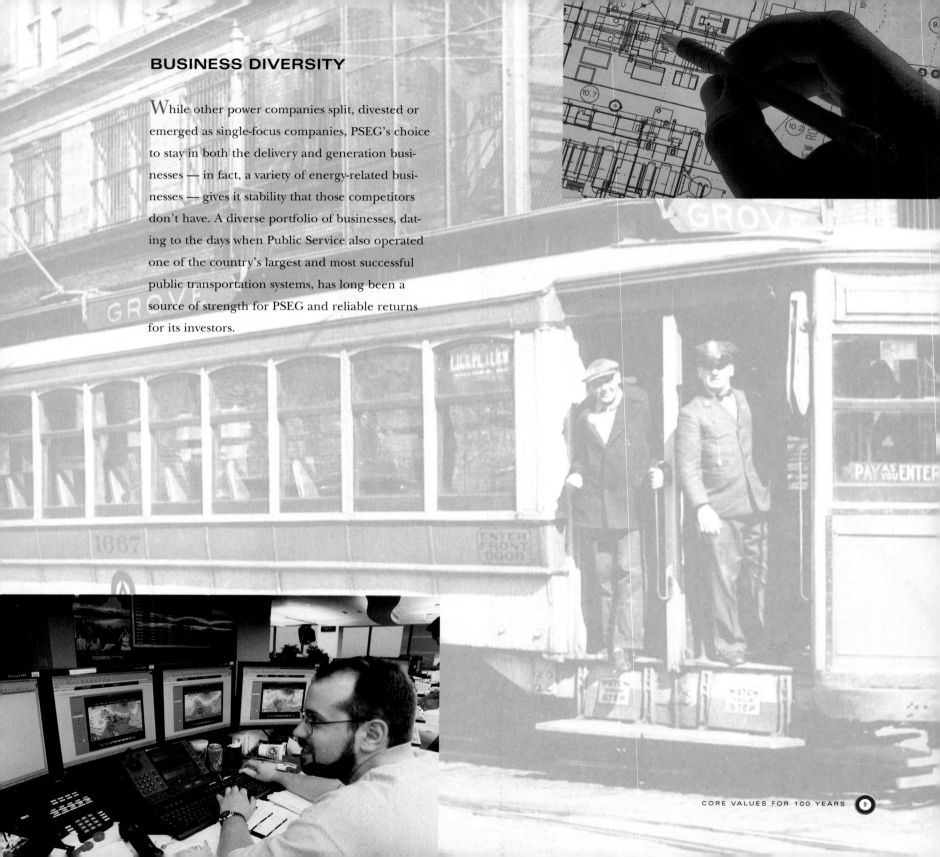

BUSINESS DIVERSITY

While other power companies split, divested or emerged as single-focus companies, PSEG's choice to stay in both the delivery and generation businesses — in fact, a variety of energy-related businesses — gives it stability that those competitors don't have. A diverse portfolio of businesses, dating to the days when Public Service also operated one of the country's largest and most successful public transportation systems, has long been a source of strength for PSEG and reliable returns for its investors.

NEW JERSEY HOME TEAM

PSEG's dedication to its home city and state has never wavered. It reaffirmed its commitment to Newark in the 1970s when it decided to stay in the city rather than follow other companies to the suburbs. Today PSEG actively partici-

pates in the public/private partnership to revitalize Newark's South Ward, as well as many other New Jersey urban initiatives. Its environmental commitment is exemplified by the award-winning Estuary Enhancement Program, which has created the largest protected wetlands area in the United States. PSEG has also been a leader on such issues as the harbor dredging referendum, New Jersey Green Acres funding, and air-quality issues.

SAFETY FIRST, WORLDWIDE

In the old days, employees donned shirts and ties for formal safety training. Today, the safety culture at PSEG reaches into every field location in New Jersey and around the world. With projects in thirteen countries on five continents, PSEG Global works to ensure that the safety, ethics and environmental responsibility of all its locations will meet its established standards. By raising the safety standards for the industry worldwide, PSEG is preparing for the future and choosing long-term success over easy, short-term profits.

Published and produced by Greenwich Publishing Group, Inc.
Lyme, Connecticut
www.greenwichpublishing.com

Designed by Clare Cunningham Graphic Design

Library of Congress Control Number: 2002117647

ISBN: 0-944641-59-8

First Printing: February 2003

10 9 8 7 6 5 4 3 2 1

The following are trademarks or registered trademarks of PSEG Corporation and its subsidiaries:
WorryFree and TradeLink

Photography Credits:
All images and artifacts pictured in the book appear courtesy of PSEG except the following images:
p. 7 (bottom right) p. 9 (top right), p. 14, p. 15, p. 104, p. 105, p. 108, p. 109 (bottom), p. 111,
© 2002 John Madere; p. 17, (top and bottom), p. 94, © Michael Melford; p. 17 (center), p. 72, p. 76,
courtesy of Craig Hammell; p. 82 courtesy of Gary Hofheimer Photography; p. 102 (left) © Richard
Berenholtz/CORBIS; p. 116 (top right) © David Street

PSEG expresses its sincerest thanks to John Masi, PSEG's creative director; PSEG photographers Mark
Lovretin, Thomas "Tom" Marren and Dave Sleeper; and other PSEG photographers throughout history
who so magnificently documented the company's first 100 years. Thanks, too, to interns Ricky Sirriani
and Bill Critchley for photographic research, and to Melissa Kern (PSEG Global) and Virginia Swichel
(PSEG Nuclear) for help with memorabilia and site research. We also appreciate the assistance of the New
Jersey Press Association, the New Jersey Information Center at the Newark Public Library, and the Rutgers
Special Collections and University Archives for their contributions to our historical and photographic
research.

Photography of PSEG artifacts by Edwina Stevenson.

MAKING THINGS WORK

PSEG'S FIRST CENTURY

Marian Calabro

GREENWICH PUBLISHING GROUP, INC.
LYME, CONNECTICUT

MAKING THINGS WORK

PSEG'S FIRST CENTURY

WE MAKE THINGS WORK

P ERHAPS YOU'RE HEADING HOME TO NEW JERSEY LATE ONE NIGHT. YOU FASTEN YOUR SEAT BELT FOR THE DESCENT INTO NEWARK AIRPORT, OR YOU PAY YOUR LAST TOLL ON THE GARDEN STATE PARKWAY OR THE NEW JERSEY TURNPIKE. AT SOME POINT, YOU REFLEXIVELY TAKE IN THE BLANKET OF ILLUMINATION THAT STRETCHES ALL AROUND YOU. YOU PROBABLY DON'T THINK TWICE ABOUT THE SOURCE, BUT IF YOU DID, YOU'D REALIZE THAT PSEG KEEPS THOSE LIGHTS LIT — THE SAME PSEG THAT RELIABLY HEATS THE HOME TO WHICH YOU'RE RETURNING. ☐ OR PERHAPS YOU RUN A SMALL MANUFACTURING PLANT IN SOUTHERN POLAND. YOU MAY NOT KNOW, OR CARE, THAT PSEG GLOBAL NOW OWNS AND OPERATES YOUR COUNTRY'S OLDEST CONTINUALLY OPERATED POWER PLANT. WHAT MATTERS TO YOU IS THAT YOUR POWER SUPPLY IS MORE DEPENDABLE THAN IT USED TO BE, AND THAT YOUR BUSINESS IS BETTER POSITIONED TO GROW.

FINDS PSEG'S WORLD
HEADQUARTERS AT 80
PARK PLAZA (CENTER
OF PHOTO) BRIGHTLY
ILLUMINATED. RIGHT:
NEW BRUNSWICK GAS
EMPLOYEE AL D'ANGELO
WELDS A PIPELINE.

PSEG is accustomed to being invisible, in a sense. And that's usually a good thing, because the company is most visible to customers during times of emergency. People tend to notice their utilities only when a storm knocks them out. The rest of the time, electricity and gas seem to flow into homes, offices and factories almost by magic — commodities with phenomenal power but no evident look or shape.

This book is not an engineering text. It won't explain the "magic" of PSEG's services in terms of kilowatt-hours and compression rates. What will become visible is the family of companies that are Public Service Enterprise Group and their remarkable century-long commitment to employees, customers, communities and investors.

PSEG's 100-year anniversary is a time to celebrate the bedrock values that remain at the heart of the company today and are guiding it into the future. The stories in this book bring to life the company's longstanding commitment to safety and the environment, shareholder value, customer service, new technologies and new markets. As the history unfolds, you'll see how PSEG has survived and thrived since 1903: by honoring its promises and making smart choices at critical times.

A HISTORY OF DEPENDABILITY

Although its founder, Thomas Nesbitt McCarter, was one of the most colorful and influential figures in New Jersey history, PSEG has traditionally shied away from blowing its own horn. "Stable, solid, dependable" is how Chairman and CEO E. James Ferland describes the PSEG culture.

Stable, solid companies tend not to make headlines. They do tend to strengthen everything they touch. At PSEG, these have been conscious

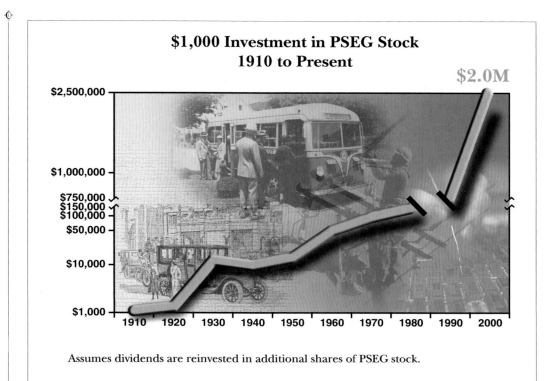

$1,000 Investment in PSEG Stock 1910 to Present

$2.0M

$2,500,000

$1,000,000

$750,000
$150,000
$100,000

$50,000

$10,000

$1,000

1910 1920 1930 1940 1950 1960 1970 1980 1990 2000

Assumes dividends are reinvested in additional shares of PSEG stock.

choices from the start.

"We've been dependable for employees as a place to work," the plainspoken Ferland says. "Dependable for customers — lights are on, gas is on — and for investors as well." In fact, auditors for the New Jersey Board of Public Utilities have singled out PSE&G as the state's "reliability leader," and PSEG stock (NYSE ticker symbol PEG) has paid dividends each and every year since the first offering of public shares in 1907.

"Since getting into the global arena, we have a lot of international partners and we're dependable for them," the chairman adds.

The company entered the global arena in the 1980s, part of an ambitious set of choices that became a turning point. PSEG chose to grow beyond its traditional borders *without* sacrificing

SHAREHOLDER VALUE HAS ALWAYS BEEN CENTRAL TO PSEG'S VISION. ON THE COMPANY'S 40TH ANNIVERSARY, PRESIDENT THOMAS N. MCCARTER DECLARED THAT PUBLIC SERVICE WOULD ALWAYS LIVE UP TO ITS "THREE-FOLD RESPONSIBILITY: TO THE CUSTOMER, TO THE EMPLOYEE AND TO THE STOCKHOLDER."

Mutual Gains in Poland

Poland is highly industrial, yet more rural and beautiful than outsiders think. The people who live and work there care about the environment and social issues. Labor unions are strong. The government is taking a responsible, economically sound approach to the restructuring of the energy marketplace.

Poland, in short, is a lot like New Jersey. Maybe that's why PSEG feels so at home there.

PSEG Global has made Poland its main target market for business development in Europe. The combined heat and power plant it is constructing in Chorzów, set to open in 2003, replaces a worn-out unit in a highly polluted region with state-of-the-art, clean-burning coal technology. In Skawina, 50 miles east, the company is upgrading a plant that supplies electricity to local power distribution companies and heat to the city of Krakow. Customers have already signed long-term agreements to purchase the output of both plants.

Successful negotiations with numerous unions have been vital to PSEG Global's success in Poland, says Nelson Garcez, managing director, Europe and North Africa region. While the projects required some downsizing from their previously state-run structures, as privatizations generally do, initial job losses were balanced by job protections and "social packages" of benefits that the unions voted to approve.

"The unions were receptive to having real conversations," confirms Matthew McGrath, vice president and general counsel, PSEG Global. "The truth is the truth wherever you are. The people in Solidarity [Poland's most famous trade union and a significant political force] told us we can count on collecting on our investment. They look at PSEG in Poland as a good thing to create jobs and bigger opportunities in the long term."

PSEG Global is building a new, efficient and environmentally advanced power plant at its Elcho site in Poland and will retire older, less efficient capacity that it acquired.

its commitment to New Jersey. By applying the expertise and values cultivated in New Jersey, it now provides safe, dependable, environmentally friendly energy service in nearly a dozen states and on five continents.

"We've successfully completed the transformation from a regulated New Jersey utility to a competitive global energy company, but PSEG is not into being big for the sake of being big," notes Robert E. Busch, president and chief operating officer, PSEG Services Corporation. "We're into being big if it can create shareholder value."

THE NEED TO GROW

The historic core of PSEG is the subsidiary PSE&G, Public Service Electric and Gas Company, which delivers energy to more than 5.5 million residents in New Jersey communities. That ampersand in "PSE&G" is important, because it differentiates PSE&G from its parent company and from PSEG's other major subsidiaries, PSEG Energy Holdings and PSEG Power.

Traditionally, most of the company's business resided within PSE&G, and therefore within the borders of New Jersey. In fact, after the company shed its transit subsidiary in 1980, PSE&G generated virtually 100 percent of earnings.

Around that time, company leaders foresaw the need to develop into new areas. The relative lack of growth opportunities in New Jersey, the most densely populated and developed state in the union, made it especially urgent to look outward for continued growth.

Moreover, the 1970s and 1980s were marked by oil embargos, ferocious inflation and a stock market crash. Many American businesses had to diversify, merge or acquire simply to survive.

One result, says Alfred C. Koeppe, PSE&G president and chief operating officer, is that "very few home teams are left in this state. Companies of great strength disappeared, or were merged or acquired. Or their global reach ended up superseding any local interest they had. By now, only a handful of major New Jersey companies have a continuous, 100-year history with essentially the same name." Koeppe is right. PSEG's's longevity places it among such esteemed New Jersey centurions as Campbell Soup, Congoleum, Johnson & Johnson, Prudential Financial and Merck & Co., Inc.

WORLDWIDE HOME TEAMS

PSEG could have chosen to grow through a merger or acquisition; possibilities have presented themselves. It could have chosen to redirect the more than $200 million it typically devotes to New Jersey each year. (In 2001 the company invested $200 million in energy conservation and education programs, and $8.3 million in economic development and charitable giving.) PSEG's choice is to remain a home team with home-team values wherever it operates.

"We keep our promises," Koeppe emphasizes.

PSEG GLOBAL AUGMENTED ITS PRESENCE IN PERU IN 2001 BY PURCHASING ELECTROANDES, AN ELECTRIC GENERATION COMPANY THAT OWNS AND OPERATES SEVERAL HYDRO-ELECTRIC FACILITIES.

■ Electric Only
□ Gas Only
■ Electric and Gas

PSE&G delivers energy to more than 5.5 million residents in New Jersey communities. The company and state developed and grew in tandem. Because its service territory includes the six largest cities — Newark, Jersey City, Paterson, Trenton, Camden and New Brunswick — PSE&G is especially committed to urban development.

Virginia Wright, a document management clerk at Salem Nuclear Generating Station, takes pride in the work her department does. Like many people at PSEG, Wright contributes to a process that is invisible to the outside world but essential to the safety and reliability of PSEG operations.

Virginia Wright

Salem's document control system is a giant electronic reference library. It contains hundreds of thousands of manufacturers' manuals and other documents — including handwritten engineering calculations — that are painstakingly scanned and catalogued by Wright and her co-workers. Engineers and technicians rely on this information, which is frequently updated, to maintain the special-ized and delicate pieces of equipment that run Salem.

"If there's a procedure, a calculation, a drawing, just about anything the technicians need to see, they can go to any computer here or off-site and call it up through our system," Wright explains. "The documents we put out are as perfect as we can make them, legible and up to date, because we realize that someone could get injured as a result of having the wrong revision of a document. Safety is all-important."

Wright's sense of purpose is matched by her enthusiasm for the work environment at Salem, where she started in 1985. "It's a desirable place to work," she says. "People fight to get jobs here."

"You can yell at us sometimes, disagree with us sometimes, but when you look around, you say, 'Hey, this is the company that hires my son or daughter, provides my service, cares about safety, is there when I need it.'"

Koeppe cites the success of New Jersey's energy restructuring as a prime example of promises kept: "We said we're going to keep reliability and service up, even as rates went down, and we have." And PSE&G's customers did not suffer the electric supply problems that occurred as a result of restructuring in other states, particularly California.

You know that PSEG is truly a home team when you hear the same message from the workers who put on their safety equipment every day and provide that reliable service. "One of the big pluses this company has is a work force that lives in New Jersey, works in New Jersey and is committed to

New Jersey and PSEG because that's our future," says Ernie Meyer, an underground division mechanic in PSE&G's Central Division in Franklin and a member of Local 94 of the International Brotherood of Electrical Workers (IBEW), the union that represents most electric workers at PSE&G.

"We know our areas, and we know the people," Meyer emphasizes. "We drive around the streets, and we know that if we do a lousy job, we'll hear about it right away." New Jerseyans are tough customers, which makes PSE&G's positive reputation even harder-earned. "PSE&G is always favorable in people's minds," he adds, "because we get the work done. Snowstorm, heat storm, we're there. *We're there.*"

PSEG transfers that New Jersey ethic to locations as far-flung as California — it worked quickly to add capacity in that state during its energy crisis of 2001 — Coyhaique, Chile, and Rades, Tunisia. By choosing to work with local partners, the company creates and supports home teams around the world.

BALANCED PORTFOLIO OF COMPANIES

The time-honored proverb "don't put all your eggs into one basket" resonates strongly at PSEG. Tom McCarter founded Public Service Corporation as a triumvirate of businesses; he even had the words *Railway - Gas - Electricity* carved into the facade of the old headquarters. In a strong parallel, Ferland now presents PSEG as a trio of businesses that can be compared to a personal investment portfolio. The analogy makes innate sense to the variety of audiences Ferland addresses, from employees to Wall Street analysts to potential global partners.

"Balance can often mean the difference between success and failure," Ferland says. "We're

fortunate to have a well-balanced portfolio of companies — PSEG Power, PSE&G and PSEG Energy Holdings — that anticipate and respond to continuing changes in the global energy marketplace." The balance is reflected in company earnings, with the three major subsidiaries contributing 50 percent, 30 percent and 20 percent respectively.

Two of the companies, in turn, have their own subsidiaries that add more diversification to the portfolio. PSEG Power encompasses:

- PSEG Fossil, which operates and maintains the company's coal, gas and oil generation plants and is leading the way toward PSEG's domestic expansion beyond New Jersey;
- PSEG Nuclear, which operates and maintains the company's nuclear plants and continues to build on its performance year over year in safety, reliability and efficiency;
- PSEG Energy Resources & Trade, which markets, buys and sells energy backed by the generation assets of PSEG Power.

PSEG Energy Holdings includes:

- PSEG Global, which has developed into one of the world's leading energy providers by being a dynamic partner and good neighbor in sustainable and profitable projects;
- PSEG Resources, which mainly invests in leveraged leases for energy-related projects.

Company leaders carefully position investments in these businesses in order to manage risks, cushion shortfalls and maximize opportunity. "We wouldn't want to invest so much capital in PSEG Power that we could not take advantage of opportunities for PSEG Global elsewhere," Ferland

WHETHER LAYING A GAS MAIN, OVERSEEING NUCLEAR OPERATIONS OR WORKING AT AN ELECTRICAL INSTALLATION, PSEG PEOPLE ARE PART OF A CULTURE WHERE SAFETY COMES FIRST.

The Amazing World of Live-Line Maintenance

Look! Up in the sky! It's not a bird or a plane or an actor impersonating a hero. That person high in the air near a high-voltage electrical tower is a true-life hero: one of PSE&G's 30 live-line workers.

Live-line work is what it sounds like — working with live, energized transmission circuits so that maintenance and repairs can be done without shutting off power to thousands of households and businesses. It's one of the ways PSE&G safely harnesses the mysterious and inherently dangerous force of electricity that touches our lives every hour of the day. PSE&G helped to pioneer live-line techniques over 25 years ago and regularly performs live-line main-tenance on its 1,200-mile overhead transmission system in New Jersey, as well as assisting neighboring utilities.

During "bare-hand" repairs, live-line workers — using the proper equipment — actually touch the circuit and become energized with it. But because they are completely separated from the ground, the electric field surrounds them harmlessly. They're like birds on a wire. In "hot sticking" techniques, they use an insulated fiberglass stick to manipulate special tools necessary for repairs.

Members of the highly skilled live-line team typically work from insulated aerial lifts. In remote areas, however, they climb towers as tall as 300 feet — the standard height of a 30-story building. But even when workers are hoisted to the top of the shortest towers, they're still 50 feet above the ground performing specialized maneuvers in the midst of live power lines carrying as many as 500,000 volts. Clearly, this work isn't for the faint of heart.

PSE&G's is the only team with this expertise in the PJM Interconnection, the electric grid operator for over 22 million consumers in Pennsylvania, New Jersey, Maryland, Delaware, Virginia and the District of Columbia. Nationwide, PSE&G is one of only about a dozen utilities that perform bare-hand live-line work.

"Live-line skills enhance our reliability to customers by keeping in service circuits that serve tens of thousands of people," notes Al Koeppe, PSE&G president and chief operating officer. "Greater availability of transmission lines ultimately lowers costs to all consumers."

Workers learn the exacting trade through formal classroom work and on-the-job training. It takes about seven years for new apprentices to become fully qualified journeymen. The hardest part, says apprentice Ryan Hill, a second-generation PSE&G live-line worker, is "just trusting yourself that you can do it."

Thanks to the Hills and their colleagues, PSE&G continues to live up to the trust placed in it by the people of New Jersey. And in recent years, PSE&G personnel have extended that trust to South America, by teaching live-line skills to partner companies in Argentina, Brazil, Chile and Peru.

explains. "At the same time, we need to carefully manage our investments in PSE&G's infrastructure to maintain system reliability."

He elaborates on the asset allocation analogy. "PSE&G, as a regulated utility, is not going to produce the highest rates of return, but it produces a steady and predictable rate of return with good cash flows. Look at that part of the company as you would at bonds in your personal portfolio," Ferland says. "PSEG Power, the domestic generation business, offers some wonderful medium-term growth opportunities." PSEG Power will add new capacity as plants under construction come on line.

Faster, more aggressive growth centers on PSEG Global, which nearly tripled earnings from $40 million in 2000 to $116 million in 2001. Higher returns indicate higher risks, of course, especially in volatile international markets. PSEG manages these risks by thorough regional analysis and project diversification. "In the long term, there are still two billion people on earth who don't have electricity," Ferland points out. "This will present investors with opportunities."

Another way that PSEG enhances shareholder value is by providing its subsidiaries with low-cost, highly valued services in such areas as human resources and information technology through PSEG Services Corporation. This subsidiary models itself on the world's top consultancies and supports the efficient operation of PSEG.

MEASURED STEPS IN A NEW ENVIRONMENT

The public perception of energy companies has whipsawed in recent years. For decades, regulated utilities were tagged as slow-moving. Then two landmark events in 2001 — the California energy crisis and the collapse of Enron, an independent energy conglomerate — made people wonder if the industry had moved too fast and too aggressively toward restructuring.

Both views are somewhat extreme. The truth lies in the middle, and PSEG illustrates it. As a regulated utility, the company not only built an energy infrastructure as reliable and efficient as any on earth, it kept up with enormous demands on the system as New Jersey grew. As parts of the industry began to deregulate, it helped write the rules for measured, responsible restructuring — creating a template that worked for New Jersey and became a model for the nation.

Also, like the vast majority of energy companies, PSEG has succeeded at building its unregulated businesses without maverick tactics or questionable accounting practices. Steven R. Teitelman, president, PSEG Energy Resources & Trade, the architect of the company's profitable trading operation, recalls a conversation that took place when Enron was flying high. It speaks volumes about the wisdom of the PSEG approach, then regarded in some quarters as overly conservative.

"An investment banker told me that to be successful in trading, PSEG would have to be national in scope," Teitelman says. PSEG trades energy only in regions where it has generation assets, roughly from New England to Virginia to Illinois. "I disagreed," he continues. "To be national in scope, for example to trade in California, we'd have to speculate. If I bought or sold power without assets to back it up, without any fuel or any generating plants, that would be pure speculation. We don't do that. PSEG trades are based on the assets we have and the knowledge that comes from operating those assets." Teitelman further suggested to the

POLE BY POLE, PSE&G LINE WORKERS (LIKE THE ONE PICTURED HERE IN 1923) BROUGHT RELIABLE ELECTRICAL SERVICE TO NEW JERSEY. IN RECENT DECADES PSEG HAS EXPANDED ITS EXPERTISE WORLDWIDE, HELPING TO MODERNIZE THE PRODUCTION AND DISTRIBUTION OF ELECTRICITY IN COUNTRIES ON FIVE CONTINENTS.

investment banker that certain companies trading nationally without assets or conventional accounting would end up in deep trouble.

Enron's downfall stunned the public. But even as the company imploded, energy supplies and energy markets held firm and have remained stable. That is a testament to the integrity of the energy industry and responsible companies like PSEG.

PEOPLE MAKE THE DIFFERENCE

In the end, a company's reputation comes from its performance over the long term. And performance doesn't come from management philosophies or balance sheets but from people. This is where PSEG really shines.

"Walk around different power plants anywhere in the United States and on one level they're essentially the same," says Frank Cassidy, president and chief operating officer, PSEG Power. "Tons of concrete, miles of wire, tens of thousands of valves, thousands of feet of pipes and sophisticated technology. What accounts for the differences in performance? The people inside and how well they work together."

Cassidy's insight can be applied more broadly to PSEG's corporate headquarters, field offices and call centers. At first glance, they seem, well, utilitarian. Look again, watch and listen, and you'll find very special people making special things happen.

McCarter's Public Service Corporation was built on the manual labor of bus drivers, ditch diggers and pipe layers. Today's PSEG is still proudly blue-collar; 66 percent of employees belong to collective bargaining units. But the mindset has changed. "'Bring me your hands and your back' was the message to workers in the old days," says Peter Cistaro,

PSE&G vice president, distribution. "Today we need your hands and your back, but we also need your mind. And, I'd even add, we need your heart."

Every day 13,000 PSEG associates use their hands, backs, minds and hearts to make things work throughout New Jersey and beyond, 24 hours a day.

They're at work using the Outage Management System (OMS), the nerve center of a complex data network that maps every single PSE&G electric customer in real time by circuit, section and branch. "OMS allows us to manage service interruptions and outages faster than ever before," says Bruce D. Cornew, emergency preparedness leader.

They're at work in towns from Willingboro to Woodcliff Lake, where appliance service technicians like Robert Mascarelli take the extra step. Kneeling in a customer's kitchen to fix a broken oven, Mascarelli doesn't just install a new igniter. He tightens the screws of the slightly wobbly oven door and advises the customer to check them herself from time to time. "It takes a minute more, but it's time well spent," Mascarelli later says. "Otherwise she might lay a pan of food on that door one day and have it crash onto her feet. We care about our customers' safety."

And they're at work around the world, wherever PSEG Global does business. "PSEG Global projects are staffed by professionals from the region," affirms B. Vanchi, managing director, India and the Middle East, "and that makes a difference."

A solid reputation cannot be bought; a company must earn it and work to enhance it. PSEG's reputation as a reliable, profitable, well-run company arises directly from its people, who began building a foundation for success 100 years ago. This is their story.

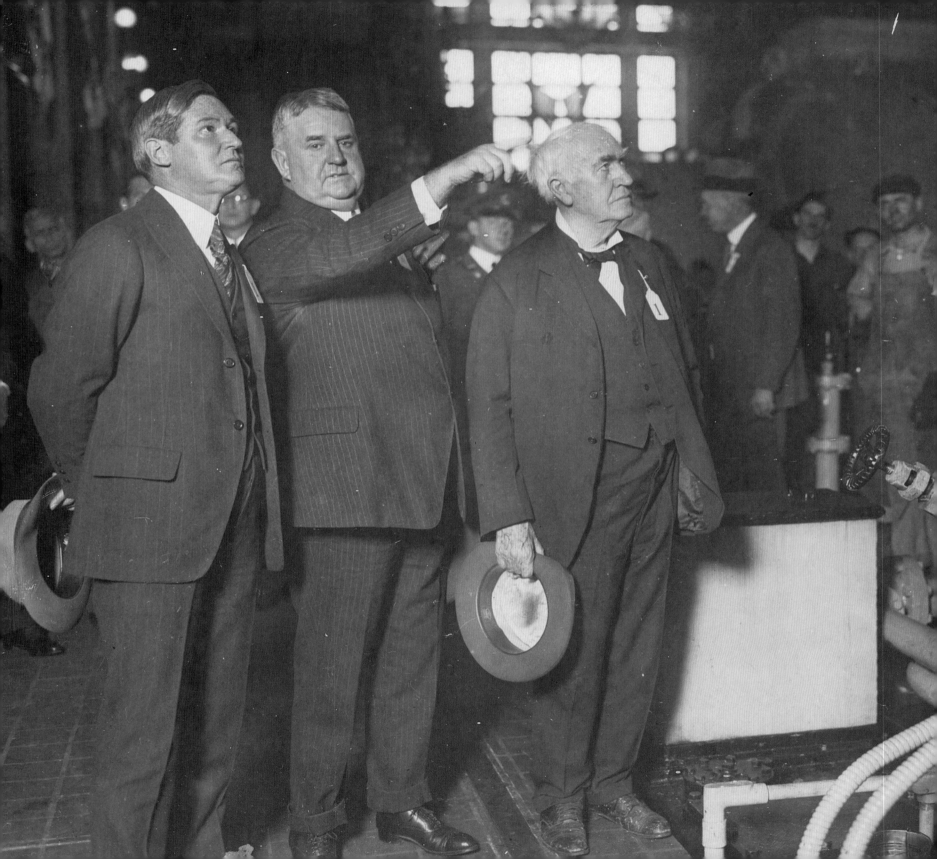

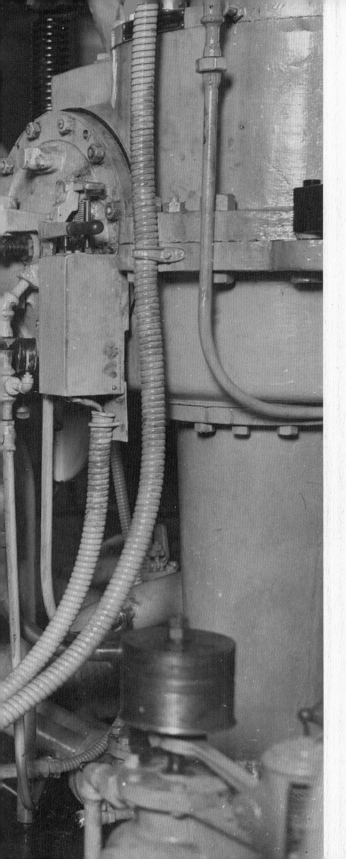

CHAPTER ONE

COMING TO LIGHT

COMPANY FOUNDER THOMAS NESBITT MCCARTER DIDN'T CREATE PUBLIC SERVICE CORPORATION OF NEW JERSEY FOR WEALTH OR PERSONAL POWER. HE ALREADY ENJOYED PLENTY OF BOTH, AS A MEMBER OF A RICH AND INFLUENTIAL FAMILY AND AS A SUCCESSFUL LAWYER. WHAT DROVE HIM, THEN, AT AGE 35, TO GIVE UP HIS POSITION AS NEW JERSEY'S ATTORNEY GENERAL FOR THE ENORMOUS WORK OF UNITING HUNDREDS OF SMALL, STRUGGLING TRANSPORT, GAS AND ELECTRIC PROVIDERS INTO A SINGLE UTILITY? ☐ MCCARTER'S STRAIGHTFORWARD ANSWER: "TO DEVELOP THE STATE OF NEW JERSEY AND MAKE IT A BETTER PLACE TO LIVE." ☐ PUBLIC SERVICE BEGAN WITH THAT MISSION IN 1903 AND HAS NEVER ABANDONED IT. THE VALUES THAT CHARACTERIZE PSEG TODAY — ESPECIALLY ITS COMMITMENT TO SAFETY, ENVIRONMENTAL RESPONSIBILITY, CUSTOMER SERVICE AND SHAREHOLDER VALUE AND ITS DEEP DEVOTION TO ITS HOME STATE — CAN BE SEEN FROM THE VERY START.

TRAGEDY INSPIRES ACTION

A tragic accident played a part in motivating McCarter to found Public Service. On an icy morning in February 1903, a Newark trolley packed with students on their way to Barringer High School collided with a train. Nine teenagers died and 20 were seriously hurt. The trolley lacked a derail switch that might have averted the catastrophe. The absence of enforced safety standards raised a public outcry — and it wasn't the first.

Safety lapses and unreliable service were common among transit providers then. The same was true for the small gas and electric providers that dotted New Jersey. Many were shakily financed and haphazardly run. McCarter sought to consolidate and strengthen them under a single corporate umbrella. The idea had occurred to him earlier, when he handled some utility deals as general counsel of Newark-based Fidelity Trust Company, a major bank headed by his brother Uzal. The trolley accident set the stage for action.

Resigning his other connections, McCarter quickly raised $100,000 in seed capital. No one had done exactly what he was proposing to do; *Fortune* magazine later called it a "daring experiment." Larger utilities were typically found only in big cities. But the business community and the public saw the wisdom of McCarter's vision. New Jersey, geographically small and densely populated, was an ideal place for it to work.

VIGOROUS START

McCarter planned to call the new company Public Utilities. He was overruled by Thomas Dolan, president of United Gas Improvement Company of Philadelphia and an initial investor, who said the name suggested a series of comfort stations. Dolan countered with Public Service Corporation of New Jersey, under which name it incorporated as a publicly held company on May 6, 1903. It began operations on June 1, 1903, at 776 Broad Street in Newark.

Physically, McCarter was stout and rather slow on his feet — not surprising for someone who routinely breakfasted on cold mince pie, liver, bacon, eggs and hot rolls dripping with butter. (He also enjoyed five-course dinners.) However, as a deal maker he moved quickly. By June 3, he had acquired the securities of four trolley or "street railway" companies and one electric generating company totaling $59 million in value.

"THE STATE OF ESSEX."
Reproduced from Newark TRUTH of June 6, 1903.

Purchases continued at a steady pace until Public Service had brought 113 transportation companies and 149 gas and electric companies in New Jersey into its fold. Most continued in their original locations at first. For workers, the only change was the company name on their pay stub and the security of having a dependable employer. The corporation grew through acquisitions and expansion and at its height would employ upwards of 20,000 people.

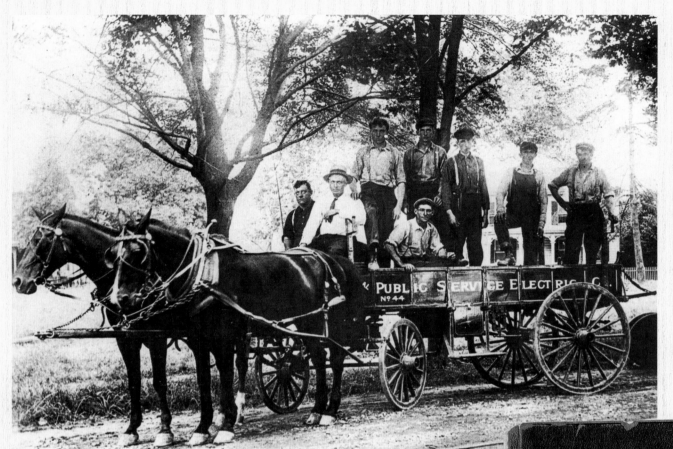

Horses provided such thrifty transportation that Public Service was reluctant to give them up. In 1924, 16 years after Model T cars went on sale, employees in Paterson asked for a small Dodge truck to replace a freight-carting horse that had died. "It will be necessary to supply very convincing arguments!" they were sternly told. Progress prevailed; they made their case and got the truck.

This "gas house gang" worked at the Newark Gas Light Company on Market Street, one of the 149 local utilities that became a part of Public Service. Newark was the first city in New Jersey to manufacture gas for street lamps and home lighting.

Second Annual Report
of
Public Service Corporation
of New Jersey

FOR YEAR ENDING
December 31, 1910

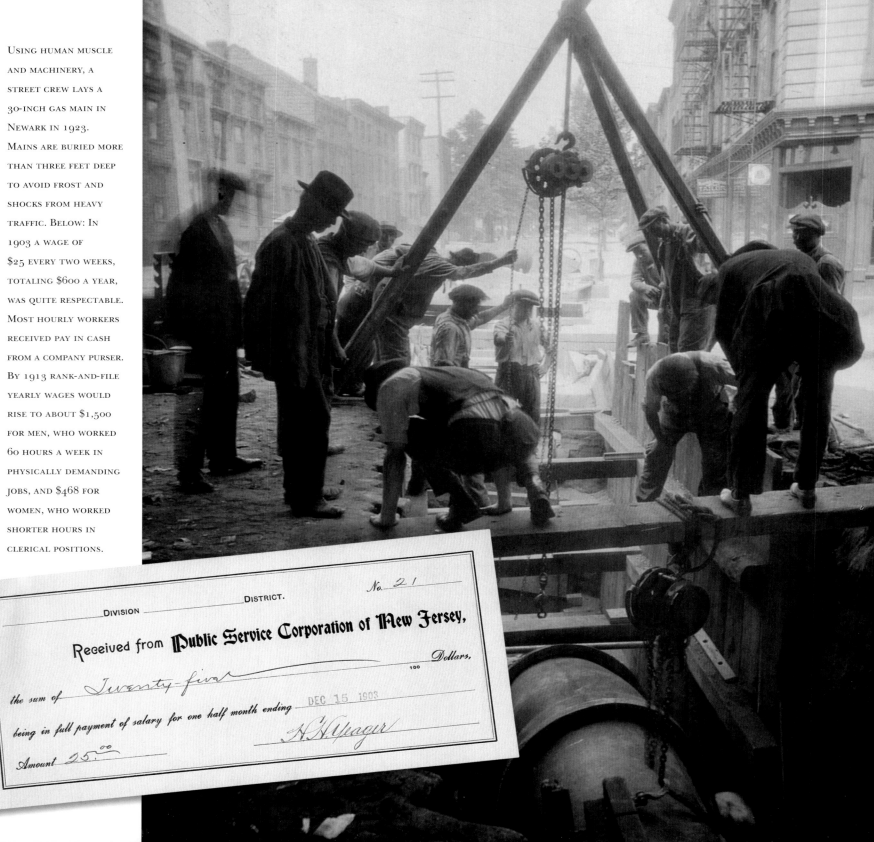

USING HUMAN MUSCLE AND MACHINERY, A STREET CREW LAYS A 30-INCH GAS MAIN IN NEWARK IN 1923. MAINS ARE BURIED MORE THAN THREE FEET DEEP TO AVOID FROST AND SHOCKS FROM HEAVY TRAFFIC. BELOW: IN 1903 A WAGE OF $25 EVERY TWO WEEKS, TOTALING $600 A YEAR, WAS QUITE RESPECTABLE. MOST HOURLY WORKERS RECEIVED PAY IN CASH FROM A COMPANY PURSER. BY 1913 RANK-AND-FILE YEARLY WAGES WOULD RISE TO ABOUT $1,500 FOR MEN, WHO WORKED 60 HOURS A WEEK IN PHYSICALLY DEMANDING JOBS, AND $468 FOR WOMEN, WHO WORKED SHORTER HOURS IN CLERICAL POSITIONS.

DIVISION _____ DISTRICT. _____ No. 21

Received from Public Service Corporation of New Jersey,

the sum of _Twenty-five_ _____ 100 Dollars,

being in full payment of salary for one half month ending DEC 15 1903

H. H. Yeager

Amount 25.00

Born in Newton, raised in Newark and educated at his beloved Princeton University (where the McCarter Theatre is named for him), McCarter knew his home state well. He shrewdly chose to focus on the most developed portion of New Jersey, the "elbow" between New York and Philadelphia, where the railroads ran and demand for utilities was strongest.

Although McCarter foresaw transit as the primary business of Public Service, gas was stronger at first. The numerous small gas manufacturing works acquired by Public Service operated at "a high state of efficiency," according to the first annual report, published in 1909. (From 1903 to 1908, Public Service filed financial statements and thousands of legal documents but no written summaries of its business.) Gas was not yet used for home heating, but it was still a common source of light. And it was the chief energy source for the power-intensive shipyards, silk mills, foundries and machine shops that made New Jersey an industrial giant. Gas operations generated $5.4 million in revenue in the company's first full year of operation.

Transit did generate higher revenue, $8.4 million in the first year, but also demanded far more capital investment. "The street railway properties acquired...were completely run down and demoralized, and required complete rehabilitation," the 1909 report explained.

And what of electric, especially in the state where Thomas Alva Edison had invented the incandescent light bulb in 1879? In 1903, electric was still the kid brother along for the ride. In the company's first year, it struggled to bring in $3.5 million, mostly from street lighting. But its standing would change dramatically just a few years later

80,000 Keys

Meter readers have always been the eyes and ears of PSE&G. For Mr. Pembleton in 1903, that meant reading and collecting payments from "the 360 beer gardens" of old Hoboken — a route, he wrote in an early *Public Service News*, "of considerable color and interest, offering a fine opportunity for one to exercise his utmost ability as a collector." For Pete Danyo, currently based in Union County, it recently meant descending to a basement and finding it submerged in a foot of water. Danyo donned safety gear, waded in, shut off the water main and averted further damage for the grateful customer.

Every day, PSE&G's 450 meter readers do much more than record numbers from a dial. They turn their trained eyes on the condition of the pipes and wires, alert to potential hazards. Is there a small patch of dying grass in your otherwise green lawn? If you notice it at all, you might suspect lack of fertilizer. The meter reader will have the company check the area for a possible outdoor gas leak.

Concern for safety is a two-way street. Meter readers can do their vital work unimpeded when dogs are kept under control and paths to meters kept clear.

Most of all, perhaps, meter readers embody the public trust placed in PSE&G. While most of us wouldn't give our house keys to anyone outside the family, about 80,000 New Jersey residents entrust PSE&G meter readers with their keys — a remarkable expression of customer confidence.

Left: This locker full of keys to customers' homes reflects the trust that New Jerseyans place in PSE&G. Above: Paterson meter readers in 1967.

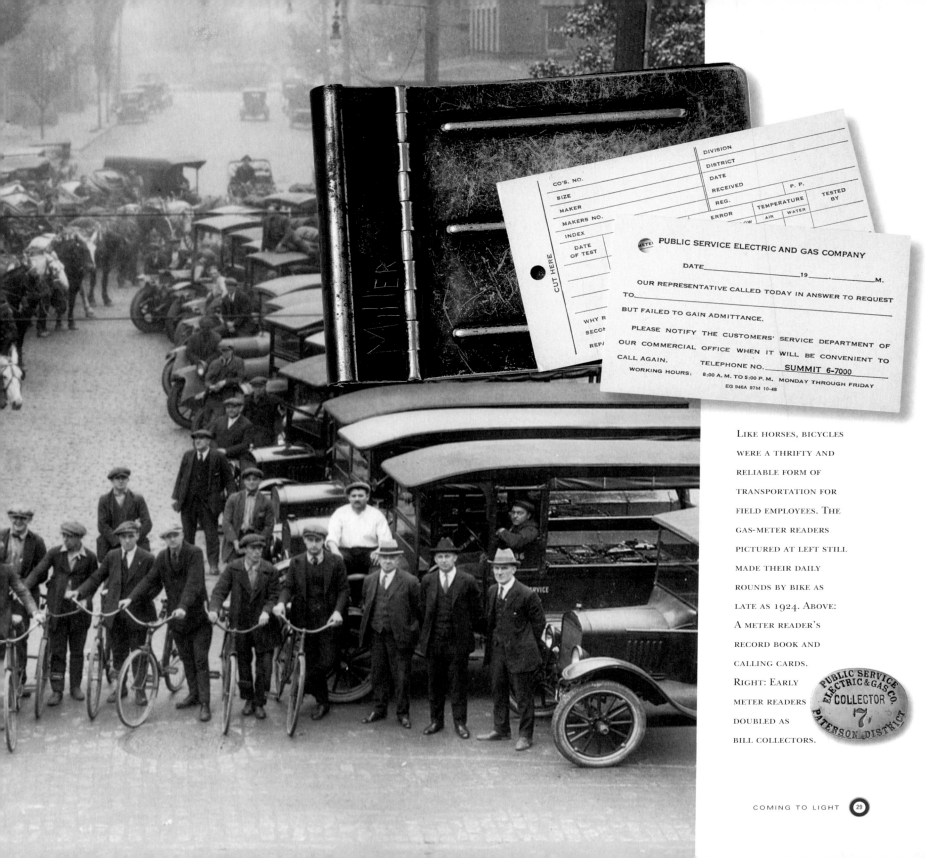

DIVISION

DISTRICT

DATE

CO'S. NO. | RECEIVED | | P. P.

SIZE | REG. | TEMPERATURE | TESTED BY

MAKER | | | AIR | WATER

MAKERS NO. | ERROR | LOW | AIR | WATER

INDEX

DATE OF TEST

CUT HERE

WHY R

SECON

REPA

PUBLIC SERVICE ELECTRIC AND GAS COMPANY

DATE_____19____,____M.

OUR REPRESENTATIVE CALLED TODAY IN ANSWER TO REQUEST

TO_____

BUT FAILED TO GAIN ADMITTANCE.

PLEASE NOTIFY THE CUSTOMERS' SERVICE DEPARTMENT OF OUR COMMERCIAL OFFICE WHEN IT WILL BE CONVENIENT TO CALL AGAIN.   TELEPHONE NO.   SUMMIT 6-7000

WORKING HOURS: 8:00 A. M. TO 5:00 P. M.   MONDAY THROUGH FRIDAY

EG 946A 97M 10-48

LIKE HORSES, BICYCLES WERE A THRIFTY AND RELIABLE FORM OF TRANSPORTATION FOR FIELD EMPLOYEES. THE GAS-METER READERS PICTURED AT LEFT STILL MADE THEIR DAILY ROUNDS BY BIKE AS LATE AS 1924. ABOVE: A METER READER'S RECORD BOOK AND CALLING CARDS. RIGHT: EARLY METER READERS DOUBLED AS BILL COLLECTORS.

PUBLIC SERVICE ELECTRIC & GAS CO.
COLLECTOR 7
PATERSON DISTRICT

as Public Service built the infrastructure necessary
to expand electrical services. Marion Generating
Station in Jersey City, completed in 1906 and now
the site of Hudson Generating Station, holds pride
of place as the first power plant built by Public
Service.

STRONGER, SAFER TRANSIT

Unlike some predecessor transit companies, Public
Service chose to invest heavily in safety. It constructed shops to build and service trolleys, equip-
ping its stock with such essentials as new derail
switches. The addition of "cow catchers," upswept
metal grates that acted as bumpers, reduced the
chance of severe injury if a pedestrian stepped in
front of a trolley. A pay-as-you-enter system, introduced in 1907 and revolutionary for its time,
relieved conductors of the need to handle fares.
That left them free to attend to the safety of passengers boarding and leaving the car, which virtually eliminated platform accidents.

The people of New Jersey appreciated the
enhancements. At its height, transit usage would
grow to 450 million passengers per year at an economical nickel per fare, later rising to seven cents.
The system encompassed 1,897 trolleys running on
695 miles of track, serving communities from
Bergen County to Camden.

By the 1920s, thanks in part to Henry Ford's
Model T, automobiles would become affordable.
But they were still too impractical and expensive
for many suburban New Jerseyans to use for com-
muting. Besides, jobs were mainly concentrated in
the cities. Therefore Public Service Coordinated
Transport, as the transit arm of the company was
eventually named, remained a lifeline of the state
for decades. Its fleet would change and grow with

THE ONLY "BEST WAY TO COOK",

—And that way is to use a Cabinet Gas Range and to have a gas water heater to provide hot water for cleaning cooking utensils and dishes afterwards.

This is the best way to cook, because it is the cleanest, the quickest, the easiest, the most convenient, the most comfortable, and, last but not least, the cheapest way.

EXPLANATION OF THE GAS METER.

Thousands of our ... cook cheaper with 90 C...

Let us convince yo... Water Heater in your ... Sold on our Servi... month—Water Heater...

ALL BILLS ARE DUE AND PAYABLE UPON PRESENTATION. IF NOT PAID BY THE 10th OF MONTH IN WHICH BILL IS PRESENTED THE SUPPLY OF CURRENT MAY BE DISCONTINUED WITHOUT FURTHER NOTICE.

Received Payment

For the Company

ELECTRIC DEPT.

Brook Bound DISTRICT

The Public Service Corporation of New Jersey, Dr.

222 EAST MAIN STREET, BOUND BROOK, N. J.

COMMERCIAL LIGHTING SERVICE
For Electrical Energy consumed as follows:

State of Meter	1910	243 000		000
	1909	244 000		000
	CONSTANT	47 000	CONSTANT	000
	Watt Hours	00.		00
		490 00 watt hours at 10c. per thousand		490

COPPER BOILER

KOMPAK

BY THE MID-1920S PUBLIC SERVICE HAD INSTALLED 3,500 MILES OF GAS MAINS, THEN ONE OF THE LARGEST SYSTEMS IN THE WORLD. THIS ALLOWED NEW JERSEY HOMEMAKERS TO HAPPILY ABANDON THEIR COAL-FIRED APPLIANCES FOR GAS STOVES AND HOT-WATER HEATERS. THE APPLIANCES PICTURED HERE WERE SOLD IN PSE&G SHOWROOMS. OPPOSITE: IN MAY 1928 THIS AD APPEARED IN *CHARM* MAGAZINE.

Safety First

Safety First isn't just a familiar phrase. It was an organized effort in accident prevention, begun by the railroads in the early 1900s and adapted by other industries. Public Service championed Safety First. The company has always realized the dangers inherent in handling gas and electricity. The Safety First movement took special interest in "preaching the gospel of safety" to immigrant laborers, perhaps especially important to Public Service because immigrants were a vital part of its workforce from the start.

The company also issued its own safety manuals to employees. These exemplify the old command-and-control culture. For example, a pocket-sized 1927 handbook for transit operators spelled out 134 rules to be obeyed. One even described how to handle inebriated passengers. "In the McCarter era, employees were told to 'do it right or else,' follow procedures, don't ask questions," notes PSEG Services Senior Vice President and General Counsel R. Edwin Selover, who oversees PSEG's overall safety efforts.

While following proper procedures remains paramount, the safety culture is now open and collaborative. Safety Councils in each location, headed by bargaining unit associates, meet monthly to discuss and resolve issues. Pete Cistaro, PSE&G's vice president, distribution, captures the core principles: "Our promise to our families and our coworkers is that we do the job right — safe and smart. We take care of each other and speak up whenever we need to.

Associates know they have the right to stop any job where safety is in question until the issue is resolved."

Statistics show that the participative approach has truly put safety first: PSEG has reduced its OSHA-reportable incident rate, an industry-wide measure, from 3.7 in 1996 to 1.34 at the end of the third quarter of 2002. (The figure measures the number of serious accidents per 200,000 hours worked.) Through the Safety Councils, employees also share information about "Near Misses" — an innovative and effective practice. As Selover says, "If you can get people to examine what almost happened, then by definition you're going to make accidents less likely to happen."

Motorman and conductor pose before their Public Service trolley. A nickel-ready rider waits at the rear. The car is fitted with a "cow catcher" front fender, a safety device that minimized pedestrian accidents on busy streets. The Public Service trolley system, which extended from Newark to Camden, served 450 million passengers a year at its height.

Pedestrian isles, like the one pictured below, were another safety innovation. At the company's start, trolleys superseded horse-drawn carriages as public transportation. In the 1930s, buses and autos began to make trolleys obsolete. The primary rule for all Public Service transit operators was always "Safety First."

the times, encompassing ferries and taxicabs as well as trolleys, trains, buses and the Newark City Subway.

THE TERMINAL BUILDING

The dominance of the transit business, in fact, led Public Service to build its unique Terminal Building — a Newark landmark for 64 years.

The corporation originally leased space at 776 Broad Street and then at 759 Broad Street, where its landlord was the Prudential Insurance Company. It outgrew those locations, despite the fact that most employees worked in the field. A permanent head-quarters would serve two purposes: the first two

PUBLIC SERVICE RAILWAY COMPANY

PUBLIC SERVICE RAILROAD COMPANY

PUBLIC SERVICE TRANSPORTATION COMPANY

PUBLIC SERVICE

RULES AND INSTRUCTIONS FOR BUS AND CAR OPERATORS

SAFETY FIRST

THE FIVE-CENT FARE
BECAME A BONE OF
CONTENTION. WHEN
MCCARTER TRIED RAIS-
ING IT TO SEVEN CENTS,
PUBLIC SERVICE LOST
BUSINESS TO UNLICENSED
JITNEYS. HE LOWERED
FARES BACK TO A NICKEL
FOR ANOTHER FEW
YEARS. RIGHT: OPENING
DAY OF THE PUBLIC
SERVICE TERMINAL IN
NEWARK IN APRIL 1916.

levels would function as a full-service, 24-hour
terminal for Public Service transit users and the
eight floors above would be the corporation's
"general office." (That phrase, never "headquarters" or "home office," is still used by employees
around the state.) No doubt McCarter, who ran a
famously thrifty operation, also wanted to stop
paying rent.

The Terminal Building at 80 Park Place opened
to great fanfare in 1916. It shared its inaugural
spotlight with Newark itself, which celebrated its
250th anniversary that year with a grand parade.
The company pointed to the $6 million building as
"a notable public improvement, made available to
the public without a cent of cost to the city." The
busy transit concourse housed a florist, shoe repair
shop, men's clothier, bakery, lunch counters and
other services for the thousands of commuters who
passed through daily.

The offices above were the stuff of legends.
Although the Terminal Building was demolished in
1981, everyone who worked there remembers it
vividly. "It had different names: the ivory palace,
the big house," recalls Paul Cafone, manager, system operations, electric systems. The top floor,
which housed executives' offices and the library,
resembled a gentleman's club, complete with
leather chairs and a few brass spittoons for the
men who chewed tobacco. Retired Library
Director Florine Hunt recalls passing one spittoon
"with a paper towel discreetly placed over the top"
as she left work each day.

Employee workspaces, however, were metal-desk
utilitarian: "A bullpen atmosphere," according to
Cafone. As the company grew, it added adjacent
buildings on Raymond Boulevard and East Park
Street. Obviously McCarter did not lavish money

FROM ITS CORNERSTONE TO THE COMPANY NAME BEAMED FROM THE ROOF IN LETTERS EIGHT FEET HIGH, THE TERMINAL BUILDING SYMBOLIZED SOLIDITY. THE OFFICES SPORTED LOGOED BRASS DOORKNOBS. THESE BECAME SOUGHT-AFTER OBJECTS WHEN THE BUILDING WAS DEMOLISHED IN 1981.

Public Service Terminal, Newark, N. J. Opened April 30, 1916. Capacity 360 Cars an Hour.

on the architecture, because the floors didn't quite line up. The eighth floor in one building was the ninth floor or the eighth mezzanine floor in another, making for some confusion and not a few dead-end hallways. "You had to have a roadmap to get around," says John Scarlatta, general manager of gas systems and supply operations.

Holland Tunnel

Until 1927, the only way to reach Manhattan from New Jersey was by ferry. Public Service, in fact, ran ferries to the city from Edgewater. But the rise in car traffic demanded an alternative mode of travel. The answer was the Holland Tunnel.

A less progressive company might have lobbied against the building of tunnels and bridges, because vehicular routes to Manhattan were bound to make ferry service obsolete. But Public Service, from its earliest years, has welcomed new ideas that have a potential to benefit its customers. The company played key roles in the creation of the Holland Tunnel, a technological landmark.

For starters, Public Service engineers helped investigate the tunnel's feasibility. No one had ever built such a long vehicular tunnel — the Hudson River is one-and-a-half miles wide at that location — because they couldn't figure out how to vent away poisonous auto exhaust fumes. The tunnel's chief engineer devised the solution, a system of 42 huge blowers and 42 exhaust fans that exchange the air every 90 seconds.

Electricity from Public Service powered the rock-blasters, caissons, hydraulic jacks and other behemoth machines used in the tunnel's seven-year construction. The company still supplies the power that lights the Holland Tunnel and keeps its landmark ventilation system running smoothly.

A. Harry Moore, then acting mayor of Jersey City, at the controls of the steam shovel that broke ground for the approach to the Holland Tunnel. Public Service Production Company built the double-decker road, while PSE&G powered the tunnel-construction machinery.

CAFETERIAS AND "COMMAND-AND-CONTROL"

Old-timers are full of stories about the hierarchical culture of the old Public Service. In an era of autocracy, it was more autocratic than most companies. This reflected its origins; McCarter had purchased hundreds of small utility and transit companies with the express purpose of organizing them into a whole and imposing uniform standards upon them. Autocracy also reflected the personal style of McCarter, who grew up in a very wealthy family and enjoyed giving orders.

For a colorful glimpse of the hierarchy, consider lunchtime in the Terminal Building. The employee cafeteria was crowded and "always noisy with the sound of metal trays hitting metal tables," Cafone chuckles. "It was a great place to eat, though. For 25 cents we got a full lunch from soup to nuts. Boy, did people complain when the price went up to 35 cents." While all employees ordered from the same menu at the same prices, junior and senior executives lunched apart from the rank-and-file in separate, club-like dining rooms where waitresses served them. The executives sat at assigned tables and ate at assigned times. "What a way of working," muses John Anderson, vice president, customer operations, PSE&G, who observed the executive dining rooms from a distance in his first years. "Imagine saying 'sorry, I have to leave this urgent meeting, I have to go to lunch.' In our general office today, everyone eats in the same cafeteria. That's the right way in today's environment."

Just as the different levels didn't mix at meals, they worked according to a strict chain of command, both in Newark and in the field. McCarter created top-down hierarchies that persisted for decades. As Regulatory Leader Willard S. Carey describes, "When I came in 1963, 'the field districts reported to divisions. The division managers were very powerful gentlemen who ran their divisions like fiefdoms. The first gas division I was in, you couldn't even talk to the division manager. When you spoke of him, you called him 'Mister.' The culture was one of command-and-control. In today's culture, we empower our employees. We're not out to watch them and try to catch them … and we're far better off for it."

Though Public Service was notably "dogmatic and authoritarian and structured," in Carey's words, the system of command-and-control "was put in place for historically good reasons," notes Domnick Facchini, director, customer services and customer relationships. "We deal with gas and electric, commodities that are inherently dangerous, so you have to make sure the right procedures are in place and you have to follow them." Of course that is still true. What has changed radically, as Facchini is quick to add, is the recognition that the people who *do* the work know the most about the work; their input is now solicited and relied upon.

FROM FAMILY PICNICS TO BASKETBALL AND OTHER INTRAMURAL SPORTS, PUBLIC SERVICE WORKERS ENJOYED LEISURE TIME TOGETHER. BOWLING WAS A DRAW IN 1909 (ABOVE) AND REMAINS POPULAR TODAY, WITH AN ACTIVE EMPLOYEES CLUB LEAGUE IN CENTRAL NEW JERSEY.

On typical days, the work of PSEG is invisible. But when natural disaster strikes, the world realizes just how remarkable the people of PSEG are.

That was as true in 1903 as it is today. It was true for George S. Curtis, who worked for Paterson & Passaic Gas & Electric, which almost went bankrupt fighting the massive fire and floods that devastated Paterson in 1902. Curtis was relieved to have his company become part of Public Service so he could continue helping his neighbors. The city of Paterson not only recovered, but figured prominently in the company's growth. "The electric meters on our lines [in 1903] numbered 3,600; we

Bob Blache

have now 93,000 connected," Curtis recalled with pride on Public Service's 25th anniversary in 1928.

When Paterson, Bound Brook and other New Jersey locations were inundated by Tropical Storm Floyd in 1999, PSEG rushed to help customers recover. The flooding of gas mains required crews to assess damage and painstakingly restore service house-by-house in many areas. "There was a lot of mud and water, but we worked at a good pace," recalls Bob Blache, dispatching department head at that time. Crises, he says, bring out "the spirit of teamwork between the people working on the frontline, as well as those supporting them."

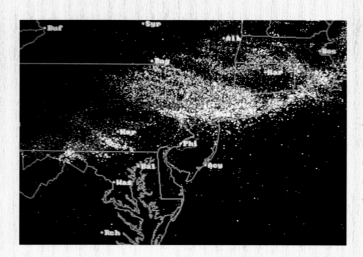

PSE&G has always reacted instantly to the tropical storms, hurricanes, blizzards and floods that periodically inundate New Jersey. Today, state-of-the-art warning systems help crews mobilize and be as ready as possible for heavy weather.

COMPANY CRUSHED ITS OWN STONE

Looking back at those dining rooms and field fiefdoms, another characteristic of the old Public Service emerges: it was a self-contained world, or a collection of them. For example, the food service workers in the Terminal Building, from cooks to waitresses, were company employees. Transit not only built its own trolley cars but bought a quarry in Fairview so it could "turn out crushed stone at minimum cost" to improve road conditions. The company even ran its own telephone system.

In the same vein, each arm of the corporation was a world unto itself. Some call it "the old silo mentality." McCarter wanted his top executives to mind their own businesses, which they did extremely well. Decades later, as the world changed, Public Service would begin to tear down its silos, looking outside and sharing expertise and services across its own disciplines — a hallmark of Jim Ferland's leadership.

Again, however, those early choices made sense. Public Service kept tight vertical control in order to run its operations more safely and cost-efficiently, to the great benefit of New Jerseyans and company shareholders. Entrusted with the complexities of building an energy infrastructure, often literally from the ground up, the corporation took full responsibility for its work. If each location was somewhat insular, it was also a center of lifelong friendships: employees played on sports teams together, formed social clubs and musical bands together and supported each other in times of crisis. Today, clubs are fewer but the tradition of camaraderie is alive and well: "The attitude out in the field is that this is our own family," says Simon "Sam" Blom, office administrator, Gas Distribution, Clifton/Orange.

BENEFITS, RAISES, SHORTER WEEKS

The McCarter-era culture may have been quasi-military, but Public Service was never the army. The company was built on the backs of no-nonsense New Jerseyans who, unionized or not, knew their worth and got their due. As early as 1910, when employee benefits were rare, Public Service voluntarily introduced an "insurance, sick benefit and pension fund." One year later, the annual report noted that "this fund has worked to advantage, even beyond our greatest expectations…. [One result] has been the creation of a better feeling between the Corporation and its employees."

Similarly, when New Jersey enacted its first workmen's compensation law in 1911 but made it optional for employers, Public Service "in contradistinction to many other large companies, immediately accepted the provisions of the act," regarding it as "the enlightened policy of the day," according to the 1911 annual report.

Various unions represented transit employees in the early years. Negotiations with them resulted in three wage increases in 1912. "First-year men" joined at 23 cents per hour, second-year men earned 24 cents and the rest 25 cents based on a six-day week of 10-hour days. Extra runs paid time-and-a-half. "This is regarded as a fair, liberal wage scale and has been received by the men in a manner most gratifying to the corporation," the 1913 annual report said. Future pay increases would be more of a battle; in 1923, for example, striking transit workers would halt Public Service trolleys for 51 days. Jitneys, or unregulated car and bus services, quickly filled the void. Despite a 20 percent increase in labor costs after the strike, McCarter lowered his seven-cent fares to a nickel to win back commuters. The public was starting to prefer buses, so he added hundreds of them to the fleet.

Quite early on, Public Service also voluntarily granted an across-the-board raise to women, most of whom were clerks. "The Board of Directors decided, as of January 1, 1913, to put all female employees upon a minimum wage basis of $9.00 per week," the annual report said. "While the increase involved in many cases was more than the positions merited, the Corporation feels that it is doing that which is eminently fitting in vouchsafing to all its female employees *a decent living wage*" (italics added). The attitude was a bit grudging, but the money showed that the corporation valued its women.

Although six-day weeks were the norm for transit workers and general office employees, gas and electric employees in the field worked seven days a week until 1923. Public Service was an innovator when it announced that "for the first time since the inception of the gas and electric industries in this state, men working in the Public Service gas-making plants and electric power stations and sub-stations will be…on a six-day basis, with no reduction in wages…. For many years the plants were manned with two sets of employees on 12-hour shifts, but Public Service long ago discarded the 12-hour day and substituted three shifts of eight hours each. Now the seven-day week will be abandoned and sufficient additional help engaged to continue the eight-hour day and give every man one day off in seven."

The people of Public Service put McCarter's vision into action. In the corporation's first quarter century, they had helped make New Jersey a better place to live. Having earned the toughest currency of all — the trust of the public — they would go on to greater achievements in more difficult times.

"To Faithfully Serve the People of a Great and Progressive State" was Public Service's stated mission in this 20th anniversary booklet. The cover captures the spirit of New Jersey when the state's top three industries were shipbuilding, silk goods, and foundry and machine-shop products.

CHAPTER TWO

TAXPAYING SERVANT OF A GREAT STATE

I N THE FIRST QUARTER CENTURY OF PUBLIC SERVICE, MCCARTER HAD BEEN THE ARCHITECT AND 20,000 EMPLOYEES THE BUILDERS. TOGETHER, THEY HAD CONSTRUCTED A CORPORATION WITH A SOLID FOUNDATION. DURING THE 40 YEARS THAT FOLLOWED, PUBLIC SERVICE WOULD STAND FIRM AND HELP CARRY NEW JERSEY THROUGH FINANCIAL DEPRESSION, THE CHALLENGES OF WORLD WAR II AND EXPONENTIAL POST-WAR GROWTH. MCCARTER WOULD BECOME THE IMPASSIONED SPOKESMAN FOR THE U.S. UTILITY INDUSTRY, AND THE WORKFORCE WOULD STRENGTHEN THEIR OWN VOICES AS THE GAS AND ELECTRIC BUSINESSES UNIONIZED.

Through it all, Public Service would meet its obligations to employees and shareholders. And such steady performance would win national approval. An analyst at Merrill Lynch, Pierce, Fenner & Beane offered an appraisal of the company during World War II that might have been written today: "Well managed and well integrated, Public Service is one of the soundest of U.S. utility companies, and has built up an enviable record of profits and common dividends (every year since 1907)."

INNOVATIVE POWER GRID

A pioneering move by Public Service still helps to ensure energy security, not just for New Jersey but many other states. In 1928 the company initiated the regional electrical power pool or grid now called the PJM Interconnection, creating it in cooperation with the Philadelphia Electric Company and the Pennsylvania Power & Light Company. The PJM name originally stood for "Pennsylvania Jersey Maryland," but in successive decades the pool added investor-owned utilities throughout the mid-Atlantic region and beyond. Today it is the largest organization of its kind in North America and the third largest in the world, exceeded only by power pools in France and Japan.

Until PJM, the only U.S. energy interconnections had been found in the wide open spaces west of the Rocky Mountains. The pool concept seemed wrong for the East, where population density and home rule were the norm. Certainly McCarter and his counterparts treasured their independence and preferred not to go outside their respective companies wherever possible. However, they foresaw the benefits of regional collaboration. By pooling readily accessible energy, member utility companies are better able to meet sudden spikes in demand wherever they occur, such as on very hot days, thus minimizing outages. The creation of PJM — and the steady growth of PSEG's participation in it — has indeed brought customers more reliable and affordable electric power. It's another example of how PSEG has always been open to innovations that benefit customers and enhance shareholder value.

In addition, Al Koeppe, PSE&G's president and chief operating officer, credits the strengths of PJM for helping New Jersey avoid the energy shortages suffered in California in recent years. "PJM has much higher reserve requirements than California," Koeppe points out. "It has a more diverse fuel mix, which stabilizes prices, and it can bring generation online quicker." PJM served as a model for the New York Power Pool and later regional grids, which in turn formed a strong energy infrastructure for much of the United States. These are enduring legacies of a wise choice made by Public Service decades ago.

DEPRESSION-ERA STABILITY

The Roaring Twenties were a lot like the 1990s. Americans lavished money on new homes, fancy cars and good times. Speculation in stocks was rampant, with many investors buying on margin.

On October 29, 1929, "Black Tuesday," the bubble burst. The stock market plunged and soon dragged down much of the U.S. economy with it. As the Great Depression stretched through the 1930s, Public Service shareholders could be grateful that their stock never missed a dividend. And although unemployment reached 40 percent in many areas, no one at Public Service was laid off. McCarter was proud of that record. "We in the utility business practically have no unemployment

problem," he told shareholders at the 1939 Annual Meeting. "Take Public Service. It has 20,000 employees, and its turnover is practically nil. Again, like the franchise taxes, we are paying unemployment taxes. But we have no unemployment to amount to anything. It has been my pride that through these whole 36 years we have come through in the sunlight." The company tried to make up for flat revenues by vigorously promoting the sale of appliances and improved lighting for homes and businesses.

McCarter seized every opportunity to remind the world of the taxes paid by Public Service. Each annual report carefully charted the exponential rise. McCarter accepted the necessity of taxes; as a future tagline would have it, Public Service was the "Taxpaying Servant of a Great State." What outraged the chairman was government intervention that seemed to threaten free enterprise. "His innate belief is that public utilities are ministers of public improvement and should be treated as such, with profits," the Merrill Lynch analyst wrote.

McCarter reserved special venom for President Franklin D. Roosevelt and the Public Utilities Holding Company Act (PUHCA) of 1935, a cornerstone of FDR's New Deal. PUHCA dissolved the 18 unregulated utility holding companies then in existence. These were financial conglomerates, not power dispatching pools like PJM. Although Public Service had become part of the giant United Corporation holding company in 1929, United had never owned more than 21 percent of Public Service stock. McCarter believed the Roosevelt administration had no right to dissolve such an affiliation. He would have to content himself with the fact that FDR couldn't break up the holding companies overnight. The full dissolution

PREVIOUS PAGES: PUBLIC SERVICE DID NOT LAY OFF A SINGLE EMPLOYEE DURING THE GREAT DEPRESSION, PROVIDING SECURITY FOR WORKERS SUCH AS THIS GROUP PICTURED IN 1934. MCCARTER SET OUT IN 1937 TO PERSONALLY INSPECT A NEW UNDER-GROUND TRANSIT TUNNEL. LEFT: A WORKER "LIGHTS A BURNER OFF" ON A STEAM BOILER. ABOVE: PUBLIC SERVICE WAS A FOUNDING MEMBER OF PJM, WHICH SINCE 1928 HAS FORMED A STRONG ENERGY GRID FOR THE REGION.

AIR CONDITIONING WAS A NOVELTY IN 1934, WHEN PSE&G HELPED SHOWCASE THE NEW-FANGLED TECHNOLOGY. COMING FULL CIRCLE, THE COMPANY NOW SERVICES AND REPLACES CENTRAL AIR-CONDI-TIONING SYSTEMS IN HOMES. A 1949 AD PRO-MOTED HOME FREEZERS AS TIME SAVERS. REDDY KILOWATT, THE CAR-TOON FIGURE WITH THE LIGHT-BULB NOSE, WAS USED BY 200 ELECTRIC UTILITIES FROM 1942 TO 1973.

of United Corporation took 10 years.

Speaking for the industry, McCarter also thundered against the New Deal's push for additional government-subsidized power systems modeled on the Tennessee Valley Authority and Bonneville Power Administration. He argued that the growth of subsidized power would spell the death of shareholder-owned utilities. It was unfair competition because the government could finance its projects with cheap government debt, while companies

such as Public Service were subject to the realities of the financial markets. On this subject, McCarter's viewpoint prevailed.

PUBLIC SERVICE GOES TO WAR

Japan's surprise attack on the American fleet at Pearl Harbor, Hawaii, on December 7, 1941, swept the country into World War II.

New Jersey, small in size but huge in industrial might, played a key role in the war. It ranked

Appliance Allegiance

For decades Public Service sold appliances. Each commercial office, or customer service center, doubled as a showroom for the latest gas stoves, electric irons and other labor-savers. An in-house sales training publication called *Service* recommended this sales pitch in 1917, when coal stoves were common: "Of course, all-gas kitchens primarily appeal to the housewife, but the husband, who totes the coal bucket and the ash pan, will be strongly influenced in favor of the new home that promises freedom from his thralldom!"

To uphold its reputation for dependability, Public Service wouldn't sell any model of appliance until company engineers had tested and approved it. Word quickly spread that the sturdiest, most reliable appliances were found in PSE&G showrooms.

Although the company stopped selling appli-

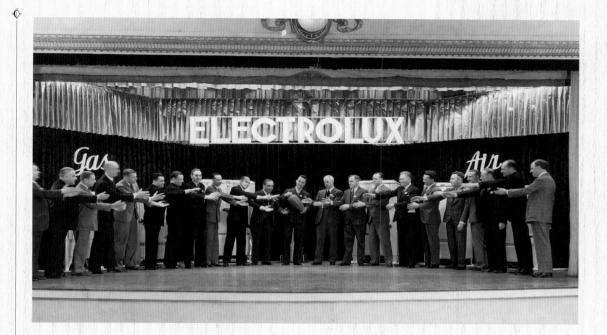

ances, it never stopped servicing gas stoves, furnaces and boilers. In the 1990s it expanded this business, which had been a hidden asset,

When Public Service began selling appliances, even wringer washing machines were considered tremendous conveniences.
Above: Salesmen get the lowdown on a line of Electrolux products. Public Service tested all brands for reliability before agreeing to carry them in the showrooms.

into the popular *WorryFree Repair Service*. In 2001, the highly trained specialists of PSE&G made 1,255,756 visits to fix refrigerators, ranges and stoves, washers, dryers, dishwashers and central air conditioners, and to arrange for replacement of hot water heaters.

Before launching *WorryFree*, PSE&G asked customers what really mattered to them about appliance repair. "They told us a simple thing," recalls Frank Cielo, who headed the company's appliance service business. "They said we want you to show up on time and fix it right the first time." According to surveys taken after service calls, PSE&G meets those expectations 87 percent of the time — a pretty solid measure of "worry free."

number one among the 48 states in wartime production. Public Service power reliably kept hundreds of defense plants working around the clock. Public Service transit also played its part, adding special streetcar lines to federal shipyards in Kearny and Camden. "Public Service is proud of its wartime record," *Public Service News* reported on August 15, 1944. "Since Pearl Harbor our riders have increased by nearly three-quarters of a million. It has been impossible for us to increase our facilities accordingly. We cannot get new equipment. Yet some 500,000 war workers are carried to and from their shops every day."

Upwards of 3,000 Public Service employees, about one in six, went to war. McCarter periodically wrote them formal but heartfelt letters. "It is gratifying to report to you that not once has there been a serious interruption to the supply of our services to [wartime] industries," he noted. "Civilian needs are also being met adequately." Each letter reassured soldiers that they would return to their "old job with the Company or a job of like seniority, status and pay, with credit in full for time spent in the service in determining pensions and other benefits."

FERTILE GROUND FOR UNIONS

Despite such assurances, blue-collar workers in the military and on the home front worried about postwar job security. Hundreds of thousands of returning GIs would soon flood the market. There was also speculation about changes in corporate structure as United Corporation disbanded. If Public Service acquired or merged with an adjacent utility company, would layoffs follow? ("After World War II we were constantly making studies to acquire other companies," confirms retired

Chairman Harold W. Sonn. Ultimately no acquisitions were made.) Not least, after giving their all in the war effort, American workers were looking forward to a relatively new benefit — the two-day weekend. The normal schedule at Public Service had been six days a week for field employees and five-and-a-half for those in the general office.

With these issues in mind, Public Service gas and electric employees began to unionize in the mid-1940s. The process would take nearly 10 years. One by one, divisions and districts joined local chapters of the International Brotherhood of Electrical Workers (IBEW) and the United Association (UA) of Journeymen and Apprentices of the Plumbing and Pipe Fitting Industry, which represents gas workers. Today the IBEW and UA are the chief unions within PSEG, although the numerous locals of old have been replaced by the

LEFT: WOMEN JOINED MEN IN DOING MECHANICAL ASSEMBLY WORK IN THE PUBLIC SERVICE TRANSPORT SHOP WHEN 3,000 EMPLOYEES LEFT TO SERVE IN WORLD WAR II. ABOVE, A DISPLAY IN A PSE&G COMMERCIAL OFFICE ENCOURAGED NEW JERSEYANS TO DO THEIR PART IN THE WAR EFFORT.

TO YOU ON THE WAR FRONT:

PUBLIC SERVICE

EMPLOYEES FORMED
"RED FEATHER" FUND-
RAISING TEAMS AND SENT
WARM WORDS OF SUPPORT
TO COWORKERS ABROAD
THROUGH MESSAGES IN
PUBLIC SERVICE NEWS.
RIGHT: IN 1940 THE
THEATER CLUB PER-
FORMED "HMS PINAFORE"
IN THE TERMINAL
BUILDING AUDITORIUM.

statewide bargaining units IBEW Local 94 and UA Local 855.

Public Service was no stranger to organized labor because its transit workers had always been unionized. McCarter regarded unions as he did taxes — a necessary evil — and was far more consumed by his continuing New Deal clashes. He railed against Secretary of the Interior Harold Ickes's attempt to woo the city of Camden with $6 million in Public Works Administration funds for a municipal power plant. Camden was squarely in Public Service territory. The plant never materialized, but the threat of it became a lever that forced Public Service to reduce its rates. Similarly, McCarter single-handedly took on the Federal

Power Commission (FPC), which sought to slash Public Service's property valuations by $68 million and thus seriously devalue the $573 million corporation in the financial markets. "The rafters still ring from the verbal broadside loosed at the FPC by New Jersey's perennial utilityman — fast-acting, fast-tempered Thomas Nesbitt McCarter," reported Merrill Lynch's *Investor's Reader* magazine. "Less-daring utilitymen shuddered, wondering how any tycoon could use such talk before the all-powerful FPC."

After the war's end in 1945 — a year also marked by the death of Roosevelt and the retirement, at age 78, of McCarter — Public Service was able to return its full attention to its original

FORM 1824
REV. AUG. 1943

AMERICAN RED CROSS
WAR FUND
CONTRIBUTORS' LIST

DATE March 7 19 44

FIRM OR DISTRICT SOLICITED

...ity Dept.   FIRM DEPT.

A. Gallagher   DIV. NO.

...m 8306   TEAM NO.
                                      TEL. NO.

STREET	HOME ADDRESS CITY OR TOWN	AMOUNT
	Newark	1 00
	Newark	1 00
	East Orange	1 00
	Newark	1 00
	Newark	1 00
	Morris Plains	2 00
	Plainfield	5 00
	Caldwell	25 00

WE GAVE

12

13

THE TERMINAL BUILDING
FEATURED A TRAVEL
AGENCY, PICTURED IN
1938. THIS 1954
MANUAL WAS GIVEN TO
NON-TRANSIT EMPLOYEES
WHOSE JOBS REQUIRED
DRIVING. KEY ADVICE:
"WHEN IN DOUBT ABOUT
THE RIGHT OF WAY, LET
THE OTHER FELLOW
HAVE IT."

MANUAL
FOR
AUTOMOBILE
DRIVERS

mission. Postwar growth would provide new opportunities to develop New Jersey and make it a better
place to live.

ENGINEERS AND LINEMEN TO THE FOREFRONT

Fears of unemployment were unfounded: Public
Service needed every person it had, and more.
"The state went bananas after the war — new housing, new office parks, phenomenal growth," says
Patrick J. Downes, vice president, delivery operations support, PSE&G. New Jersey grew twice as
fast as the rest of the nation; its population
reached 6 million in 1960, a 50 percent rise from
1940. At the same time, the state added over
400,000 jobs, a 25 percent expansion.

"Our people were able to stay on top of that
growth," Downes notes. Both the gas and electric
businesses of Public Service, which in 1948 were
grouped under the new PSE&G umbrella, were
known for engineering excellence. But not since
designing the original energy infrastructure had
company engineers enjoyed such a chance to
shine.

For the gas business, the emergence of inter-
state pipelines was a turning point. Earlier
pipelines couldn't extend far from the gas fields of
Texas and Louisiana, mainly because cast iron and
wrought iron pipes couldn't withstand the pressure
necessary for transporting gas over long distances.
The development of high-tensile, thin-walled, large
diameter pipe solved the problem, permitting the
safe and economical flow of natural gas across
thousands of miles. As pipeline suppliers extended
their lines into New Jersey, Public Service began
connecting to them. Gradually, one by one, it
closed its own gas manufacturing plants. The shift

Betty Crocker, Jersey-style

The tremendous popularity of radio in the 1920s and 1930s led Public Service to create its own Radio Cooking School. The host was Ada Bessie Swann, director of the company's home economics department. Through her twice-weekly program, which "symbolized the spirit of cheerful service of this great organization toward its many homemakers," Swann became a local celebrity — New Jersey's own real-life version of the mythical Betty Crocker.

Tens of thousands of listeners wrote in regularly for Swann's recipes, designed to take advantage of the gas stoves and electric refrigerators that were modernizing American kitchens. A dinner menu from 1931 featured baked shad with roasted onions, moulded pineapple and cucumber salad and lemon icebox cake.

Swann and her staff presented free classes throughout the state on "home management, household hygiene and home lighting," as well as cooking. In succeeding decades, Public Service home economists evolved into consumer advisors who educated New Jerseyans on energy conservation, safety and the facts of nuclear power. Although PSEG cooking schools are a relic of the past, the company continues its tradition of energy education at its 16 customer service centers and through informative community programs such as In Concert with the Environment, Energy Choice and Fires & Wires.

Some looked skeptical, others bemused, but all appliance salesmen took cooking classes to better understand the products they sold. Public Service taught cooking to homemakers for decades.

BETWEEN 1950 AND 1960, NEW JERSEY GREW TWICE AS FAST AS THE NATION. PUBLIC SERVICE MET THE INCREASED DEMAND FOR POWER BY LAYING THOUSANDS OF MILES OF GAS MAINS AND BUILDING GENERATING STATIONS SUCH AS THIS ONE AT MERCER (RIGHT).

to natural gas allowed the company to vigorously promote gas heating and to lay its own, smaller pipelines across the Watchung Mountains to towns like Chester, which had never had gas.

The electric business enjoyed unprecedented expansion. In the postwar years it built five generating stations: Sewaren, Linden, Mercer, Hudson and Bergen. When the Sewaren plant in Woodbridge opened in 1948, it earned remarkable acclaim. *Power Generation* magazine praised it for "marking an important point in the history of power development, because in its design are

meet the huge, new number five unit at SEWAREN

FAR RIGHT: FROM THIS SPOTLESS CONTROL ROOM AT THE KEARNY GENERATING STATION, AND OTHERS LIKE IT THROUGHOUT THE SERVICE TERRITORY, PSE&G WORKERS MONITORED THE GENERATION AND DISTRIBUTION OF ELECTRICAL POWER. THIS PHOTO WAS TAKEN IN 1953, WHEN PSE&G ACHIEVED A WORLD FIRST BY ADVANCING TURBINE STEAM TEMPERATURES TO 1100 DEGREES FAHRENHEIT AT KEARNY.

POINT OF PRIDE

Charlie Wolfe

"It makes for a good feeling, starting as a custodian, becoming a lineman and ending up as president of IBEW Local 94," says retiree Charlie Wolfe, who worked for PSE&G in Burlington County for 44 years.

Thanks in large part to union leadership, PSE&G has achieved excellent labor relations. The key was Wolfe's willingness, and that of other union leaders, to try a process called mutual gains. "What it means is both sides were finally putting all their cards on the table and trying to make things work," he explains. "Once we got established in that mode, it became a viable force."

Early in his career, Wolfe worked on the crews that ran electric lines to tens of thousands of new homes in Willingboro and Cherry Hill. He also spent 12 years as a troubleshooter, a tough but rewarding job. "You're the first on call during storms, when poles get hit or wires are down," he says. "Your job is to go out, get things cut and clear, make them safe, get the people back in service as quick as you can. PSE&G is there to help people. It makes you feel good about what you do."

embodied nearly all of the new ideas that have been accumulating during and immediately after the war." Public Service pioneered in raising turbine steam temperatures, a benchmark of electrical generating efficiency: Sewaren's 1050-degree Fahrenheit unit and the 1100-degree unit at Kearny Generating Station in 1953 were both world firsts.

All that electrical power had to go somewhere, and a memorable generation of Public Service linemen made sure it did. In those days before bucket trucks and other equipment made line work less labor-intensive, line gangs consisted of eight workers: a foreman, a driver, four linemen (two for each pole) and two ground men (one for each pole). Line gangs had a culture all their own, one that William Walsh Jr., director, corporate responsibility, and a third-generation employee, knew from childhood. His late father was a lineman and union vice president in Trenton.

"Dad lived through the roaring years when the company was growing at 5, 6, 7 percent a year," Walsh recalls. "Linemen were very much a breed unto themselves, especially at that time — a very close, tight-knit bunch of people who looked out for one another. I remember my father coming home in tears one night when one of his friends was burned by a flash on the job. The potential dangers, I think that's what really fused that family feeling among all of them. Lifelong friendships were made."

CADET PROGRAM

The renewed focus on engineering created a need for additional talent. The result was the Cadet Program, a strong force in the development of Public Service management. The military-style name is no accident, as the program was designed by company leaders who had served as U.S. Army officers. It exemplified, and extended, the traditional move-up-the-ladder culture.

Cadets were the cream of the engineering crop. Recruited fresh from college, they generally spent 18 months learning the ropes. There were gas cadets, electric cadets and commercial cadets. Donald W. Weyant, currently regulatory leader, state/delivery operations support, joined the company in the electric cadet class of 1959. He explains: "We spent a few weeks in commercial operations, six months in a generating station, about four months in a distribution location, a month at the Maplewood test lab and the rest of the time in Newark in departments such as engineering and system planning. It was an especially

good course if, like me, you didn't really know what you wanted. At the end of the course, you could select where you wished to go. Then you learned the business from the bottom up. You learned operations, the geography of the divisions, the union contracts, how to become an efficient operating person. Then you'd spend a few years in the engineering, substation and line departments, then the line department. By that time, you were pretty much ready to become a group head. That was the path."

MANY COMPANY LEADERS CAME UP THROUGH THE CADET PROGRAMS FOR COLLEGE GRADUATES. PICTURED ABOVE IS THE 1926 CLASS OF ELECTRICAL ENGINEERING CADETS. LEFT: THE HUDSON DIVISION LINE SCHOOL AT THE OLD HUDSON GENERATING STATION IN OCTOBER 1947.

100 Years of Green Vehicles

Energy-efficient and safety-enhanced vehicles may seem like recent innovations, but PSEG has always supported them enthusiastically.

The company's very first fleet included battery-powered wagons that Public Service acquired along with the company that made them, United Electric. In the 1920s, Public Service introduced 49 electric vehicles to the fleet. Limited to a top speed of 15 miles per hour and a 100-mile range, they were perfectly suited to urban uses such as street lighting maintenance in Jersey City.

The company's transit business got a boost during the Great Depression when Public Service engineers helped to develop the diesel-electric bus. Twenty-seven of these fuel savers were placed in service, the first such bus fleet in the world. And PSE&G vigorously promoted seatbelt usage before it was the law. "Do You Buckle Up?" was the message of a safety campaign in 1976. It featured Plainfield-based service specialist Bill Sederman, who escaped uninjured from an overturned van because he had buckled up.

PSEG currently operates more than 6,100

vehicles, ranging from construction equipment to the familiar *WorryFree* appliance service vans. Several hundred are powered by natural gas, an environmentally friendly alternative to standard gasoline. PSEG's fleet maintenance professionals keep all company vehicles running at optimum performance. They also retrofit them at each servicing with any applicable safety enhancements, such as the high-visibility lights now found on all PSE&G utility service trucks.

Battery-operated line trucks, like the one pictured at left, were a familiar sight on urban streets in the 1920s. In terms of minimal environmental impact, their contemporary counterparts are PSE&G's vans powered by natural gas, above.

The program eventually tapered down to nine months, then six, then four. Reborn as the Management Training Orientation Plan (MTOP), it dropped most of its military vestiges. These early recruitment programs were later criticized for keeping the company management insular and lacking diversity. Nonetheless, they did cultivate talent that would carry Public Service into a new era. Many cadets rose to influential positions; for example, Robert J. Dougherty Jr., president and chief operating officer, PSEG Energy Holdings, was an MTOP finance cadet in 1973. ("My MTOP class provided the greatest amount of four days of information packed into 16 weeks I've ever seen in my life," Dougherty quips.)

Current recruitment programs redress the old drawbacks. Today PSEG actively recruits a diverse mix of high academic achievers and MBA graduates, and while it continues to rotate them through different areas, it places them into decision-making positions from day one. Thomas R. Smith, president of PSEG Fossil and executive vice president, operations and development, PSEG Power, champions the approach. "Young MBAs aren't wedded to old ideas," says Smith. "These are eager people. Mix that with experience, and it's a powerful combination."

"EVERYONE'S DARLING"

The postwar era was generally easy and prosperous for Public Service. Certainly, as Frederick D. DeSanti, vice president, external affairs, says: "The price of energy was low, the company and state were building like crazy, we never had an energy crisis, there were no legislative issues. Your residential bill was $10 a month, and it never went up." In general, he adds, "we were everybody's darling."

However, one issue did cloud this otherwise bright period. Relationships between management and the nine unions that then represented workers tended to be "very acrimonious and adversarial," says M. Peter Mellett, retired vice president, human resources, and a 41-year company veteran. Disputes over pay and benefits erupted in a major strike in 1959. Mellett recalls it as "a very, very bitter event in this company – there was shooting at the picket lines." That strike ended after six weeks, but not much was resolved. Strikes would continue to flare up, including a wildcat walkout in the late 1960s that led to two-week suspensions for union officials.

These growing pains were inevitable. Although Public Service outwardly looked like the same utility it had always been, the original order had gradually reversed. By McCarter's death, in 1953, electric had become the fastest-growing business, gas a strong second and transit a lagging third.

McCarter had been such a commanding presence that his successors seemed mild by comparison. Without question, all were fiscally cautious and committed to the growth of New Jersey: Edmund W. Wakelee, president, 1939-1945; George H. Blake, president, 1945-1954; Lyle C. McDonald, chairman, 1954-1958; Donald C. Luce, president 1954-1965 and CEO 1958-1965; Watson F. Tait Jr., chairman 1965-1968; and Edwin H. Snyder, president 1965-1972 and chairman 1968-1972. Their low-key leadership was appropriate. But Edward R. Eberle and Robert I. Smith, who took the reins after Snyder, would be far more visible and vocal. The crises of the 1970s would demand it.

Licensed for use by electric utilities until 1973, Reddy Kilowatt put a friendly face on electricity throughout the world. Europeans called him "Don Kilovatio" or "Le Bon Genie d'Électricité." His image now belongs to Northern States Power Company. In his honor, more than a few PSE&G employees named their dogs Reddy.

CHAPTER THREE

MEETING CHALLENGES WITH COMPETENCE

AMERICAN SOCIETY CHANGED RADICALLY IN THE 1960S AND 1970S, TRANSFORMED BY POLITICAL ASSASSINATIONS, DISSENT OVER THE VIETNAM WAR AND BATTLES FOR EQUALITY BY MINORITIES AND WOMEN — TO NAME JUST A FEW OF THE FACTORS. ☐ PUBLIC SERVICE SEEMED OUTWARDLY UNAFFECTED, ALTHOUGH THE GENERAL OFFICE DID CLOSE FOR BRIEF PERIODS DURING NEWARK'S CIVIL UNREST IN 1968. THE CITY AND NATION MAY HAVE BEEN TROUBLED, BUT THE COMPANY STILL INSISTED ON PROPRIETY. PAUL CAFONE, MANAGER, SYSTEM OPERATIONS, ELECTRIC SYSTEMS, RECALLS SEEING AN EMPLOYEE ESCORTED OUT OF THE TERMINAL BUILDING BY POLICE FOR HAVING WORN JEANS TO WORK. RETIRED CHAIRMAN HAROLD SONN RECALLS WITH AMUSEMENT A REVEALING ANECDOTE FROM HIS DAYS IN MIDDLE MANAGEMENT: "I WORKED FOR ED EBERLE, THEN A VICE PRESIDENT, WHO ONCE ASKED ME TO SIT IN FOR HIM AT THE WEEKLY MEETING OF THE COMPANY'S OPERATING COMMITTEE. I WORE A VERY PALE BLUE SHIRT. STANDARD DRESS WAS A WHITE SHIRT AND DARK SUIT. THE VP OF COMMERCIAL OPERATIONS TOOK ME ASIDE LATER AND SAID, 'I REALLY ADMIRE YOU FOR WEARING THAT SHIRT. THAT'S WHAT WE NEED, SOME YOUTHFUL THINKING AROUND HERE.'"

The choice to abandon the triangle-in-a-circle logo must have been a tough one, because New Jerseyans had long known and loved the original emblem. The sunburst, and the fresh white-and-orange color scheme that surrounded it, better reflected the company's commitment to nuclear power and a healthy environment.

The change in logo symbolized a time when the giant had to stir, spurred by the Mideast oil embargo, energy crises, sky-rocketing costs and controversies about the company's ambitious plans to build nuclear plants. Public Service rose to these challenges by making some of the toughest choices of its history. It drew on the "something" it had cultivated since 1903: technical expertise and commitment to New Jersey and the public trust.

"GENERATING STATIONS ON EVERY CORNER"

Many of PSE&G's choices arose from the steady growth in the demand for electricity. For years, demand had grown by 7 percent annually, theoretically doubling every decade. "At that rate we'd have needed a generating station on every corner in about 30 years, but that was evident only in retrospect," notes Frederick W. "Fritz" Lark, PSE&G vice president, business analysis. While additional generating stations built across the Northeast in the 1950s were vital in meeting the demand, systems were still strained and major, multi-state blackouts occurred in 1965 and 1967.

The answer, for PSE&G and other utilities, was nuclear power. Introduced in the United States in the 1950s, it had proven a safe and reasonably

PREVIOUS PAGE:
THE ELECTRIC SYSTEMS
OPERATIONS CENTER IN
NEWARK, 1974. ABOVE:
PSEG BROUGHT NEW
JERSEY INTO THE
NUCLEAR AGE WITH
SALEM AND HOPE CREEK
GENERATING STATIONS.
RIGHT: A CARTOON BY
HENRY MARTIN INTRO-
DUCED THE SUNBURST
LOGO IN 1971.

Sonn was in his middle 40s then. Some 20 years later, PSEG would appoint a chairman of that age — unthinkable in the 1960s but recognized as the right choice in 1986 — and employee engagement at all levels would become the norm.

While dress codes and hierarchy still ruled on the surface, Public Service was also poised to change radically. In 1971 it signaled a major commitment to change by introducing the sunburst logo, still in use today. Curiously, no one knows who created the original Public Service logo or where it first appeared. Old-timers agree that the triangle symbolized the three sides of the business — transit, gas, electricity — within the circle of the corporation.

priced source of electricity. PSE&G procured a site on the Delaware River in Salem County and partnered with three other utilities in the PJM Interconnection to build Salem Nuclear Generating Station. As the principal owner, PSE&G would oversee the construction and eventually operate the plant. Fieldwork started in January 1968.

Always capital-intensive and time-consuming, plant construction was becoming extremely expensive due to rising costs and more sophisticated technologies. Where would the money come from, especially when electric and gas revenues could not begin to cover spending? As retired PSE&G President Larry Codey puts it: "By the early 1970s, Bob Smith [then president] recognized that he had to do more than just build plants; he had to pay for them." PSE&G considered acquiring Atlantic City Electric Company (now part of Conectiv) to gain efficiencies of scale, but the merger never materialized.

"Alvin, come quick! A new day has dawned!"

The *Second Sun*

When PSE&G made the commitment in the 1960s to develop nuclear power for New Jersey's future, it also committed itself to educating the public on the subject. Many nuclear education programs took place aboard a refurbished ferry, the *Second Sun*. Retired Chairman Harold Sonn explains the source of the name: "The most promising long-term source of bulk power production is nuclear fusion, which duplicates the process continually occurring in the sun."

From its home port on the Delaware River, close to where PSEG's Salem and Hope Creek nuclear generating stations now stand, the *Second Sun* traveled New Jersey's waterways. For several years it provided information that helped dispel misconceptions and fears about nuclear power. One of its most popular offerings was a film in which *Star Trek* celebrity William Shatner helped PSE&G present the case for nuclear energy.

The sun symbolism made a lasting mark when the company adopted the sunburst logo in 1971. Passage of the Clean Air Act that year also brought a heightened public awareness about air pollution, which stimulated a new look for the company fleet. PSE&G's vehicles went from gray or black to white-and-orange, the color scheme that is now central to the company's visual identity.

Tens of thousands of New Jersey schoolchildren received this educational comic book as a souvenir of their visit to the *Second Sun*. The floating information center is also pictured in the photo, opposite.

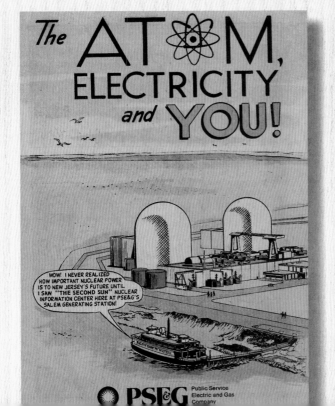

Debra Thomas has experienced many of PSE&G's changes first-hand. As a clerk hired in 1971, she recorded incoming bill payments by hand. Later she dispatched service orders by teletype. Those jobs are now handled by computers. Thomas was also a meter reader back when customers were surprised to see a woman in that role.

Thomas's career progression led to customer service, a move that perfectly suits her knowledge of PSE&G operations and her warm personality. Thomas works the busy day shift at the Northern Inquiry Center in Cranford, where she typically answers 120 customer calls each day. She and 300 other customer service professionals (CSPs), some based in the Southern Inquiry Center in

Debra Thomas

Bordentown, fielded more than 5 million calls around the clock in 2002.

"You never know what the next call will bring," Thomas says. She's proud of her ability to handle difficult issues: "I like solving things." She finds special satisfaction in being a peer coach to new CSPs.

In its ongoing commitment to world-class service, PSE&G recognizes that the people who actually do the work are the best ones to improve it. In 2000, Thomas contributed her know-how as part of the Voice Response Unit Enhancement Team, which identified and implemented new technologies to handle customer calls even more efficiently. The team's efforts earned a Corporate Team Excellence award, another point of pride for Debra Thomas.

WALL STREET ACUMEN

Smith made a revolutionary choice in 1972: he hired William E. Scott as vice president, finance, a title equivalent to today's chief financial officer. Formerly an executive at Irving Trust Company, Scott was the first "outsider" recruited at such a high level. Furthermore, Smith quickly appointed Scott to the Board of Directors and continued to promote him (he retired as senior executive vice president). This ruffled some feathers, but everyone knew that Public Service urgently needed Scott's Wall Street experience.

"Bill really understood capital markets," Codey emphasizes. Scott focused like a laser on maintaining PSE&G's AA or better bond ratings to ensure access to capital. He also sought to facilitate relations with the New Jersey Board of Public Utilities (BPU), the regulatory body that hears the cases by utilities for rate changes. To support this focus, Scott hired Everett L. Morris as comptroller. As a former accountant for the Federal Power Commission (now the Federal Energy Regulatory Commission) and the former chairman of New York's equivalent of the BPU, Morris thoroughly understood every aspect of utility financing and regulation. He would go on to serve PSE&G in executive positions in corporate development and customer operations, on the Board of Directors and as the president of an unregulated subsidiary.

Codey, another outsider, joined as a trial attorney in 1973 and was promoted within two years to corporate rate counsel. He was instrumental in streamlining the rate case process, an enormous step forward for PSE&G and the BPU. "Instead of having 20 witnesses, we streamlined it to six or seven who covered broader subjects," Codey recalls. "We looked for regulatory and accounting mechanisms to help match and explain revenue and expenses. We focused on giving the BPU everything it needed, speeding up the process and working our tails off so we weren't responsible for one minute of delay." Codey himself, a skilled communicator and natural negotiator, specialized in "explaining regulation to finance and finance to regulation." Though they hadn't always understood each other, Codey says, "Both communities were indispensable to PSE&G."

LONG GAS LINES, SHORT TEMPERS

These moves, as it turned out, could not have been timelier. Public Service had positioned itself to navigate a long and stressful period of financial challenges. The company would not escape pain, but it would survive better than many other utilities did.

August 1973 marked the start of the Mideast embargo, in which Saudi Arabia and certain other Middle East nations stopped exporting gas and oil to the United States for political reasons. Today the period is chiefly remembered for the gasoline rationing it necessitated: drivers waited in long lines to fuel up on odd- or even-numbered days, depending on the last digit of their license plate. But the embargo caused a negative ripple effect on the economy that lasted for years. It sent prices

soaring. Rudely awakened to the drawbacks of depending on foreign resources, Americans began clamoring for energy independence.

The utility industry soon felt deep shock when Consolidated Edison of New York did not pay shareholders a dividend in 1973. Such a step was truly startling because utility stocks were regarded as reliably sound "widow and orphan" investments that always paid dividends. (By and large, they still are; in 2001, half of the 25 highest dividend-paying stocks on the Standard & Poor's 500 Index were energy companies, including PSEG as number 18.) The move sent Con Ed's stock price on a downward spiral to $4 per share from a high of about $30. Public Service, which never omitted its dividend, suffered less; its share price dropped from about $30 to $11.

"Con Ed's move was absolutely huge," Codey emphasizes. "Con Ed was basically saying to the regulatory community: 'We're really in trouble and you guys don't recognize it.' And with the quadrupling of oil prices, we had the beginning of inflation."

The federal government tried to fight inflation by raising interest rates, which backfired. Most businesses cut back on expansions; spending was flat to negative. However, utilities in the midst of building nuclear plants didn't have that option. "We were operating in an environment with slow regulatory responses, huge cost increases, rampant inflation and extremely high interest rates — and

THE OBSERVATIONS MADE IN THIS 1976 NUCLEAR EDUCATION AD REMAIN TRUE TODAY. THE U.S. STILL RELIES ON IMPORTED OIL. THE ROUTE TO ENERGY INDEPENDENCE DOESN'T LIE SOLELY IN THE INCREASED USE OF COAL OR SOLAR POWER, WHICH ALONE CAN'T GENERATE ENOUGH ENERGY FOR THE COUNTRY'S NEEDS. NUCLEAR ENERGY HAS INDEED PROVEN TO BE RELIABLE, NON-POLLUTING AND AN EFFICIENT WAY TO GENERATE ELECTRICITY ON A LARGE SCALE.

The 60-Foot Revolution

One of the most dependable sights in New Jersey is the familiar white-and-orange PSE&G bucket truck, on the scene whenever an employee is replacing a street light or servicing a line. These unheralded trucks may not seem like cutting-edge technology, but their introduction in the 1960s was a turning point in utility history.

Bucket trucks and diggers made pole-setting much safer and easier. "Before we had them, to set a pole, you physically had to put a boom together," recalls retired IBEW Local 94 President and PSE&G Chief Lineman Charlie Wolfe. "Then the work gang had to dig the hole and set the pole." With a reach of up to 60 feet, bucket trucks almost eliminated the need for pole climbing, which also enhanced safety. By reducing the typical line crew from eight people to two or three, PSE&G could redeploy much-needed personnel as New Jersey was busy expanding its suburbs, office parks and malls. And bucket trucks made it possible for PSE&G to build its 13kV electric distribution loop system, an invaluable fallback that automatically provides a second source of power if the primary source goes out.

In recent years PSEG Global has exported this innovation to partners in other countries. Brazil's Rio Grande Energia (RGE), for example, had only two bucket trucks for a territory seven times the size of New Jersey. When PSEG Global became a co-owner of RGE, it promptly helped the company add more trucks to improve on-the-job safety and system performance.

The nonconductive fiberglass bucket is a vital safety component of the bucket truck. These trucks are so symbolic of PSE&G that the company sells toy models at Christmas, with the proceeds earmarked for charities. The limited-edition toy trucks have become collector's items among employees.

we couldn't take the medicine we were told to take, which was to cut construction costs," Codey says. Public Service was a champion at controlling costs, but it could not tame inflation single-handedly. "We had to keep building, because the drive for energy independence called for it," he points out. "It was a huge financial problem with no easy remedy, and it generated rate case after rate case after rate case." Costs to consumers began to rise.

FIRST-EVER LAYOFFS

In 1974 the brilliantly illuminated "Public Service" sign atop the Terminal Building, long a beacon on the Newark skyline, was turned off. Darkening the sign saved energy, but it also captured the bleakness of the times.

Across the nation, companies retrenched. Public Service had to resort to layoffs for the first time, an agonizing choice. Lifetime employment at many major U.S. companies had been the unspoken contract, so much so that "downsizing" was not yet a common term. But economics at Public Service demanded that about 1,200 people, almost 10 percent of the workforce, be let go. This figure was roughly in line with national statistics — by 1975 about eight million of America's 94 million workers were out of work — but that was no consolation to anyone.

"What a rotten time," says Pat Downes, PSE&G's vice president, delivery operations support, who still winces at the memory of personally having to lay off 70 associates. Union contracts, which have since changed, dictated the terms. The last hired were the first laid off. Others were demoted, based on seniority. Those with at least 10 years were guaranteed a position, not necessarily at their former pay. Describing a grim scenario that was repeated

in many locations, Downes continues: "My boss and I sat at a table with everybody's name on index cards. We worked down to the pool of people who weren't going to be here anymore. It hurt. PSE&G took five years to come back from that. By 1979 the economy had changed, and by 1980 we were hiring again." By that time the company was actively recruiting a more diverse workforce as well. It had adopted an Affirmative Action plan in 1976 and was making special efforts to hire and promote more women — efforts that continue today.

Both union and management employees felt threatened by the 1976 merger of gas and electric. Although the two businesses had been united in name under the PSE&G structure since 1948, they had operated separately. According to company veterans, each was a "fiefdom" with distinct and territorial cultures. Uniting them made financial and strategic sense, because it allowed for economies of scale and cross-pollenization of talent. But it inflamed existing turf battles. Short strikes also flared up periodically, as union/management relations remained tense.

THE ENERGY PEOPLE

At the same time, customers suffered mightily. The cost of living had skyrocketed, and "rate case after rate case" had raised utility rates. Taxes figured into the upward spiral: more than half of PSE&G's 1974 rate increase request for $257 million was earmarked for federal, state

Public Service Electric and Gas Company

EMPLOYEE INFORMATION CARD
1968
(Dec. 31, 1968, Year 1968, or as noted)

Service Area:	Munici-palities	Square Miles	Population
Electric Only	33	200	735,210
Gas Only	72	1,000	704,630
Electric and/or Gas	295	2,400	5,663,830

Per cent of State's population served . . . 79%
Salaries and Wages
Employees—December 31 . . . . $143,860,807
Employees with 25 or more years of service 3,302
Retired Employees 14,393
(Includes 70 beneficiaries receiving benefits under survivorship options) 3,291
Total revenue—Electric and Gas . . $635,996,770
Taxes charged to Operating Expenses $121,123,349
Stockholders (all classes) 154,343
Shares of Common Stock 31,004,216
Dividends paid per share of Common Stock $1.61
Earnings per share of Common Stock:
  Before extraordinary items $2.57
  After extraordinary items $2.60
Taxes per share of Common Stock $3.91
Utility plant—total $2,577,619,063
Utility plant—per employee $179,088
Gross additions to utility plant $223,333,748
Commercial offices 18
Commercial branch offices 12

IN THE 1970S, PSE&G
INSTALLED SOLAR
ENERGY AT ELEVEN NEW
JERSEY HOMES AS PART
OF A THREE-YEAR
ANALYSIS OF SOLAR'S
POTENTIAL IN THE
STATE. THE $600,000
STUDY FOUND THE
SYSTEMS TO BE VIABLE
FOR CERTAIN INDIVIDUAL
HOMES BUT GENERALLY
UNFEASIBLE FOR
GEOGRAPHIC AND
FINANCIAL REASONS.

and local taxes. In the 1976 case, the BPU granted PSE&G a 25 percent increase to cover its costs. A cycle of anger began. Customers vented their displeasure on meter readers and service representatives, themselves still angry from the layoffs and restructuring.

In short, the utility that had been everyone's darling in happier decades became everyone's punching bag. As a humanizing gesture, corporate leaders adopted a new tagline — "The Energy People." They wanted customers and employees to appreciate that Public Service was not a faceless entity or a mindless monopoly, but an organization made up of New Jerseyans who were playing by the rules and doing their best in a troubled era. The tagline debuted in 1971 along with the sunburst logo.

A utility lives up to the public trust by communicating with customers and employees, especially

in difficult times. Public Relations General Manager Arthur F. Lenehan and his staff kept their audiences informed through media as varied as bill stuffers, good will advertising campaigns and *The Energy People,* a print and video magazine for employees. The anonymous author of one consumer pamphlet on rising prices captured the sheer frustration of the times in the title: *We don't like it any more than you do!*

PLASTIC PIPES, POWER TOWERS AND FISH FARMS

PSE&G engineers did not simply wring their hands and wait for the bad times to pass. To supplement the supply of natural gas from pipelines in the Southeast, the company built two synthetic natural gas plants. It also arranged to import and store liquid natural gas from Algeria, an innovative plan thwarted by political controversy. Less dramatically, the company steadily replaced the aging cast iron and steel gas lines typically found in New Jersey, a process facilitated by the introduction of polyethylene piping. "In the past, if a cast iron gas line to your house corroded, we would run a new copper line through it, which was expensive," explains Will Carey, PSE&G regulatory leader. "With polyethylene we can do it very economically and we don't have to excavate what's there." Similarly, the arrival of trenchless technology facilitated new construction by making it possible to run gas lines under the street without digging up the street.

The company also invested millions of dollars into alternative energy research. It yielded some interesting results, but no viable, long-term sources of bulk power production. One solar concept involved "Power Towers," in which tower-mounted mini-generators were surrounded by special mirrors to capture the sun's rays. It was found that to match the output of a conventional fossil plant, a Power Tower required 66 square miles of open land and continuous sunny days, at odds with the realities of New Jersey.

To make use of waste heat from generating stations, PSE&G even experimented with fish farms and hydroponic greenhouses for growing tomatoes. The company tried to sell the goods commercially, but lacked the marketing clout. Old-timers look back on these minor ventures with major amusement. As Lark wryly observes: "Public Service really didn't know how to do business at the Fulton Fish Market."

What did make a major difference was an unglamorous innovation — high efficiency, gas-fired heating systems — by which homeowners and business owners *consumed* less energy every day. Carey, who advised on these systems as a member of the Gas Research Institute's Appliance Project Advisory Group, notes that gas-fired hot-water heaters and clothes dryers are also more energy-efficient than ever. The same is true for refrigerators, dishwashers and other electrical appliances. Since the 1970s PSE&G and other utility companies have actively promoted energy conservation and offered rebates to customers who install energy-efficient heating systems and air conditioners. It may seem odd for a company to promote *less* use of its product, but again, PSEG believes that what is good for the customer is ultimately good for the company and its shareholders.

NUCLEAR ADVANCES AND SETBACKS

Despite the financial traumas of the 1970s, Salem One Nuclear Generating Station went online as planned in 1977. It had been 11 years in the mak-

ing. Construction of Salem Two and two neighboring nuclear units at Hope Creek continued. The people of Public Service were rightfully proud of these achievements, which helped ensure New Jersey's energy future.

However, in a choice almost as agonizing as the layoffs had been, the company cancelled another, more unusual nuclear facility. Atlantic Generating Station was to have been a floating nuclear plant moored three miles east of Atlantic City. Eminent scientists hailed the concept as an imaginative resolution of the conflict between the demands for energy and a cleaner environment. Indeed, between 1967 and 1973 alone, Public Service invested $4.1 million in nuclear-related environmental studies concerning marine biology, meteorology and other areas. But a few years after Atlantic was commissioned, demand for electricity began to

So innovative was the conception for the Atlantic Generating Station that Pulitzer Prize-winning writer John McPhee wrote about it for *The New Yorker*. However, plans for this floating nuclear power plant were cancelled in 1978 when the energy crisis abated.

THE IMPLOSION OF THE
TERMINAL BUILDING IN
1981 MARKED THE END OF
AN ERA. DURING PRELIMI-
NARY DEMOLITION WORK,
CONTRACTORS LABORED
FOR DAYS TO BLAST OUT
THE TERMINAL'S REIN-
FORCED TRANSIT LANES.
"THEY WERE BUILT LIKE
THE PYRAMIDS," ONE VET-
ERAN EMPLOYEE SAID.
PSEG'S ROBERT I. SMITH
AMPHITHEATER, AN AIRY
SITTING AREA ADJACENT
TO 80 PARK PLAZA, NOW
OCCUPIES THE SPACE.

flatten considerably, partly as a result of energy conservation efforts. Bill Scott came to the conclusion in 1978 that the company couldn't afford Atlantic. (The concept of a floating plant eventually took a new form — in 2001 PSEG Global and project partner GMR began operating a barge-mounted fossil plant on the Gurupur River in Southern India. PSEG sold its interest in the project in 2002.)

Nuclear energy leapt into the spotlight after a major accident at the Three Mile Island (TMI) plant near Harrisburg, Pennsylvania, in 1979. Public Service had no connection with TMI, but like all other utility companies with nuclear plants, it was affected. "The crush for public information became extraordinary," says Fred DeSanti, vice president, external affairs, who represented

PSE&G at numerous forums around New Jersey. "One Sunday morning I showed up to speak at a program at a Paterson church. There were 2,000 cars there. I said 'What's this about?' They say 'Don't you know? You're going to be debating Dr. George Wald.'" Wald, a 1967 Nobel Prize laureate for his work on the human eye, was a vocal opponent of nuclear power.

"To make a long story short, we had the debate, and I can't say I did a better job; Dr. Wald was an awesome individual, but basically I made the necessary points," DeSanti says. "I closed my remarks by saying that the greatest fear we should have about nuclear power is the fear of facing the future without it." That defining quote, which was highlighted in boldface type in the next day's *Star-Ledger*, perfectly captured the company's ongoing commitment to nuclear power.

SHEDDING OLD SKINS

Long-time employees agree that the 1970s were the toughest time in the history of Public Service. The company survived as well as it did, they say, because the people of the company made the necessary choices, transitions and sacrifices. An important turning point came in 1977, when eight unions, representing 8,000 employees, signed three-year contracts — a company first.

As if to turn the corner on the decade for good, Public Service shed two pieces of itself, pieces that had virtually defined "the old PS." The money-losing transit business was sold to New Jersey Transit Corporation, a state agency. And the outmoded, energy-inefficient Terminal Building was demolished to make way for 80 Park Plaza, the 26-story headquarters that the company has leased since 1979.

It was a fresh start for a new decade.

100 Years of Commitment

Public Service "walked its talk" to Newark in the 1970s. Having outgrown its outmoded Terminal Building headquarters, the company could have moved out of the city altogether or in part. Some old-time Newark companies did just that, following the civil disruptions that rocked New Jersey's cities in the 1960s. But then-Chairman Bob Smith and the Board of Directors "refused to take PS to the suburbs," recalls Pete Mellett, retired vice president, human resources. Despite the numerous economic difficulties of the time, Smith steadfastly turned down incentives from areas that hoped to lure an employer as attractive as PSE&G.

The company's loyalty to its home city did not go unnoticed. When PSE&G moved into its newly built Newark headquarters at 80 Park Plaza in 1980, the Newark-based *Star-Ledger*, the state's largest newspaper, praised the decision as one that "tells a tale about the hope of New Jersey's cities…[and] perhaps best exemplifies the kind of commercial development so desperately needed by the state's urban centers."

PSEG continues to be one of Newark's biggest employers and most dedicated supporters. The company helped launch the remarkable South Ward Urban Initiative, a public/private partnership that has improved job opportunities and the quality of life in an inner-city neighborhood, and supports programs offered by the Urban League of Essex County, United Way of Essex and West Hudson, the Clinton Hill Health Care Initiative, the Business Technical Assistance Forum, Newark Public Schools and numerous private schools, the Newark Museum and the New Jersey Performing Arts Center.

Groundbreaking for 80 Park Plaza took place on April 17, 1978. The heads of the companies involved in the project, as well as city and state leaders, all turned out. From left: Alton G. Marshall, president, Rockefeller Center, Inc.; Anthony J. Peters, chairman, Cushman & Wakefield, Inc.; PSE&G Chairman Robert I. Smith; Newark Mayor Kenneth A. Gibson; Robert V. Tishman, president, Tishman Realty & Construction Co., Inc.; State Energy Commissioner Joel Jacobson; and Newark City Council President Earl Harris.

CHAPTER FOUR

SHAPING AN ENTERPRISE

PUBLIC SERVICE ENTERED THE 1980S AS A TRADITIONAL, REGULATED UTILITY AND EMERGED AS A DIVERSIFIED ENTERPRISE WITH FOOTHOLDS IN SEVERAL ADDITIONAL, UNREGULATED BUSINESSES. THE EVOLUTION WOULD CONTINUE INTO THE 1990S, FEELING MORE LIKE A REVOLUTION TO SOME AND CONTINUING TO DEMAND TOUGH CHOICES EVERY STEP OF THE WAY.

PREVIOUS PAGE LEFT:
PSE&G ASSOCIATES
SERVICE A POLE-TOP
TRANSFORMER. PREVIOUS
PAGE RIGHT: PSE&G
EMPLOYEE BUNDLED
AGAINST THE ELEMENTS
WHILE ASSISTING
UTILITIES IN CANADA.
RIGHT: THE CONTROL
ROOM AT SALEM
GENERATING STATION.
LIKE ALL NUCLEAR
PLANTS, SALEM DIFFERS
FROM CONVENTIONAL
POWER STATIONS ONLY IN
ITS SOURCE OF HEAT. IT
USES THE CONTROLLED
FISSION OF URANIUM TO
MAKE HEAT, WHILE A
CONVENTIONAL PLANT
BURNS FOSSIL FUEL SUCH
AS OIL OR COAL.

NUCLEAR ADVANCEMENTS

The nuclear program continued to dominate the company's resources. Salem One Nuclear Generating Station had been in commercial operation since 1977. But the opening of Salem Two — and of every other nuclear plant under construction in the United States — had been delayed by changes mandated by the Nuclear Regulatory Commission following the Three Mile Island accident in Pennsylvania in 1979.

When Salem Two finally went online in 1981, bringing the company's installed electrical capacity to 9,101 megawatts, there was cause for celebration. It was tempered, however, by the difficult decision to cancel one of two nuclear generating stations under construction at the adjacent Hope Creek site. The company was careful to point out that economics drove the decision, not lack of confidence in the value of nuclear power. The reality was that electrical demand was lower than anticipated, while construction costs continued to rise.

According to retired PSE&G President Larry Codey, then-Chairman Smith agonized over the move. "Bob believed we would need this power by the late 1980s," Codey recalls. "But he also knew we ultimately couldn't afford it. And frankly, if we had not cancelled one unit at Hope Creek, I don't believe we would have ever finished the other."

Codey, then PSE&G rate counsel, and his team negotiated innovative terms for discontinuing the second Hope Creek plant from the BPU and former public advocate Al Nardelli, a critic of nuclear expansion. All parties agreed that the costs of dismantling the plant, which was 18 percent completed, would be amortized over 15 years in order to reduce the burden on both the company and ratepayers. In addition, the state passed legislation requiring cost containments on the construction of the remaining Hope Creek plant. Cost overruns would incur penalties. PSE&G, in effect, agreed to have its feet held to the fire.

TIDE OF NEW EMPLOYEES

Everyone involved in completing the Hope Creek station recalls the tremendous four-year push. Pete R. Landrieu, currently vice president, electric transmission, oversaw the effort. "He ate, slept and drank Hope Creek, as did his team," Codey says. Stanley M. Kosierowski, currently president, PSEG Energy Technologies, handled the centralizing of nuclear operations. That involved moving the nuclear engineering group from Newark to Salem, recruiting 2,200 new employees and coordinating 8,000 contractors on site. Challenges at Salem One, where failure of a relay had necessitated a precautionary four-month shutdown in 1983, created additional pressures for PSE&G's nuclear team.

"This was not the old PS; we were creating a whole new culture," Kosierowski emphasizes. That culture was arising out of "a sea of mud and people," recalls Virginia Wright, document management clerk, who came to work at Hope Creek in 1985. "I'd leave work, and people would be waiting for my parking space. At one stretch, I worked 31 days in a row. I didn't mind. We all did it. Together." Anyone who thought that utility workers were strict nine-to-fivers would have been quickly divested of that notion. The people at Hope Creek understood loyalty and sacrifice. Pulling together to overcome obstacles, they made it possible for the plant to begin commercial operation in 1986.

Though PSE&G did pay a small penalty for slight cost overruns, the cost-containment proviso

TECHNICIANS PERFORM MAINTENANCE ON A TURBINE ROTOR AT HOPE CREEK GENERATING STATION.

had been a beneficial discipline. "We listened to what the state and the consumer advocate had to say," Codey says. "We came up with a solution. And I dare say it was good for the company and good for society. We kept the price of Hope Creek down and we expanded energy resources for customers."

The project also benefited the environment. In return for its use of seven acres of wetland to create an access road to the site, PSE&G restored an equivalent seven acres of wetlands area. In a preview of the larger Estuary Enhancement Program to follow, this effort greatly improved breeding areas for the horseshoe crab and thus ensured an essential supply of food for the tens of thousands of migratory birds that pass over southern New Jersey each spring and fall.

TECHNOLOGY AND FIEFDOMS

The U.S. economy improved by fits and starts in the early 1980s, but inflation remained a problem. In this environment, emerging technologies helped the company maximize its resources.

"The engineering side of the house was pretty sophisticated in the use of computers for work such as pipe stress analysis," says Bob Dougherty, president and COO, PSEG Energy Holdings, who worked in systems analysis then. "But this was a company that had done its general ledger accounting with paper and pen until 1973." The automation of accounting had been a boon, and by the

1980s, the obvious next step was to centralize and automate customer accounting.

That marked a turning point for the fiefdom culture of PSE&G. For decades, districts and commercial offices had been self-contained in terms of customer service. Each had its own set of billing records and its own telephone operators. It was an efficient system but hardly cost-effective, given a base of almost two million customers.

The first step was to move all account data to a mainframe. Then the company created centralized call centers in Newark and Bordentown with terminals linked to the mainframe. Telephone representatives enjoyed instant access to records and could also automatically transmit service orders and emergency calls to field locations. Soon the technology that had seemed so revolutionary was commonplace: "mini-computers" appeared on desktops and meter readers began using automated, handheld devices to improve their productivity.

FATHER VERSUS SON

A bitter strike tore at the fabric of PSE&G in 1982. Union/management relations were still somewhat adversarial, typical for the times. Both sides were experiencing intense economic pressures, as business costs, interest rates and the cost of living continued to rise. At issue were benefits for new hires and other changes. The adversity erupted into a 42-day work stoppage by the IBEW and the Office and Professional Employees International Union

Hand-held computers add speed and efficiency to the meter-reading process. The computers are downloaded at night with the following day's route information. This technology allowed PSE&G to institute home-based reporting for meter technicians (and appliance service technicians as well). By starting their work day from home rather than a dispatching center, they can cover more territory — a labor efficiency for workers and customers alike.

(OPEIU), which represents clerical and technical workers in electrical distribution.

John "Chip" Gerrity, now president of IBEW Local 94, headed IBEW Local 1576 at the Salem Generating Stations at that time and participated in negotiations. His father, Nick Gerrity, worked at Salem as a watch engineer in supervision. "There was a time during the strike that my father and I couldn't even talk to each other," Chip Gerrity says. "He was on the inside. And they were helicoptering the supervisors in and out. We finally agreed just not to talk about work or the strike."

The 1982 strike eventually was resolved after intervention by federal and state mediators, but not before it had inflicted "definite wounds," according to PSE&G Vice President Pete Cistaro, then an industrial relations manager. The memory of this divisive episode would later help inspire new thinking on both sides. "Subsequently, we started to make changes in how we dealt with each other and came into the era of win/win," he says.

A leader in that progress was Charlie Wolfe, a 44-year veteran of PSE&G who retired as president of IBEW Local 94 in 1999. Wolfe sums up the difference between the divisive labor relations then and the cooperative ones now: "We learned what it was like not to work together and then what it was like to work together."

ENVISIONING THE FUTURE

By the mid-1980s, company executives were able to catch their breath, so to speak, for the first time in years. The nuclear program had finally come to fruition. No new fossil plants were planned. Natural gas prices had dropped and the pipeline supply had stabilized after the federal government lifted its controls, enabling PSE&G to close its gas manufacturing plants. Cogeneration – which for the first time enabled non-utilities to sell power – was gaining momentum as a competitive force.

"It became necessary for the company to start thinking about what its future would be," Codey says. He and the two heads of finance, Bill Scott and Everett Morris, urged then-Chairman Harold Sonn to undertake some formal strategic planning for the first time. Sonn had become chairman in 1983 upon Bob Smith's retirement.

A handpicked task force of up-and-comers took on the challenge in 1984 and 1985. They brought youth, talent and ambition to the project. Indeed, all four would go on to become senior executives: Frank Cassidy, Bob Dougherty, Mort Plawner and task-force chairman Pete Mellett. Their charge, Dougherty recalls, was to "take a broad, long-range view in terms of PSE&G not just being a utility anymore. 'Why would we want to do that? What are we going to be?' Those were the questions."

Cogeneration had raised the notion of "not being just a utility anymore." After the wakeup call of the Public Utility Regulatory Policy Act of 1978 (PURPA), a few industrial customers — small in number but major in size and impact — had seized on cogeneration opportunities. They installed their own generating equipment or entered into arrangements whereby they swapped the waste heat from their processes for electricity from a supplier other than PSE&G. The concept itself was not new; PSE&G had pioneered it as early as 1957, when the Linden Generating Station began exchanging energy with the nearby Bayway Refinery, then operated by Esso. But the 1980s brought cogeneration into the mainstream, thanks in part to federal and state subsidies and tax incentives. Those subsidies couldn't last forever, but the

Sam Blom feels good every time he sees a Call Before You Dig bumper sticker. And he sees lots of them, because every utility truck in New Jersey has to have one. That valuable safety initiative came out of an idea from Sam, who joined PSE&G in 1968 and is currently office administrator, Gas Distribution, Clifton/Orange.

Whether contractors are laying a building foundation or homeowners are planting a tree, they must check in advance for the existence of underground utility lines or cables. One call to 1-800-272-1000 notifies all the local utilities of their plans. The utilities respond by "marking out" the location if necessary, with flags and paint, so the contractor or homeowner can dig or drill safely.

The One Call program began in New York in the 1970s. After it reached New Jersey, Blom says, "I suggested we publicize it by putting bumper stickers on all PSE&G vehicles."

The Board of Public Utilities eventually mandated all state utilities to follow PSE&G's lead. You might say Sam has 483,964 reasons to be proud — that's the number of calls handled by New Jersey's One Call center last year.

Thanks to an idea from PSE&G's Sam Blom, every utility truck in New Jersey now sports a Call Before You Dig bumper sticker. Company employees also distribute the stickers at community events statewide, along with safety literature on many topics.

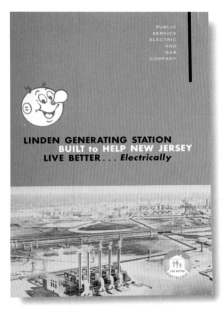

LINDEN GENERATION STATION HAS ALWAYS BEEN A PIONEER. IN 1957 IT BECAME ONE OF THE NATION'S FIRST COGENERATION FACILITIES; IT EXCHANGED STEAM FOR FUEL WITH THE NEIGHBORING ESSO (NOW BAYWAY) REFINERY UNTIL 1995. PSEG POWER IS CURRENTLY REPLACING LINDEN'S STEAM UNITS WITH A HIGHLY EFFICIENT, COMBINED-CYCLE GAS-FIRED FACILITY.

PSEG GLOBAL CO-OWNS AND MANAGES THE KALAELOA COGENERATION PLANT NEAR HONOLULU, HAWAII. POWER PRODUCED HERE IS CRITICAL FOR MEETING THE ENERGY NEEDS OF THE HIGHLY URBANIZED ISLAND OF OAHU. BY PIONEERING THE USE OF RECLAIMED WATER RATHER THAN DRINKING WATER, KALAELOA ALSO CONSERVES PRECIOUS RESOURCES. RIGHT: KALAELOA'S CONTROL ROOM, WHERE GENERATION EQUIPMENT IS STARTED, SECURED AND MONITORED.

model was in place. "The genie was out of the bottle," Codey liked to say. "Some companies in the industry didn't start to ask strategy questions until the 1990s. So we were a bit ahead."

The strategy group recommended two changes, both significant. "The first thing we said was that we needed to form a holding company for legal and financial flexibility to grow," Dougherty says. That structure would allow the company to act on the second recommendation: to diversify into non-regulated businesses with the potential for earning higher returns on investments.

THE BIRTH OF ENTERPRISE

The board of directors, the BPU and company shareholders approved the restructuring. May 1, 1986, was the official birth date of Public Service Enterprise Group Incorporated, or PSEG. Retaining the ampersand that still distinguishes it from its parent, PSE&G became a wholly owned subsidiary and continued as a regulated entity. It would be joined by nonregulated siblings, including a few already in very early stages.

Officially, the first new subsidiary was PSEG Resources, a financial investment organization. Now headed by Eileen A. Moran, president and chief operating officer since 1990, Resources initially seized such opportunities as investing in a leveraged lease of the RCA satellite launched in 1985 aboard the space shuttle Atlantis. Today it manages a diverse portfolio of more than 60 investments in energy infrastructure.

Community Energy Alternatives (CEA) followed. Founded in 1984 to pursue the independent power production opportunities presented by PURPA, it began to take shape under the direction of President Arthur S. Nislick in 1985. Eventually

the domestic market driven by PURPA evaporated, and so CEA, under the leadership of Michael J. Thomson, looked to apply its knowledge internationally. Thus it evolved into PSEG Global, with Thomson as its president. Domestic innovations launched by CEA — such as a hydroplant in Maine, a woodchip-fired generating plant in New Hampshire and several large cogeneration projects in New Jersey — helped to create a cash flow that still contributes to PSEG Global's earnings.

Thomson developed this subsidiary into an aggressive growth engine for the shareholders of PSEG. PSEG Global supplies and/or delivers energy in more than a dozen countries on five continents. Rather than investing in random projects, it chose to build sustainable, long-term businesses in selective markets. This disciplined strategy enabled PSEG Global to grow tenfold from 1996 to 2001, from $300 million in investments to $3 billion. The earnings of the subsidiary have more than quadrupled in recent years — from $28 million in 1999 to $116 million in 2001.

JIM FERLAND COMES ABOARD

Jim Ferland joined PSEG as president on June 1, 1986, and added the roles of chairman and CEO one month later when Sonn retired. His arrival was a groundbreaking event: in 83 years, the board of directors had never gone outside company ranks for a chief executive.

According to most observers, Everett Morris, executive vice president, finance, had been the leading inside candidate. But Ferland's remarkably broad experience won out. Since his college graduation in 1964, Ferland had built his career at Northeast Utilities (NU) in Connecticut, working his way up from an entry-level mechanical engi-

Speaking the Same Language

From Chile and China to Tunisia and Oman, the sustainable businesses cultivated by PSEG Global speak the same language as all PSEG operations. "We bring 100 years of technical skills and expertise that help countries develop more reliable, efficient energy services," President Mike Thomson says. "Certain values transfer very well," adds Ozzie Cano, general manager, governmental and regulatory affairs, PSEG Global. "We're dedicated to service 24/7. We believe that a strong electrical infrastructure is essential to improving the economic conditions of developing economies. And we bring a strong emphasis on safety. Safety is the number-one priority."

Drawing on the talents of many long-time PSE&G safety experts, PSEG Global created an Environment Health and Safety (EH&S) team that has regularly traveled to all locations since 1996. Team members work with local partners to assess safety conditions and implement key practices, such as the daily use of insulated gloves, fire-retardant clothing and other protective equipment. PSEG Global also promotes safety through pay incentives within its foreign assets; for example, the compensation of local CEOs may be partly tied to safety results, which in turn encourages the companies to make safety a part of their employee performance appraisals.

This exporting of PSEG's safety culture can be measured in accidents avoided and lives saved. "PSEG Global has a strong commitment to insuring that its associates worldwide return

In Peru, PSEG Global introduced the use of two key safety devices — flame-retardant clothing and rubber-glove inflators — to the live-line crews of Luz del Sur. The insulating gloves are inflated before use to detect leaks.

home to their loved ones at the end of the day," notes Al Matos, vice president, distribution performance and EH&S. "Delivering electricity is extremely dangerous and requires that each person is equipped with the mental attitude, training and tools to continuously make safety first at all our international operations. Our safety-first philosophy is based on a long PSEG tradition of targeting a zero-accident work environment, and hence has produced world-class results at Global's generation and distribution businesses. Our generation and distribution results speak for themselves. Worldwide we've reduced the number of recordable injuries by 46 percent in 2001 compared with 2000."

"One thing that especially helps us in every aspect of our business is that we perform with polyglot teams, all with different cultural and functional backgrounds," adds Matthew McGrath, vice president and general counsel. "What we all share cross-culturally is the commitment to growth and to safety." Interestingly, PSEG Global is no longer regarded in other countries as an American company but a multinational one.

PSEG Global is increasingly the full or majority partner in its projects, a factor that controls financial risk. But regardless of how much equity it holds in any project, it respects local cultures and takes a team approach. "Our approach to doing business is not that we're a great big American company that knows everything," Thomson emphasizes. "We say to partners that we have certain areas of expertise and they do, too; together we can make it work."

neering job to station superintendent of the nuclear unit Millstone 2, then becoming NU's chief financial officer, then president.

Not only was the Maine-born Ferland an "outsider," but he assumed the leadership of PSEG at the ripe young age of 44. That piqued employees' curiosity even more. "My first impression was he was the same age I am," says Paul Cafone, manager, system operations, electric systems. "So you certainly focused on who this man was and what his skills and abilities were."

Then as now, Ferland was what Al Koeppe, PSE&G president and chief operating officer, calls "a look-'em-in-the-eye fellow." He got out and circulated — and encountered the company's classically hierarchical culture.

"When I first came, people were almost afraid to talk to senior officers," Ferland recalls. "That changed fast. I don't think the change was so much my doing. Whoever was going to be CEO would have done that, because times were changing."

At first, Ferland's direct style could throw old-timers "into a tizzy," according to Cafone. He relates one of the early company legends about Ferland: "One afternoon Jim sent word that he wanted to meet with me at 8 a.m. the next morning. I had never met him. No one knew what he wanted." Cafone wasn't upset at the prospect of Ferland approaching him instead of going through established channels, but his managers were. "They called me at home that night and questioned me for four hours. This was the cultural atmosphere. They felt very slighted."

"It turned out Jim had met the owner of a cogeneration project PSE&G was involved in and sought out the project manager — that was me," Cafone chuckles. "It didn't matter that he didn't

know me from Adam. He had some technical questions he wanted to ask, and I was the logical person to answer them."

Ferland is a questioner. His primary question for his new company was how it would grow. "It was apparent that New Jersey was a very mature service territory, growing at only 1 to 2 percent a year," he says. "We needed to do something creative, develop some new opportunities." With the holding company structure already in place, PSEG was well positioned to do just that.

TIGHTER, LEANER ORGANIZATION

There were already stirrings within the energy industry about deregulation, which had begun in major industries such as air transportation, banking and telecommunications. "One of the first things

JIM FERLAND HAS BEEN CHAIRMAN, PRESIDENT AND CEO OF PSEG SINCE 1986. HE INTRODUCED A MORE DIRECT MANAGEMENT STYLE AT A TIME WHEN STRICT HIERARCHIES WERE THE NORM. FERLAND HAS GUIDED PSEG'S GROWTH IN ITS NEW JERSEY HOME TERRITORY AND ITS EXPANSION INTO EMERGING ENERGY MARKETS AROUND THE WORLD.

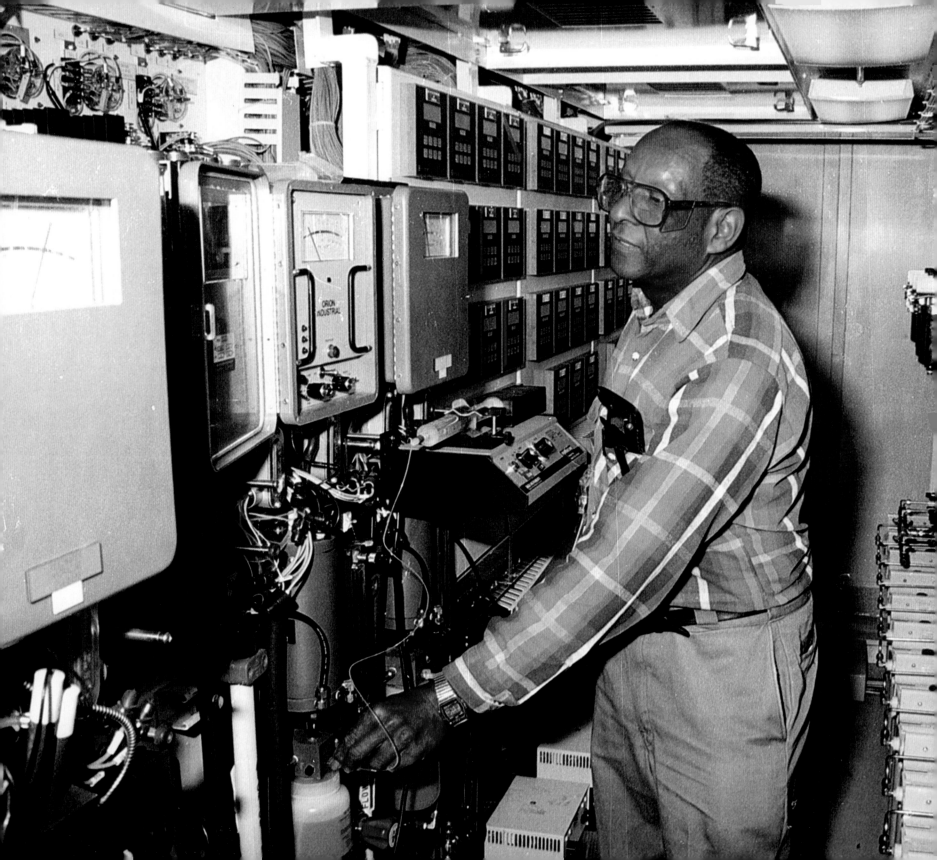

we had to do, all of us, was to say that while we don't exactly know what form this restructuring might take, we know there's going to be competition out there," Ferland continues. "We had to focus on getting competitive, getting changes in productivity, doing things better and smarter."

Working with consultants from McKinsey & Company, PSEG spent a year analyzing the cost and value of each and every work process. All 12,000 employees took part. Fred DeSanti, vice president, external affairs, who devoted almost a year to the project, calls it "an unbelievably painstaking process, never before done at that level of detail." One result was that almost 800 people — all management, no union associates — chose to leave the company with a modest attrition package. Between that and the streamlining of work processes, PSEG reduced expenditures by about $80 million. "This effort really represented Jim's way of bringing PSEG together as a tighter, leaner organization with great focus," DeSanti continues. "It was invigorating for the organization, a watershed moment." It was also the first of several significant initiatives that reshaped PSEG.

The next was the reorganization into business units. For the first time, subsidiaries and key divisions within them were accountable for their own business plans, income statements and balance sheets — in short, for their bottom-line performance. "Goals weren't soft anymore; they were hard," DeSanti says.

Lorraine Mnich, at the time PSE&G manager of employment and placement, captured a typical reaction in a 1989 article in *Management Quarterly,* an internal magazine: "People learned to be successful under the old system — stay in line, don't make waves, wait your turn," she observed. "They're

SAFE AND RELIABLE NUCLEAR OPERATIONS CALL FOR CHEMICAL AS WELL AS ELECTRICAL EXPERTISE. IN THIS 1992 PHOTO, FORMER CHEMISTRY DEPARTMENT ASSOCIATE JAMES CUNNINGHAM IS INSIDE THE ONLINE MONITORING PANEL IN A LABORATORY WITHIN THE TURBINE BUILDING AT SALEM GENERATING STATION UNIT 2. HE IS OPERATING A CHLORIDE ANALYZER FOR THE ROUTINE "BLOWDOWN" OR CLEANING OF A STEAM GENERATOR.

Customer Service 24/7/365

A century ago, many companies were happy to have a single telephone line — but not Public Service. Realizing that "the nature of our business brings us face to face with accidents and emergencies of every nature," the company from its earliest years maintained its own private telephone system and staffed it around the clock. With 33 exchanges and 146 operators, this system covered the entire service territory. It ensured that customers could always reach Public Service and that employees could always reach each other. The "telephone order table," an early call center, was a special source of pride. According to the March 1, 1928, issue of *Public Service News*, its operators deftly handled 736,000 calls a year: "All calls are completed at the table and the annoying practice of transferring [has been] eliminated."

This commitment has not changed, although call volume has multiplied to more than 5 million calls a year. Today, PSE&G is New Jersey's only utility with customer service professionals on hand 24 hours a day, every day of the year, to respond to any inquiry. "That's what customers need and want," says John Anderson, vice president, customer operations. And first-call resolution, to use the modern catchphrase, remains the goal: "Our priority is to satisfy the customer the first time."

In addition to around-the-clock telephone customer service, PSE&G maintains 16 Customer Service Centers (CSCs) throughout New Jersey. The centers are widely used, especially by urban customers. CSC professionals handle about two million transactions a year.

saying 'I did what I was told and now you say I'm not proactive enough.' The culture is certainly changing, but it is a difficult period."

This more proactive culture slowly began to take root. Some people found it liberating, including veterans who had been successful under the old system. Bob Metcalfe, formerly vice president, construction, PSEG Power, was one. As a cadet and then as a manager, he had obediently hewed to the command-and-control culture for years. "But I didn't like it," he says, "and so once I was in a position to influence change, it came very naturally …to have our employees take ownership in projects, and to coach them rather than have managers make every decision."

NEW AVENUES OF INCOME

The utility, PSE&G, still accounted for the majority of business, but PSEG was making good on its promise to shareholders to develop new avenues of income through unregulated subsidiaries. It consolidated them under a single structure, Enterprise Diversified Holdings Inc., in 1989, but eventually dropped the EDHI name in order to reemphasize the subsidiaries' connection to PSEG.

The original non-utility subsidiaries, PSEG Resources and Community Energy Alternatives, had been established in the mid-1980s and were doing well. A few subsequent ones, however, encountered struggles directly related to the ups and downs of any unregulated marketplace. Energy Development Corporation (EDC), involved in gas and oil exploration, faced weakened revenues when the price of natural gas dropped after the federal controls of the 1980s were lifted. The market for natural gas, as a consequence, grew soft. Choosing to look beyond the United States

for growth possibilities, EDC invested in an oil production field in Argentina. This represented one of PSEG's first forays beyond domestic borders and helped lay some groundwork for the South American expansions by PSEG Global in the later 1990s.

PSEG Energy Technologies, created in the 1990s to provide energy management solutions for regional businesses, also struggled. In 2002, the company announced that it was exiting this business.

Like many corporations, PSEG, through its Enterprise Group Development Company, has invested in commercial real estate. This area seemed a "sure thing" in the mid-1980s, but years of overbuilding led to an ample supply and thus to

FROM ITS HIGH-TECH
TRADING FLOOR IN
NEWARK, PSEG ENERGY
RESOURCES & TRADE IS
AT THE FOREFRONT OF
ANTICIPATING TRENDS IN
THE WHOLESALE ENERGY
MARKET.

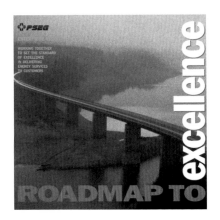

PSEG AFFIRMED ITS
COMMITMENT TO TOTAL
QUALITY AND EMPLOYEE
DIVERSITY IN THE
1990s. THE MULTI-YEAR
QUALITY JOURNEY, AS
IT WAS CALLED, HAD
ITS OWN ROAD MAPS
OF OBJECTIVES. RIGHT:
AL KOEPPE (LEFT),
PRESIDENT AND CHIEF
OPERATING OFFICER,
PSE&G, ACCEPTS
CONGRATULATIONS FROM
NEW JERSEY GOVERNOR
JAMES E. McGREEVEY
ON PSE&G'S RECEIVING
THE PRESTIGIOUS
RELIABILITYONE AWARD
FOR SUPERIOR ELECTRIC-
SYSTEM RELIABILITY IN
THE MIDATLANTIC
REGION.

a leveling of prices, a trend supported by the relative lack of inflation in the 1990s. In a manner typical of the corporation, PSEG never put too many eggs in this one basket. It protected shareholders against major losses by making relatively modest investments. And when company leaders decided to withdraw from active real estate investment, they made the prudent choice not to sell off the holdings all at once or at fire-sale prices. Instead, they slowly harvested them as market conditions improved. In 2002 PSEG still retained a small exposure to real estate, part of its diversification strategy to maximize shareholder value.

The utility was also finding innovative ways to grow. In the 1980s, it wisely chose to enter into energy trading, then in its infancy. The growth of technology and computer networks had made it possible for utilities to buy and sell wholesale blocks of energy; the ever-shifting forces of supply and demand made it advisable. Two PSE&G electric systems operators, Earle Britten and George Graham, changed hats and used their extensive knowledge to begin trading energy for the company. They weren't called traders but "economy men," a title that reflected PSE&G's straightforward, money-saving approach to the practice. By selling PSE&G's excess capacity at a profit, and by supplementing it with cheaper energy from other sources, they saved the company $14 million in their first full year of trading — a strong start for a

fledgling business. In 1996, Steve Teitelman, who had directed Sun Oil's international trading operations, took that business and began growing it. PSEG Energy Resources & Trade, of which Teitelman is president, has succeeded beyond all original expectations. It is a disciplined, highly respected organization whose earnings increased from $23 million in 1999 to $83 million in 2001.

up some interests. You go from tolerance to respect to comradeship."

Soon after becoming president and chief operating officer of PSE&G in 1991, Codey championed total quality management (TQM) because "it gave us a framework, a common language" for breaking down the walls.

Cistaro, who helped steer the multi-year effort,

Diversity

TOTAL QUALITY AND "BREAKING DOWN THE WALLS"

In keeping with these strides toward a more competitive future, PSEG accelerated its quest for cultural change. Larry Codey stresses that the company needed to "break down the walls, the fiefdoms, even the wall between bargaining units and management." He points out that the prevailing feelings weren't those of "a hostile relationship, but of tolerance. 'You do your job and I'll do mine and don't bother me.' We had to get over that…in order to develop a culture and camaraderie that would give us the best chance to excel. We started with respect. You know what the other guy does, they know what you do and you respect each other for that. From there, you start to build

explains that it focused on "quality with a big Q versus small-q quality, which we already had. Big-Q quality puts the customer at the center of the business model. What do your customers want? What are they looking for? You find answers to those questions and then you develop your strategies to meet them. Then you engage the people to change the process to better serve the customers."

Widespread participation was crucial. Union associates were skeptical at first, but they gave TQM a try and soon committed to the process. The "them and us" mentality was disappearing, as team members truly listened to each other and worked together to use their knowledge to improve processes. "Say we were looking for a different approach to an operating problem," says Pat

PSEG IS BROADLY COMMITTED TO DIVERSITY. IN 2001 PSE&G'S DIVERSITY COUNCIL BEGAN OFFERING CAREER DEVELOPMENT WORK-SHOPS THROUGH LOCAL NONPROFIT ORGANIZA-TIONS TO HELP MEET THE CHALLENGE OF EMPLOYING A WORK-FORCE THAT MIRRORS THE DEMOGRAPHICS OF NEW JERSEY'S CUS-TOMERS AND MARKETS.

Environmental Leadership

From its relatively small New Jersey footprint, PSEG has taken giant steps in improving air quality for the entire country.

This David and Goliath story starts with the Clean Air Act and Amendments of 1970. Those laws allowed for different levels of compliance. PSEG chose, voluntarily, not just to meet the toughest standards but to exceed them. "We decided to be the forerunner," says Larry Codey, retired PSE&G president, "because the resources of this industrialized state are under constant pressure and because New Jerseyans have an environmental ethic second to none." In the 1990s alone, the company invested more than $1 billion on cutting air pollution; this included repowering the Bergen and Burlington Generating Stations to double their efficiency and specifically reduce nitrogen oxide (NOx) and sulfur dioxide (SO2) emissions.

However, the patchwork quilt of regulations meant that utilities in other states could shirk such investments. Codey and PSEG believed strongly that freedom to pollute the air should *not* be a competitive advantage — and that utilities in New England and the mid-Atlantic shouldn't get stuck cleaning up Midwestern pollution after the prevailing winds carried it eastward. Working with the Northeastern States Committee of Air Directors, then-President George Bush's Clean Air Act Advisory Commission and the National Resources Defense Council, they set about equaling the rules.

Codey half-jokes that the battle made him the most hated man in the Edison Electric Institute, the national organization of utility companies. But PSEG and its allies won out. The Environmental Protection Agency, Codey proudly notes, now applies the rules "more stringently to the Midwest than we could have imagined." And the movement to reduce NOx and SO2 has expanded to address other pollutants that contribute to acid rain and greenhouse gases.

In addition, PSEG has spent nearly $1 billion on energy efficiency and load management efforts in New Jersey in the past two decades — investments that have reduced system-wide peak demand by 700 megawatts, the amount of energy supplied by a large power plant. These efforts have helped avoid releasing 2.2 million tons of carbon dioxide, 5,600 tons of nitrogen oxide and 11,000 tons of sulfur dioxide into the air.

The company reinforced its industry leadership in 2002, when PSEG Power committed to a 10-year plan to invest $337 million in cleaning up coal-burning plants in New Jersey. The move earned national praise and these editorial kudos from the *Star-Ledger*, New Jersey's largest newspaper: "The prospect of a regulatory rollback has prompted many utilities to snub a longstanding government push to install expensive clean-air upgrades to their old generating plants. Why bother when Washington soon may make the costly rules go away? PSEG Power is different…. It is a major victory for the environment…. Pressure will mount to clean up the power plants, and eventually the utilities will have to do it. PSEG recognized this and decided to move forward now. If utilities in other states followed this lead, we would all breathe easier."

The choice to voluntarily set and meet tough, costly, aggressive goals for cleaner air has made PSEG a national environmental leader. Its reputation, in turn, has made it a welcome neighbor in New York, Ohio, Indiana and Texas, where PSEG has built or is building new generating plants.

PSEG's award-winning Estuary Enhancement Program, described on pages 112-113, exemplifies the company's commitment to environmental action.

Downes, vice president, delivery operations support, PSE&G. "With TQM, the folks who sat down to work on it would be from all levels; there might be one engineer and three associates who do the work. Before TQM, it would have been three engineers, some supervisors and no hands-on workers."

IBEW Local 94 leader Chip Gerrity confirms: "Nobody had solicited our input at that level before." "The move on quality," as Gerrity terms it, has yielded many results. One result is apparent to any customer who calls in with a service order.

"We respond so much faster now," Cistaro notes. "We created a system that is accessible to anyone in the process. Any associate, from the customer service professional on the telephone to the technician in the field, can see exactly where the order is. They know exactly what's happening at all times. We're giving customers more definite time frames in which their work will be done."

Total quality practices have also led to fewer electrical outages, as the squirrels of New Jersey can attest. Squirrels? Yes, these bushy-tailed rodents are among the top causes of outages. They climb trees, contact pole equipment, gnaw into circuits and cause havoc. PSE&G can't change animal behavior, of course, but it can and does equip pole tops with animal guards and also trims trees on streets where circuits run. These remediation plans, as they're called, take place on a regular schedule. This system of keeping squirrels and lines apart came out of TQM and it continues to help prevent outages before they can happen. PSE&G's overall level of reliability, already the highest of any utility in the state, has improved as a result.

Less visibly, employees took the TQM approach in redesigning system maintenance for PSE&G's electric generating stations and substations. This involved the development of a highly specialized group of mechanics who travel to sites as needed. By expertly handling regular maintenance as well as major projects, such as turbine overhaul, this group has displaced $30 million a year in costs formerly paid to outside contractors.

The total quality model is now embedded in PSEG culture. Perhaps the most lasting result is that while employees no longer talk about big-Q quality, they think and act in the language of quality — a sign of the movement's success. Quality practices are second nature. "Quality is the way we do business," summarizes Dom Facchini, director, customer services and customer relationships.

RENEWED COMMITMENT TO SAFETY

Dating back to the creation of Public Service Corporation, in part motivated by McCarter's desire to prevent trolley accident deaths, PSEG has been proactive about safety. Long in advance of emergency medical training programs, Public Service trained key workers in emergency procedures and created the McCarter Medal for Resuscitation to honor those who saved lives. Similarly, before OSHA mandated that anyone who works with electricity must wear fire-retardant clothing, PSEG required it and issued it to employees. The company also provides essential personal protective equipment such as hard hats, reflective vests, rubber gloves and dielectric footwear that insulate against shock.

However, electricity and natural gas are inherently dangerous. Like every utility in the world, PSE&G has suffered fatalities. The death of two associates in 1997 galvanized the company. "We put a stake in the ground and said we're not going to accept this anymore," Cistaro recalls.

SAFETY GLOVES ARE ESSENTIAL PIECES OF PERSONAL PROTECTIVE EQUIPMENT. LEFT: KEARNY GENERATING STATION, 1994. WHEN THOMAS A. EDISON HELPED INAUGURATE THE STATION IN 1926, IT WAS ENTIRELY COAL-FIRED. TODAY ITS POWER UNITS ARE FIRED BY OIL OR NATURAL GAS. PSEG POWER BELIEVES IN THE ENVIRONMENTAL AND ECONOMIC BENEFITS OF USING EXISTING SITES AS LOCATIONS FOR NEW, EFFICIENT AND CLEAN ELECTRIC GENERATING CAPACITY.

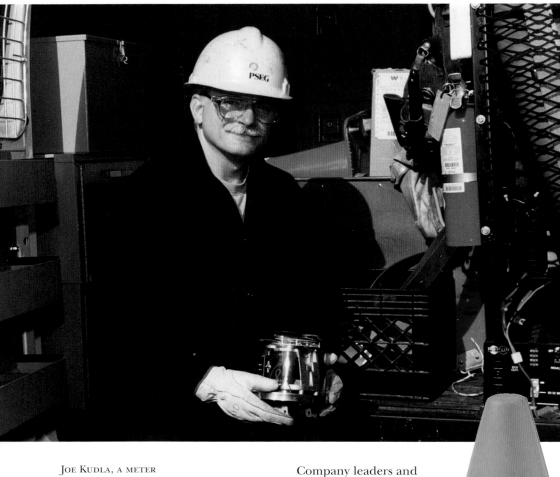

an end. It is woven into the worklife of PSEG.

At the center of the safety effort are the local Health and Safety Councils, which meet monthly in every location that has at least 50 employees. The role of council members, who are primarily bargaining unit associates, is to examine and resolve safety issues. A council at an electric division, for example, might consist of a line worker, an underground technician, a meter technician, a system maintenance professional, an equipment operator, an engineer or supervisor, and experts in materials, transportation and industry standards. Each local council also has a safety coordinator who is an expert in OSHA rules and regulations. The council chairperson serves as a representative to the next-level council, which examines safety issues across lines of business. That level, in turn, takes part in a PSEG council, effectively linking all levels and locations.

The ultimate goal, of course, is to eliminate accidents and injuries. And that takes more than the right equipment and procedures. It requires an open environment where employees can raise concerns and share knowledge, an environment the councils have created. "The biggest improvement is that everyone has the right to speak up at any time about any safety aspect of a job," Cistaro says. That right was once the exclusive province of the supervisor. Pre- and post-job briefings are also critical. "We communicate information about accidents and prevention measures to all parts of the company now, a big plus," Chip Gerrity says. It has also become part of the culture to discuss near-misses, a valuable tool for learning.

"Safety is truly a case where the unions and the company have worked well together," says Bob Callahan, former president and now

JOE KUDLA, A METER TECHNICIAN IN THE PALISADES DIVISION, IS AN EXPERT ON SETTING AND REPAIRING THE MANY DIFFERENT TYPES OF METERS FOUND THROUGH-OUT PSE&G'S SERVICE TERRITORY. THE COMPANY PERIODICALLY REPLACES METERS TO ENSURE THAT CUSTOMERS HAVE ACCURATE READINGS.

Company leaders and employees committed themselves to strengthening the safety culture of PSEG. They started with the same "ask the people who do the work" approach that characterized the successful implementation of total quality management. Like quality, safety is a movement without

Health & Safety
The Only Choice

business manager of UA Local 855. "The associates on the councils put in a lot of their own time, as well as time supplied by the company. The results have showed themselves." PSEG's OSHA incident rate, which measures serious accidents per 200,000 hours worked, has dropped from 5.26 in 1994, to 2.16 in 1998, to 1.34 at the end of the third quarter of 2002. Callahan emphasizes that "the real bottom line" is measured daily, when "everybody goes home safely to their families at the end of the day."

RESTRUCTURING: INTO UNCHARTED TERRITORY

In breaking down the walls on so many fronts, PSEG was also readying itself for its biggest challenge yet: the restructuring of the electric industry in New Jersey.

PSEG chose to be a leader, not a follower, in this historic process. It envisioned the ideal outcome — one that would benefit the numerous constituencies affected by restructuring — and worked diligently to bring that outcome to life. New Jersey, in turn, made the right energy restructuring choices and became a model for other states. This part of PSEG's history deserves a book of its own, but the following summary highlights what set PSEG apart from other companies faced with this challenge.

No blueprint or roadmap existed initially; the rules for restructuring utilities had to be written from scratch. PSEG had laid some important groundwork in the late 1980s and early 1990s, when Dougherty joined with his counterparts at other New Jersey utilities to explore how restructuring might work. Their findings, published in a white paper, became the basis for discussions by business executives, legislative leaders and members of former governor Thomas H. Kean's staff,

Hurricane Gloria

When Hurricane Gloria hammered New Jersey in September 1985, cutting off power to 14 percent of PSE&G's customers, a columnist for the *Trentonian* criticized the company's response times. "Waiting game!" he accused. "One would think that those running a company called 'Public Service' would at least attempt to practice a little public relations."

Gloria had snapped 126 electric poles and toppled 1,159 trees onto live lines. Yet PSE&G crews restored electricity to every customer within 48 hours.

Another *Trentonian* columnist, Ann Rinaldi, happened to be the wife of a grade-one lineman, Ron Rinaldi. Like every PSE&G family member, Ann understood the true extent of PSE&G's efforts during natural disasters and the dangers inherent in restoration work.

She publicly set her colleague straight: "Ron went in at 4 a.m. Friday morning, the day Hurricane Gloria hit. He worked all day in the storm, soaking wet, repairing lines. When the rest of us make a mistake, we correct it immediately. If Ron and the other linemen at Public Service make a mistake on the job, they don't get a second chance. It could mean their death."

As Gloria stormed northward, 48 PSE&G crews kept pace. After three consecutive 16-hour days in New Jersey, Ron Rinaldi and his fellow workers labored five days straight to help relight millions of households in Rhode Island, Massachusetts, Connecticut and Long Island. They returned home to find hundreds of letters of gratitude from customers who, unlike the columnist, understood what public service really means at PSE&G.

Gloria ranked as the century's most powerful Atlantic hurricane when it hit in 1985. As PSE&G crews worked around the clock to restore service to 239,000 households, customer service professionals in the Newark and Bordentown Inquiry Centers handled up to 1,500 calls an hour.

The Power of Giving

In this age of mergers and conglomerates, few New Jersey companies have the same track record of community involvement and continuing concern as PSEG. Each year for 100 years, the company and its employees have invested countless dollars and thousands of hours to improve their home state.

Maria Pinho, who spent several years as general manager, corporate responsibility, says: "Every company chooses priority areas to fund. We have chosen areas we think are critical to the long-term success of both our company and our state: education, with an emphasis on families and children; economic development, especially for our cities; and the environment." In 2001, the dollar amount of this commitment totaled $8.3 million.

PSEG actively rewards employee involvement. Through the annual Recognizing Excellence in Volunteerism program, the company provides competitive grants of up to $10,000 to qualified nonprofits on behalf of exemplary volunteers. It also funds up to 200 Dollars for Doers grants, at $250 each, to nonprofits where PSEG employees donate at least 50 hours of volunteer time a year. The recipient organizations are as diverse as New Jersey and have included the American Cancer Society, Chinese American Cultural Association, Passaic Youth Empowerment, Salem County Humane Society and numerous emergency squads and volunteer fire departments statewide.

And, when disaster strikes, the people of PSEG immediately rally to help. Following the

tragic events of September 11, 2001, employees and retirees raised $328,000 for the PSEG Power of Giving World Trade Center Disaster Relief Fund. The company matched those contributions dollar-for-dollar and then brought the total up to $1 million. More than half of the

donations went to the families of New Jerseyans who died in the attacks on America; the remainder was donated to appropriate New Jersey service organizations. As part of this effort, the company directly sent $1,000 in assistance to the New Jersey victims' families. A thank-you letter from one recipient, whose mother died on Flight 93, said: "Of all the support that my family has received since September 11, PSEG's is the first to arrive from the business world. I applaud PSEG's decision to directly contact the families, ensuring that the money from its employees, its retirees and the company's matching funds gets into the right hands.... Thank you all for helping my family deal with our loss. It is comforting knowing we are not alone."

Nearly 200 PSEG associates personally volunteered in the relief efforts immediately following September 11. Thousands more gave of their time and support in myriad ways. Above: The March of Dimes is a beloved cause for many at PSE&G. No other utility in the country has raised more funds for the organization. In honor of this, PSE&G received the Crystal Award in 1996.

including Christine Todd Whitman, then president of the New Jersey BPU. The issue lay somewhat dormant under James Florio, who succeeded Kean. It came to the fore when Whitman became governor in 1994 and culminated in her signing of the Electric Discount and Energy Competition Act in 1999. Those five years, according to those who lived them, were exhilarating, exhausting, tough, productive and deeply satisfying.

PSEG charted the course for the utility industry, applying some useful lessons from recently deregulated industries. Koeppe, who had joined PSE&G in 1995 as senior vice president of external affairs, had helped shape the restructuring of the telecommunications industry as the president of Newark-based Bell Atlantic (now Verizon). From that experience he knew that "unless you have your blue-collar labor force aligned with the fundamental goals of any public policy change, you're not going to get to square one."

Through PSEG's total quality initiative and renewed commitment to safety, labor and management had achieved excellent partnerships. As a result, the largest unions — IBEW, UA Local 855, OPEIU and UWUA/UCA Local 601 — were willing to negotiate unprecedented six-year contracts early in the restructuring process. "The company recognized they needed our support, so they had to give us some guarantees for some stability" during those years, explains the UA leader Callahan. PSEG's goals for restructuring were consistent with the goals of its unions, which allowed the company to speak with one voice throughout the process. It is no accident, then, that when New Jersey's Energy Master Plan legislation was finally written, it contained what is perhaps the strongest set of labor protections in any restructured industry.

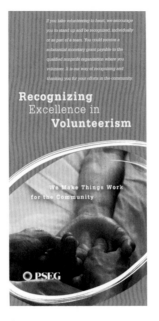

"RECOGNIZING EXCELLENCE IN VOLUNTEERISM" GRANTS ARE PSEG'S WAY OF THANKING EMPLOYEES WHO DONATE THEIR TIME AND TALENT TO COMMUNITY ORGANIZATIONS. EACH YEAR PSEG PRESENTS UP TO 17 AWARDS TO QUALIFIED NONPROFITS, RANGING FROM $1,000 TO $10,000, ON BEHALF OF EMPLOYEE VOLUNTEERS.

POWER FLOWED AS
RELIABLY AS EVER
DURING AND AFTER NEW
JERSEY'S RESTRUCTURING
OF THE ELECTRIC
INDUSTRY. FOLLOWING
THE PROCESS, PSE&G
CUSTOMERS ENJOYED
THE LOWEST RATES IN
THE REGION AND THE
LOWEST IN THE
COMPANY'S HISTORY.

ALL VOICES HEARD

Restructuring took shape through a three-part legislative effort. First, PSEG with other utilities presented the BPU with alternative regulatory scenarios. DeSanti describes these as trial runs designed "to find the right set of criteria." The overriding purpose was to ensure consumer protection and fair competition. This part of the process took 18 months. Out of it came certain incentives and penalties that would be written into law, as well as the decision that restructuring would ultimately be introduced in phases — a sensible choice given the uncharted territory.

Next, PSEG and other utilities worked to level the playing field regarding taxes. PURPA-era cogeneration had been popular among industrial customers because it exempted them from the 13.5 percent utility consumption tax then levied by New Jersey. Legislators ultimately replaced that tax structure with an across-the-board 6 percent tax. That achievement took two years because the process was fraught with objections from the parties that had enjoyed the tax exemption. The lower, fairer tax was essential because it put everybody on an equal footing: cogenerators, independent power producers (IPPs), utilities and anyone getting involved in the generation business going forward.

The third step, actually hammering out the public policy, was the longest and most vociferous. Multiple parties staked out different interests: politicians, the business community, environmentalists, IPPs and utilities. Governor Whitman and BPU President Herbert Tate encouraged all voices to join the debate, and the process lasted for almost two years. Participants recall public hearings attended by as many as 600 people and testimony on a single subject that lasted for days. "Very, very convoluted, complicated issues," DeSanti says. "In the end, the legislature had to balance one set of interests against the other. They had to develop a market structure that made sense. They had to meet their own political goals to reduce energy costs. We had to find ways to find policies to accomplish the goals and then afford all of this. It was just incredible."

One of PSEG's chief concerns was that the playing field be kept level and fair. Unlike potential competitors, it had invested billions of dollars on behalf of the people of New Jersey to build and upgrade generating plants. Such investments had always been recouped through capped and regulated rates of return. However, some potential competitors wanted to see PSEG stranded with those costs. The company would end up defending the issue all the way to the New Jersey Supreme Court in a separate case and it would win.

Throughout the years of discussions on deregulation, PSE&G also worked closely with the National Resources Defense Council (NRDC) to ensure that conservation would have a prominent place in the restructuring of the state's energy markets.

LOWEST RATES IN COMPANY HISTORY

Following years of hard work, a new era began when the restructuring of New Jersey's energy market took effect on August 1, 1999. The state's plan proved to be fairer than those adopted elsewhere, where bigger customers with more bargaining clout got larger savings. New Jersey's rate cuts of 13.9 percent over three years ensured that residential customers, as well as industrial and commercial ones, benefited from restructuring. "New Jersey's rates became the lowest in the region, and PSE&G's rates the lowest in New Jersey," Codey notes. The savings was equivalent to a 2 percent cut in the state's sales tax. In fact, restructuring brought PSE&G customers the lowest rates in the company's history, adjusted for inflation.

Restructuring has allowed customers to choose a supplier other than PSE&G to provide their electricity. PSE&G, meanwhile, continues to deliver the commodity to the home or business while also maintaining the safety and reliability of the system.

Central to the restructuring was the critical fact that, unlike other New Jersey utility companies, PSEG chose not to sell its generation assets but to retain them as part of the larger parent company. Before restructuring, PSE&G owned its generating stations. After restructuring, it spun off those units into PSEG Power, a separate unregulated entity. PSEG Power now generates the electricity, and PSE&G distributes it to homes and businesses. PSE&G continues to be regulated by the New Jersey BPU. The nuclear plants continue to be regulated by the Nuclear Regulatory Commission.

Although this division of functions makes no practical difference to the end user, it is a major reason why PSEG has prospered and why New Jersey's restructuring succeeded where other states have had difficulties. California's restructuring plan, for example, required all utility companies in the state to leave the generation business. Those utilities also had to guarantee a fixed rate to customers, even though they lacked control over the generation to carry out that promise. So when energy prices soared on the open market, in winter 2001, California's utilities had to pay far more for energy than they were collecting in rates. Additionally, in anticipation of deregulation and

Red, White and Blue-Collar

The unions and management of PSEG spoke in a unified voice throughout the multi-year process of energy restructuring. Working together, they say, is a key reason why New Jersey's energy transition has been a success and a model for other states.

Concerned that restructuring might result in job loss and a weakened PSEG, union members lobbied, testified and attended hearings from the start. "Our political action committees (PACs) met with management, state lawmakers and regulators to share our views," says Bob Callahan, former president and current business manager of UA Local 855. "It was important for all of us to have a stable company."

As part of restructuring, many utilities sold their generating stations to function solely as distributors of energy. For some, such as GPU in New Jersey, this was a corporate choice; for others, notably in California, it was mandated by state law. PSEG decided it would be in the best interests of associates, customers and shareholders to keep its generating capacity. Union activism helped achieve that outcome.

"We supported keeping the generation, and the company, in turn, supported our issues about job protections, which were ultimately written into law," says Ernie Meyer, underground division mechanic, Central Division, and IBEW Local 94 PAC member. Fortunately, no associate has had to invoke those protections.

"There's no better job protection for anyone," Meyer adds, "than having a job in a strong company."

Former New Jersey Governor Christine Todd Whitman signed the Electric Discount and Energy Competition Act into law on February 9, 1999. The act took effect on the following August 1, ushering in a new era of energy for the state.

Liberty's Light

The Statue of Liberty is PSEG's most famous customer. PSEG powers her elevators, her air conditioning and the dramatic lighting that renders her a beacon of freedom in the eyes of the world.

A customer since 1916, Lady Liberty underwent a complete restoration and repowering for her centennial in 1986. Former PSEG Chairman Harold Sonn led the Statue of Liberty/Ellis Island fundraising campaign in New Jersey. The effort held special meaning for Sonn because he had studied thermodynamics in France, the country that donated the statue to the United States, and had fought there in World War II.

Careful and loving detail went into the repowering. The Okonite Company of Paterson, N.J., a PSE&G customer, constructed a 57,000-pound submarine cable. IBEW workers at Simplex Wire & Cable Company in New Hampshire, volunteering their time, wrapped the cable in an armored sheathing of red, white and blue.

The 4,000-volt line, which draws power from the Bayonne substation, stretches about one-half mile from Liberty State Park to Liberty Island. The experience gained in supplying power to the statue recently helped to guide the design of PSEG Power's proposed eight-mile "extension cord" from New Jersey to Manhattan, targeted for completion in 2005. After decades of dependable service to Lady Liberty, PSEG is hopeful it can play a part in serving her uptown neighbors as well.

Restored and renovated from torch to toe for her 100th anniversary, the Statue of Liberty gets her power through 1,300 feet of underwater cable powered by PSE&G. Above: a cross-section of the patriotically colored cable.

tougher environmental laws, the industry had added no new generation capacity in more than a decade. Because of the resulting shortages, customers were forced to endure rolling blackouts and utility companies suffered a financial crisis with ongoing reverberations.

"Herb Tate, the former head of the BPU, has been very proud to say that New Jersey's restructuring process worked because we kept the generation with the company that was guaranteeing the rate," Tom Smith points out. PSEG shareholders can be proud, too, because PSEG Power — a product of restructuring — now accounts for half of the earnings of its parent company.

"WE'RE ALL BUSINESS PEOPLE"

A program called PowerMaps, which ran from 1998 to 1999, helped PSEG employees prepare for life after restructuring. It brought small groups together to discuss PSEG's future and their role in it. "I think PowerMaps was one of the best things we ever did, because it showed a lot of us that there's another world out there," says Sam Blom, Clifton/Orange office administrator, Gas Distribution, who facilitated many sessions. "We discussed why we don't spend money on what doesn't add value to the company and the impact of capital expenditures versus expenditures for operations and maintenance. We talked about how, when New Jersey was growing, PSEG could make all its money here. Now we have to go outside to survive, and that has proved the right thing to do."

Jim Ferland has encouraged that mindset all along. He likes to know what the people of PSEG are thinking, and so he talks with them regularly, at small-group breakfasts and annual Town Hall-style meetings. One message he always emphasizes is

that "in this environment, we all have to be business people, not just engineers or scientists or operators."

Ferland speaks with quiet satisfaction of how deeply the message has spread. He says: "I can go to our generating stations and walk around and talk to anybody" — something he also regularly does — "and they understand the economics. The level of knowledge has impressed me."

That knowledge has carried PSEG into a new century of energy leadership. The people of PSEG drew on a history of engineering excellence, financial acumen, legislative savvy and employee teamwork to make restructuring work for New Jersey. At the same time, they carefully built new and sustainable businesses separate from the traditional electric and gas utility. The result is a company well prepared to compete on all fronts.

THE POWERMAPS PROGRAM HELPED EMPLOYEES ANALYZE THE EFFECTS OF INDUSTRY RESTRUCTURING. THROUGHOUT PSEG, PEOPLE UNDERSTAND HOW THEIR PART OF THE BUSINESS IMPACTS THE COMPANY'S OVERALL BOTTOM LINE.

CHAPTER FIVE

21ST-CENTURY POWERHOUSE

P SEG HAS SET ITSELF THE AMBITIOUS GOAL OF ACHIEVING A 7 PERCENT COMPOUND ANNUAL GROWTH RATE. DESPITE FACTORS THAT HAVE AFFECTED THE GROWTH OF THE ENERGY INDUSTRY AT LARGE IN THE PAST FEW YEARS — DEREGULATION-RELATED CRISES IN CALIFORNIA, CONTROVERSIES OVER FEDERAL ENERGY POLICIES, TURMOIL IN ARGENTINA AND THE COLLAPSE OF ENRON — PSEG IS ON TRACK TO MEET THAT GOAL. ☐ "GROWTH PROSPECTS ARE STRONG," DECLARES CHAIRMAN JIM FERLAND. DRIVING THE GROWTH IS THE COMPANY'S ABILITY TO MAKE SMART CHOICES, DEVELOPED OVER 100 YEARS AND HONED IN THE COMPETITIVE GLOBAL MARKETPLACE OF THE TWENTY-FIRST CENTURY.

PLANS TO INCREASE ELECTRIC CAPACITY

PSEG Power plays a major role in the company's overall growth. It is the largest power producer in the PJM Interconnection and is adding more than 3,000 megawatts of electric capacity to its already healthy base of more than 13,000 megawatts (a megawatt is enough power for about 1,000 homes). Strategies for growth include redeveloping existing power plants with new, cleaner generating technology in New Jersey and Bethlehem, N.Y.; purchasing plants nationwide; and building new plants in the Midwest, with construction under way in Ohio and Indiana. In 2002, the company entered the New England wholesale market by purchasing two primarily oil- and coal-fired electric generating stations, in New Haven and Bridgeport, Conn.

"Our power generation fleet is one of the most diverse in the nation in terms of fuel, technology and market segments," notes Frank Cassidy, president and chief operating officer, PSEG Power. "This mix gives us the flexibility to meet the energy needs of the marketplace efficiently and to leverage our energy trading capability at every hour and in every season."

As PSEG Power grows, its trading operation will expand in tandem. Choosing to trade only regionally, in areas where PSEG Power has electric generation, the trading organization is nonetheless among the most successful in the country. George Henderson, a former oil trader who is now PSEG Energy Resources & Trade's managing director, marketing and origination, believes the trading organization has helped transform PSEG into a leading twenty-first-century competitor.

Since joining PSEG in 1997, Henderson has observed in the parent company "a very, very interesting evolution" toward the acceptance and man-

PREVIOUS PAGE: A PSEG ENERGY TRADER AT WORK. ABOVE: ONE OF PSEG GLOBAL'S PLANTS IN CALIFORNIA. IN 2001, PSEG GLOBAL BUILT THE HANFORD ENERGY PARK IN HANFORD, CALIFORNIA, A 90-MEGAWATT NATURAL GAS-FIRED POWER PLANT. THE PLANT WAS CONSTRUCTED IN RECORD TIME FOR NORTH AMERICA — LESS THAN 90 DAYS — TO MEET CALIFORNIA'S URGENT ENERGY NEEDS IN SUMMER 2001.

agement of risk through a disciplined and rigorous process. The trading operation helped push the company in this direction. "Any management has difficulty dealing with uncertainty and risk," Henderson says. "You can't describe the future on an Excel spreadsheet. You can maybe get it 70 percent right; then you just have to go with your best decisions."

Tom Smith, PSEG Power's executive vice president, operations and development, and president of PSEG Fossil, adds that PSEG has integrated "the new key success factors: more commercial savvy,

INAUGURATED IN 2001, THESE WIND TURBINES PROVIDE 16 PERCENT OF THE ELECTRIC POWER NEEDED IN A RURAL AREA OF SOUTHERN CHILE. THE THREE HIGHLY COMPUTERIZED UNITS ARE THE FIRST WIND POWER PROJECT IN THAT SOUTH AMERICAN COUNTRY. THE PROJECT WAS DEVELOPED BY THE SAESA GROUP, OF WHICH PSEG GLOBAL IS A MAJORITY OWNER.

greater analytical and financial skills, sharper risk-management skills. Operational capability is one of many success factors now, whereas as recently as five years ago it was the key factor."

PSEG GLOBAL'S GROWTH PIPELINE

PSEG's other unregulated subsidiary, PSEG Energy Holdings, has recently grown by double digits annually. PSEG Global, part of Energy Holdings, is managing the largest construction program in its history. New projects are in progress in Poland, Oman and several locations in South America. In addition,

PSEG Energy Holdings President and COO Bob Dougherty notes, "PSEG Global plants that were in development in the 1990s have come online and are producing power, earnings and cash."

PSEG pursues its goals by measured strides as well as giant leaps. A recent project in Coyhaique, Chile, is an excellent illustration. The project, Central Eolica Alto Baguales, would qualify as a modest undertaking by most measures. It consists of three wind turbines that generate just under 2 megawatts of electric power, a microfraction of PSEG's total capacity. Yet this small wind farm in

the rugged reaches of southern Chile is a historical landmark. It added wind power to the mix of fuels in the PSEG fleet — coal, oil, gas, nuclear, biomass and hydropower. (The company's interest in wind power dates back to 1932, when an ambitious experiment in Burlington County proved that New Jersey's geography makes wind power unfeasible there.) It shows how global expansion helps PSEG take advantage of geographical opportunities not present in highly developed areas of the U.S. And it demonstrates PSEG's commitment to the growing Latin American energy market and the global environment; the project replaced diesel generation and is Chile's first-ever wind generating project.

Central Eolica Alto Baguales was developed in partnership with SAESA, a leading South American energy company that PSEG Global acquired in 2001. The project reflects the ethic of thinking globally and acting locally. Although its output is minor by U.S. standards, it provides 16 percent of the energy requirements of its isolated region. The bottom line is that customers in southern Chile are paying less, enjoying more reliable service and breathing cleaner air, outcomes that PSEG pursues everywhere it does business.

NEW ERA FOR PSE&G

PSEG's 100th anniversary comes during the final year of New Jersey's four-year transition to a restructured electric market — a fact that would have pleased founder McCarter, a champion of free enterprise.

The New Jersey Board of Public Utilities designed the transition so that all of New Jersey's regulated utilities could secure their electric supply needs — and, in turn, the needs of their customers

LEFT: WATERFORD ENERGY FACILITY, AN 850-MEGAWATT GAS-FIRED COMBINED CYCLE ELECTRIC GENERATING PLANT IN WATERFORD, OHIO, IS SCHEDULED FOR COMPLETION BY PSEG POWER IN MID-2003. BELOW: SALEM AND HOPE CREEK GENERATING STATIONS. IN RECENT YEARS, PSEG NUCLEAR HAS SET COMPANY RECORDS FOR SAFETY, RELIABILITY, TOTAL OUTPUT AND TURNAROUND TIME IN REFUELING.

Ozzie Cano

On a recent Sunday night, Ozzie Cano flew from Santiago, Chile, to Washington, D.C., for meetings with the Chilean ambassador, the president-elect of Peru and his economic team, U.S. State Department officials and members of Congress. On Thursday, Cano conferred with PSEG Global colleagues at their Miami office; Friday found him at PSEG in New Jersey; and by Monday he was back in Chile for a business closing.

"All of us at PSEG Global are very agile," says Cano, general manager, governmental and regulatory affairs, PSEG Global. "We come together as teams in different countries. We weigh many factors, but also we quickly reach decisions and implement them."

Born in Cuba and raised in Bergen County, the bilingual Cano joined PSE&G in 1968. "I chose Public Service because I never wanted to leave New Jersey," he says with a chuckle. Cano now points to his six years of living and working in South America as one of the most valuable experiences of his career.

Cano is proud that PSEG Global has helped privatize formerly government-owned utilities around the world. "There is a direct relationship between the strength of an economy and its electric sales," he points out. "To meet Chile's projected economic growth, for example, electric supply must double within 10 years — the same scenario we had in New Jersey 50 years ago. It's a challenge that only private enterprise and experienced companies like PSEG Global can meet."

A representative of Chilquinta in Chile makes a personal visit to a customer. Chilquinta, an electric distribution company 50 percent owned by PSEG Global, systematically calls on customers to gather input aimed at strengthening its quality of service.

— at a competitive price. To fulfill this objective, the BPU conducted a Basic Generation Service auction in 2002. Numerous suppliers bid on contracts to determine the price at which they would supply energy during the period August 2002 to August 2003, when the transition will end. PSEG Power, as an independent power producer, did not participate directly in the auction but secured contracts to supply power to several of the direct bidders.

"The BPU should be saluted for making the transition to a deregulated market a smooth one, especially when compared to some other states," Al Koeppe, PSE&G president and chief operating officer, says. "The auction was well run and prices were determined by vigorous competition." PSE&G

agreed to pay $.0511 per kilowatt-hour to obtain electricity until August 2003.

"At the end of the transition, rates will need to rise as the costs we face continue to increase," Koeppe adds, "but we are working hard to ensure that electric rates remain below or close to 1999 levels and well below the rates of most other utilities in the region."

TECHNOLOGY DRIVES RELIABILITY

While rates are important, PSE&G customers repeatedly tell the company that they value reliability even more. And although PSE&G is already New Jersey's most reliable utility, it has not rested on its laurels. Its Outage Management System

THE INTERACTIVE, WIRELESS TECHNOLOGY OF PSE&G'S OUTAGE MANAGEMENT SYSTEM GIVES FIELD TECHNICIANS IMMEDIATE ACCESS TO DATA FROM THE ENTIRE ELECTRIC GRID — ENABLING OUTAGES TO BE IDENTIFIED MORE QUICKLY AND ACCURATELY, AND THUS REDUCING THE TIME NEEDED TO RESTORE POWER.

Estuary Enhancement Program:
An Award-Winning Environmental Solution

PSEG is honored to be a winner of the National Oceanic and Atmospheric Administration (NOAA) Excellence in Business Leadership Award for Coastal and Ocean Resource Management. The award, made in 2001, cited PSEG's Estuary Enhancement Program (EEP) as an innovative solution to an environmental issue that balances the needs of natural resources and the community's need for safe, dependable economic power. NOAA singled out the Estuary approach to complex environmental issues because it provides long-term, broad-based benefits for natural resources.

PSEG's EEP is the largest privately funded wetlands restoration program of its kind in the United States. Through it, more than 20,000 acres of degraded salt marsh and upland buffers along the Delaware Estuary in both Salem County, N.J., and Delaware are being enhanced, protected or restored to their natural condition. All lands involved in the program are preserved in perpetuity by special conservation deed restrictions. In addition, fish ladders have been installed on tributaries to the Delaware that have substantially increased spawning and nursery habitat for coastal species.

"The EEP is a model for what can be accomplished through cooperative efforts by industry, governmental agencies, academia, and conservation and public interest groups," says Ed Selover, PSEG senior vice president and general counsel. "All have played integral roles in the success of this marvelous endeavor."

PSEG invites the public to enjoy activities such as fishing, crabbing, bird watching and canoeing at several wetlands in southern New Jersey and Delaware. Many areas include nature trails and observation platforms. More information about each public use area is available on www.pseg.com.

The Cohansey River Watershed in Cumberland County offers an outdoor classroom. Families and school groups often visit the EEP's public use areas — just as horseshoe crabs congregate on the estuary's shores.

ENGINEERS JIM HUBERTUS (FOREGROUND) AND CHARLIE GENTZ PARTICIPATE IN A BPU-MANDATED OMS DRILL IN THE NEWLY RENOVATED DISTRIBUTION EMERGENCY RESPONSE CENTER (DERC), LOCATED IN NEWARK.

(OMS), introduced in late 2000, combines wireless and interactive technology to enhance PSE&G's ability to react to electric service outages.

Designed by interdisciplinary teams within PSE&G, the highly sophisticated OMS is a computerized, real-time mirror image of the PSE&G power grid. The first graphic layer consists of customized maps on which PSE&G engineers have plotted every block of the service territory. The second layer places the electric and gas grid on top of that; it is so detailed that it maps every PSE&G electric pole by its pole number.

When a customer calls PSE&G to report an outage, the data entered by the customer service representative is automatically fed into OMS and the trouble spot highlighted in flashing red on screen. OMS also automatically alerts the nearest field office — all are staffed 24 hours a day, 365 days a

year — where a service dispatcher will send a troubleshooter to the scene.

Once activity has begun, OMS displays a third layer: the placement of PSE&G people and equipment. This changes minute by minute, as crews respond to problems (or handle routine maintenance). Again, the level of detail is so fine that the system captures the radio number of the vehicle on the scene. OMS even helps PSE&G answer the question most often asked by outage-affected customers: "How soon will my power be restored?" Troubleshooters use truck-mounted computers to enter estimated times, information that is instantly available to everyone using OMS.

"OMS obviously enhances our productivity and our reaction in storms," says Koeppe. "Fundamental customer service is enhanced when the people with the skills and the knowledge are getting where they need to go with the right tools at the right time."

By converging the electric grid and the telecommunications grid, OMS also helps the company keep New Jersey's infrastructure on the cutting edge of technology — a vital component of the state's long-term prosperity and growth.

"We have a whole generation of very skilled people soon reaching retirement, people who literally built this post-World War II network," Koeppe points out. "They know this business intuitively. How do we preserve and pass along their knowledge? One way is through this virtual world that replicates the real world."

NEW MARKETS, ENDURING VALUES

PSEG believes that shareholder value is enhanced, not compromised, by corporate responsibility. As the company expands into new locations and grows in financial strength, it remains committed

Linemen's and Underground Rodeos

Baseball players have the World Series, movie stars the Oscars®. For electric overhead and underground workers, a category that covers men and women, the ultimate skills competition is the International Lineman's Rodeo.

Created by electric utilities, contractors and the International Brotherhood of Electrical Workers (IBEW) to promote safety and share job-improvement practices, the event takes place annually in Kansas City, Mo. Competitors from PSE&G stage their own rodeo every June in Edison, open to underground technicians and division mechanics as well as linemen. Working on de-energized lines, they participate in such events as hurt-man rescue, manhole rescue, pole climb, 13kV glass insulator change and half tap splice.

At the rodeos, judging is based on speed and accuracy — but safety comes first. Contestants must wear required personal protective equipment, and they lose points for any safety violations.

Participants have found that the rodeos produce lasting benefits as well as being just plain fun. Here are some examples of safety and productivity improvements that PSE&G has implemented as a result of the competitions:

- A faster and safer hurt-man rescue procedure;

- The use of one torch with improved safety features rather than two different torches for solder work and heat-shrink splices; and

- Improved hardhat visors, safety glasses and ratchet wrenches for line work.

PSE&G teams have qualified for the Kansas City championship each year, gaining international recognition for the company's quality and performance.

In addition to taking part in the International Lineman's Rodeo, PSE&G associates have yearly competitions in New Jersey. All contests emphasize accuracy and safety, then speed. The linemen at right is wiring a single-phase padmount transformer.

An Economic Engine for New Jersey

- Eighty-five percent of PSEG employees live in New Jersey.

- PSEG spends about $400 million a year with more than 9,000 New Jersey businesses.

- PSE&G has helped attract 300 companies and 65,000 jobs to New Jersey since 1991.

- PSE&G established a $30 million New Millennium Economic Development Fund, which provides gap financing in the form of loans and loan guarantees to economic development projects, with 75 percent of the fund's activities directed to urban areas. The Fund has also provided $4.8 million in seed capital for the development of Salem County's first industrial park.

- PSE&G contributes more than $125,000 to local, county and regional groups fostering economic development in New Jersey.

- PSE&G has contributed more than $1 million to the New Jersey Performing Arts Center in Newark and the Liberty Science Center in Jersey City.

- PSE&G spends nearly $200 million a year on energy efficiency programs in New Jersey.

- PSE&G provides $750,000 for environmental education annually.

- PSE&G spends nearly $2.4 million each year to support programs for New Jersey's children and families.

- PSE&G has provided over $1 million in computer equipment and funding to improve access to educational technology in New Jersey's cities.

- PSE&G provided a $1 million funding grant for the formation of NJ SHARES, a statewide program that assists people who temporarily need help to pay their energy bills.

- PSEG has spent nearly $1 billion on energy efficiency and load-management efforts in New Jersey in the last two decades, reducing peak demand by about 700 megawatts, enough to power 700,000 homes.

Location NJ is used to attract foreign investment to New Jersey.

PSEG IS A PROUD CONTRIBUTOR TO THE NEW JERSEY PERFORMING ARTS CENTER IN DOWNTOWN NEWARK.

to communities, the environment and the well-being of employees.

One example is PSE&G's Urban Initiative. It began in 1996, in Newark's South Ward, when PSE&G worked as a catalyst to bring together residents, government, corporations and a broad range of nonprofit organizations. This public/private partnership program has resulted in the creation of an industrial park, new jobs and fewer neighborhood crimes in virtually every category. Another successful initiative is the Cool Cities program, in which PSE&G partners with the New Jersey Department of Community Affairs, Fannie Mae and local lenders to provide incentives that stimulate the construction, rehabilitation and purchase of energy-efficient affordable housing. "Throughout New Jersey, the Cool Cities program is helping people realize the American dream of home ownership and contributing to urban revitalization," says Shirley M. Ward, manager, strategic urban development.

Around the country, environmental leaders

applauded PSEG's 2002 choice to spend $337 million to install state-of-the-art control systems to reduce sulfur dioxide, nitrogen oxides and mercury from older generating plants over 10 years. Frank O'Donnell, executive director of the Clear Air Task Force, a Washington, D.C.-based watchdog group, told the *Wall Street Journal:* "This agreement sets the bar for future new source review cleanup settlements."

In announcing the agreement, Cassidy echoed the beliefs that have guided PSEG in its two decades of leadership toward tougher, uniform, nationwide environment standards: "We are leading where our industry should follow if we are to help this nation meet the unrealized goals of the Clean Air Act."

The traditions of community service and life-long learning never end at PSEG. Take Edward Amerman of Doylestown, Pennsylvania, a former PSE&G commercial manager. He is almost the same age as the company itself — and he is still growing and learning. In his 80s he began taking college classes "just for the fun of it" and was still at it at age 97.

Many retirees also continue the volunteerism begun during their careers; John McClynche, for example, travels once a week from Spring Lake to Newark to volunteer at a food bank because "getting involved and staying involved is the right thing to do."

"This company recognizes the need to balance work and family issues," adds Margaret M. Pego, PSEG vice president of human resources. Pego knows the issue first-hand. After joining PSE&G in 1974, she worked full-time in a variety of HR positions while finishing her undergraduate work, obtaining a master's degree in business administration and raising three children. "We've seen a lot

of changes as our businesses have grown, but our core values haven't changed," Pego says. "Helping to improve the quality of life is what PSEG and its services are all about."

The last word should go to Tom McCarter, who envisioned the Public Service Corporation and brought it to life a century ago. Speaking to the annual meeting of shareholders in 1939, a year fraught with world tragedy and economic upheaval, McCarter chose his message carefully. He said: "From the beginning, I charged myself with the responsibility of being a trustee to see that the public got fair rates; that our employees were fairly treated; and that our security holders, past and present, should receive a fair recompense and fair return. We have never lowered that banner."

At PSEG in the twenty-first century, the banner flies higher than ever.

WITH 100 YEARS OF HISTORY BEHIND THEM, THE PEOPLE OF PSEG WILL CONTINUE TO DEVOTE THEMSELVES TO IMPROVING THE QUALITY OF LIFE IN THE COMMUNITIES THEY SERVE.

Timeline of Major Events

All locations are in New Jersey unless otherwise noted.

1816

The country's oldest utility, Baltimore Gas and Electric Company of Maryland, begins operations as the Gas Light Company of Baltimore.

1825

PSEG's oldest predecessor in New Jersey, Paterson Gas Light Company, is chartered. It begins actual operations in 1847.

1879

Thomas Edison invents the incandescent electric lamp.

1903

Public Service Corporation of New Jersey incorporates on May 3 and begins operations on June 1 under founder and President Thomas Nesbitt McCarter. He creates the corporation and its subsidiaries by acquiring hundreds of local transit and utility companies, including Paterson Gas Light. Headquarters are at 776 Broad Street, Newark, in offices rented from the Prudential Insurance Company of America.

1906

Marion Generating Station in Jersey City, the company's first self-built electrical plant, opens.

1907

A stock company since inception, Public Service Corporation pays its first shareholder dividend. It has paid dividends every year since.

To promote safety, the transit arm of Public Service introduces a pay-as-you-enter system on its 1,897 trolleys serving 450 million passengers a year. This move virtually eliminates platform accidents.

1909

The 30th commercial office opens. Designed to bring Public Service closer to the customer, these service centers/showrooms become a fixture of New Jersey's cities and larger towns.

1910

The company moves to larger quarters at 759 Broad Street, Newark; Prudential remains the landlord.

The company voluntarily creates an "insurance, sick-benefit and pension fund" for all employees.

1911

New Jersey passes a Public Utilities Law, marking the beginning of state regulation.

Company library opens.

The company voluntarily participates in New Jersey's first workmen's compensation law, then optional for employers.

1913

Public Service Railway Company achieves a milestone: the opening of New Jersey's first trans-state trolley line, running from Hoboken to Camden.

Land is purchased on Park Place in Newark for the construction of a company-owned headquarters.

The company voluntarily grants an across-the-board pay raise to all female employees.

1916

The Terminal Building opens at 80 Park Place, combining a massive transit terminal with sizable office space.

Newark celebrates the 250th anniversary of its founding.

1922

Public Service News, a twice-monthly employee newsletter, is launched.

1923

Public Service is the first New Jersey utility to voluntarily reduce the work week from seven to six days for all employees at gas plants, generation stations and substations.

Unionized transit operators win a 20 percent pay raise after a 51-day strike that cripples public transportation throughout the state. Despite increased labor costs, McCarter reduces trolley fares to a nickel to maintain ridership.

To compete with private jitneys, Public Service begins purchasing bus routes and buses.

1926

Public Service trolleys, streetcars and buses carry a record 600 million passengers. The company boasts that its transit line mileage "exceeds the distance to Mercury."

Thomas Edison helps cut the ribbon at the opening of the Kearny Generating Station.

The company's first call center handles 736,000 calls a year from a single "telephone order table."

1927

Blending environmental innovation and cost consciousness, Public Service has a fleet of 49 electrically powered service vehicles.

The Holland Tunnel opens after seven years of construction powered by Public Service electricity. The tunnel has remained a customer of PSE&G.

1928

Various transit subsidiaries are merged to create Public Service Coordinated Transport.

Public Service joins with Philadelphia Electric Company and Pennsylvania Power & Light Company to form the world's first integrated electrical power pool, the forerunner of today's PJM Interconnection. (The PJM name, an abbreviation for Pennsylvania Jersey Maryland, is adopted in 1956.)

1929

The Public Service Radio Cooking School begins broadcasting and becomes a fixture of the radio era in New Jersey.

1932

Public Service engineers conduct sophisticated power experiments in Burlington County.

1935

Federal oversight increases with passage of the Public Utilities Holding Company Act, which limits ownership of energy companies, and creation of the Federal Power Commission.

1937

Public Service introduces the world's first fleet of diesel-electric buses, a technology co-developed by company engineers.

1938

The last streetcar passes through the Terminal Building, reflecting society's shift to buses and cars.

1939

At age 72, McCarter resigns the presidency and becomes the board chairman.

1941-1945

To meet the power and transport demands of New Jersey's industries, which lead the nation in wartime production, Public Service employees work overtime and weekends.

Gas and electric workers begin to unionize.

1945

McCarter retires at age 78.

1948

The company unites its utility businesses into Public Service Electric and Gas Company, although operations and accounting are kept separate.

Sewaren Generating Station opens, the first of five electric plants built to meet the post-war growth needs of New Jersey. The others are Bergen, Hudson, Linden and Mercer.

1949

Public Service begins to shift from manufacturing its own gas to buying newly available natural gas from pipeline suppliers.

1953

Turbine steam temperatures of 1050 degrees Fahrenheit at Sewaren Generating Station and 1100 degrees at Kearny Generating Station are world firsts.

1957

PSE&G becomes a pioneer in cogeneration when it exchanges steam from the Linden Generating Station for boiler fuel and water from Esso's adjacent Bayway Refinery.

1959

A bitter six-week strike occurs company-wide.

1965

Daily manufacturing ceases at the company's six gas works.

Yards Creek Generating Station in Pahquarry Township begins operation. Built and operated in partnership with other New Jersey utilities, it is the second large-scale pumped storage electrical plant in the U.S.

A major blackout affects northeastern states in November, traced to problems in Canada. PSE&G is unaffected.

1967

At Sewaren, the company installs the first of 150 jet engines to drive electric generators.

A major blackout in June, stretching from New England to the mid-Atlantic, marks the first system-wide interruption in PJM's 39-year history.

1968

Construction of the Salem Nuclear Generating Station begins.

1971

The company replaces its original triangle-in-a-circle logo with the orange sunburst logo and adopts the tagline "The Energy People."

1973

Facing shortages and price spikes in natural gas, the company opens the nation's first synthetic natural gas plant at Harrison. Another, at Linden, opens in 1974.

An oil embargo by Saudi Arabia and other Mideast nations triggers gasoline shortages and leads to widespread inflation and higher energy prices in the United States.

1974

The worsening economy forces the company's first-ever layoffs. About 1,200 employees are let go, roughly 10 percent of the workforce.

1976

The company launches multi-million-dollar programs to assess the potential of solar energy and other alternative power sources in New Jersey.

The company adopts Affirmative Action.

The gas and electric businesses, united in name under the PSE&G structure since 1948, are merged operationally.

1977

Salem One Nuclear Generating Station begins operation. Construction of Salem Two and two neighboring nuclear units at Hope Creek continues.

1978

The company cancels plans for Atlantic Generating Station, an offshore floating nuclear plant.

In a company first, eight unions, representing 8,000 employees, sign three-year contracts.

1979

A nuclear accident at Three Mile Island, Pennsylvania, triggers increased federal scrutiny of all nuclear plants. As a result, construction slows at Salem Two and Hope Creek.

1980

Public Service's transit history ends when the remaining transit subsidiaries are formally transferred to New Jersey Transit, a state agency.

The company moves into its current leased headquarters at 80 Park Plaza, Newark.

1981

Salem Two Nuclear Generating Station begins operation.

The Terminal Building is demolished.

The company decides to abandon construction of one of its two nuclear plants at Hope Creek, then about 18 percent complete.

The U.S. Department of Energy selects PSE&G to build a $15 million test facility at Hillsborough Township to evaluate electrical storage batteries.

1982

A six-week strike occurs company-wide.

1984

An in-house task force conducts the company's first formal strategic planning, which includes hypotheses for operating in a deregulated environment.

Two unregulated subsidiaries take shape: Community Energy Alternatives (CEA), the predecessor to PSEG Global, which begins developing independent power plant projects domestically in 1985; and PSEG Resources, a financial investment organization.

1985

Salem sets a national yearly gross electric power production record of approximately 9 million megawatt hours generated.

1986

Corporate restructuring creates two holding companies: Public Service Enterprise Group Inc., of which PSE&G is a subsidiary; and Enterprise Diversified Holdings Inc. for nonregulated subsidiaries.

E. James Ferland, formerly an executive at Northeast Utilities, becomes president, CEO and chairman.

Hope Creek Nuclear Generating Station, the largest construction project in company history, begins operation.

Cogeneration emerges as an alternative to utility-supplied electrical power for some large industrial customers.

PSE&G repowers the 100-year-old Statue of Liberty.

PSE&G and IBEW jointly introduce the ChildWatch safety program.

1986-1987

After a year-long analysis of work processes, PSEG reduces expenditures by about $80 million. Subsidiaries and key divisions are reorganized into business units accountable for their bottom-line performance.

1991

PSEG voluntarily chooses to meet and exceed the toughest standards of the federal Clean Air Act and Amendments.

PSEG adopts Total Quality Management practices.

1992

Congress opens the door to deregulating the energy industry by passing the Federal Energy Policy Act.

1996

Major unions representing the majority of PSEG workers — the International Brotherhood of Electrical Workers, UA, UCA and OPEIU — negotiate unprecedented six-year contracts.

PSEG begins to build its energy trading organization.

Public Service News, the company newsletter since 1922, is renamed *Enterprise Outlook.* In 1999 it becomes *PSEG Outlook.*

1997

PSEG vigorously renews its ongoing commitment to safety with a permanent, company-wide initiative.

PSE&G's Urban Initiative program in Newark's South Ward earns national recognition when it wins the Ron Brown Award for Corporate Leadership.

The New Jersey Board of Public Utilities issues its Energy Master Plan, a blueprint for industry restructuring.

PSEG Global begins its first major expansion, in Argentina. This begins the creation of businesses in Brazil, Chile, Peru, Venezuela, China, Taiwan, Tunisia, Italy, Poland, India and Oman in addition to ongoing projects in the United States.

PSE&G wins Quality New Jersey Outstanding Performance Award.

1998

The name Enterprise Diversified Holdings Inc. is dropped and certain unregulated subsidiaries are renamed to better reflect their PSEG affiliation.

1999

Restructuring begins in New Jersey when Governor Christine T. Whitman signs the Electrical Discount and Energy Competition Act into law. PSE&G customers enjoy the largest rate reduction of any deregulated state, totaling 13.9 percent by August 1, 2002.

PSE&G establishes Safety Councils for all lines of business and at all field locations.

Repowering of the Bergen and Burlington Generating Stations doubles their efficiency and drastically reduces emissions.

With the acquisition of 10 companies, PSEG Energy Technologies becomes one of the 10 largest mechanical contractors in the nation.

The Nuclear maintenance department receives New Jersey's Continuing Excellence Award for Safety, achieving seven million hours worked without a time-lost accident.

2000

PSE&G transfers its generating station assets to PSEG Power, an unregulated subsidiary created as a result of restructuring. PSEG Power generates electricity, while PSE&G continues to deliver it to homes and businesses.

PSEG Power begins to expand existing power plants in New Jersey and Bethlehem, N.Y., and develop new plants in Ohio and Indiana.

Customer Services is the first PSE&G organizational unit to win the Quality New Jersey Governor's Award for Performance Excellence.

PSE&G is one of four utilities nationwide chosen by the U.S. Environmental Protection Agency as an "Ally of the Year" for its EnergyStar Homes Program.

PSE&G's state-of-the-art Outage Management System goes live.

2001

Electricity shortages occur in California. New Jersey's approach to industry restructuring, which contrasts sharply with California's, proves to be stable and is regarded as a model for other states.

PSEG Global helps California weather its energy crisis by completing an electrical plant in 90 days, a North American record.

2002

Following an auction conducted by the New Jersey Board of Public Utilities to determine the price of energy from August 2002 to August 2003, PSE&G customers continue to pay below-market regulated rates.

PSEG voluntarily chooses to spend $337 million to install state-of-the-art control systems to reduce sulfur dioxide, nitrogen oxide and mercury from older generating plants.

PSEG Power acquires Wisconsin Energy Corporation's Wisvest Connecticut LLC subsidiary and its two electric generating stations in Bridgeport and New Haven, Connecticut.

Acknowledgments

Researching and writing this book took many months spread out over two years. I enjoyed virtually every minute. For someone who has always lived in PSE&G territory and loves her home state as much as I do, the project was catnip.

At one point, out of curiosity, I decided to count how many times in a day my life is affected by PSEG. The count began when I turned off the electric alarm clock in the morning. It continued through turning on the lights in the house, washing with water heated by gas, cranking up the baseboard heat fired by gas, making tea on the gas stove, taking food from the refrigerator, toasting bread, switching on the radio, using an electric toothbrush, booting up the computer in my home-based office, and stealing a few minutes at lunchtime to play my electric piano. By early afternoon I lost count — and I hadn't even ventured into town, where every visit to a store and every stop at a traffic light would have offered yet more proof of how PSEG really does make things work for its customers.

Many PSEG associates pitched in to make this book possible. I thank them all: Paul Rosengren, Leslie Cifelli and Denise Jacobs of the Communications & Research Services Department, my primary contacts; Laurel Gould, Lisa Holland and Adam Barth of Libraries & Information Resources, who provided research support and encouragement right up to press time; and Emma Byrne, who helped clarify the book's themes during the planning stage.

Special thanks to my interviewees: John Anderson, Sam Blom, Andrea Bonime-Blanc, Bob Busch, Paul Cafone, Bob Callahan, Ozzie Cano, Will Carey, Frank Cassidy, Frank Cielo, Pete Cistaro, Larry Codey, Tim Comerford, Bruce Cornew, Fred DeSanti, Bob Dougherty, Pat Downes, Dom Facchini, Jim Ferland, Nelson Garcez, Chip Gerrity, George Henderson, Florine Hunt, Harry Keiser, Al Koeppe, Stan Kosierowski, Joe Krejsa, Fritz Lark, Matthew McGrath, Pete Mellett, Bob Metcalfe, Ernie Meyer, Eileen Moran, Bob Murray, Peggy Pego, Bob Peters, Maria Pinho, John Scarlata, Dave Seabrook, Ed Selover, Tom Smith, Harold Sonn, Steve Teitelman, Mike Thomson, B. Vanchi, Bill Walsh, Shirley Ward, Don Weyant and Charlie Wolfe.

My field trips provided some of the most memorable moments of this project. I thank Judith Yannarelli and Ralph Izzo in Newark for arranging my appliance service ride-along with master "fitter" Bob Mascarelli. At the Oradell shop Jim Gragnano, Pete Crecco, Dave Hayo, Dennis Jandoli, Wayne Lezette and John Panebianco fed me pizza and shared their memories. At the Cranford Inquiry Center, I enjoyed the warm hospitality of Maryann Murphy, Debra Thomas and fellow writer Steve Sharkey. Skip Sindoni gave me an in-depth tour of Salem Generating Station, answered many questions and lined up a fine group of interviewees: Virginia Wright, Robin Rhea, Tom Lake, Mike Headrick, Gary Stith, Jim Clancy, Tim Hunt, Rick Dawson and Sue Vaughan. Joe Krejsa took time to introduce me to Bergen Generating Station.

Last but not least, I extend a warm "thank you" to the scores of employees and retirees who answered the call for memorabilia. I wish I could name you all.

Making Things Work: PSEG's First Century is not a definitive history of PSEG. That would have required several volumes. But I hope it captures something of the spirit and accomplishments of this remarkable enterprise. May you enjoy reading it as much as I enjoyed writing it.

Marian Calabro
Hasbrouck Heights, New Jersey

Index

Page numbers appear in boldface for illustrations.